LIAM O'FLAHERTY THE STORYTELLER

LIAM O'FLAHERTY IN 1952

LIAM O'FLAHERTY THE STORYTELLER

A. A. Kelly

BARNES & NOBLE
BOOKS
10 East 53d St., New York 10022
(a division of Harper & Row Publishers, Inc.)

First published 1976 by
THE MACMILLAN PRESS LTD
London and Basingstoke

Published in the U.S.A. 1976 by
HARPER & ROW PUBLISHERS, INC.
BARNES & NOBLE IMPORT DIVISION

ISBN 0-06-493616-3

Library of Congress Catalog Card Number: 75-43225

Printed in Great Britain

To the memory of my father
Patrick Joseph Kelly

Contents

Acknowledgements

Permission to quote from the work of Liam O'Flaherty has been granted by the author himself, and by A. D. Peters & Company, writers' agents, London; quotations from the letters of Liam O'Flaherty to Edward Garnett are made by courtesy of the Humanities Research Center, the University of Texas at Austin.

Gratitude is expressed for advice and co-operation during the preparation of this study to:

Mr Liam O'Flaherty and Mrs Catherine Tailer, acting as his secretary; Dr Georges-Denis Zimmermann, now at the University of Neuchâtel, for extensive advice; a number of other persons who either read and criticised the draft text or helped provide bibliographic items; the staff of all the libraries visited over several years of research; the two typists of the final draft; my husband and family for their forbearance upon several occasions.

Finally I should like to pay tribute to the memory of the late Dr Hans-Walter Häusermann of the University of Geneva from whom I learned a great deal.

A. A. K.

Introduction

O Storyteller do not tire
Between the fire and the wall,
For hills are greener where the spade
Has been:

(from 'The Lad Made King' by Austin Clarke)

Liam O'Flaherty was born at Gort na gCapall, Inishmore, the largest Aran island, on 28 August 1896, the ninth of ten children and second son. He was educated at first locally, then at Rockwell College, County Tipperary, Blackrock College, County Dublin, and for one year at University College Dublin. The atmosphere of his childhood is well illustrated in two books by his brother Tom who emigrated to Boston as a young man, *Aranmen All* (London, 1934) and *Cliffmen of the West* (London, 1935). In 1915 the young Liam, then usually called 'Bill' and using his mother's maiden name 'Ganly', joined the Irish Guards, took part in the terrible battle of the Somme, and in 1917 was discharged with shellshock, having been wounded at Langemarck.

In an autobiographical note published in 1933 Liam O'Flaherty states: 'After my discharge from the army I went home to the Aran Islands and there began to write some short stories, which I read to a few friends. They were amused, but they thought nothing of them'. He then set out to roam the world, as he later described in *Two Years*, but returned weary and disillusioned. During this period, when in the United States, he wrote more stories but burnt them all after reading Maupassant and finding that his were 'Barbarous compared to those of the great master'.[1] In 1920 in London he tried writing again, and once more burnt his efforts. He forsook the Church and became a Communist, which distressed his family. Back in Dublin he became involved in the Irish civil war as a Republican, and participated in the Four Courts Rebellion, an experience which was later to be described in *Insurrection*. He wrote for Republican papers such as *The Plain People*,[2] but no fiction. After the rebellion he returned to

England, fearing arrest, and in September 1922 started to write 'definitely'.

In a few weeks he wrote a 150,000-word novel, and at the same time several stories a week. None of these stories were printed and the novel was submitted to a publisher but not accepted. The typescript of this first novel has since been lost.

Liam O'Flaherty's first short story to attract attention was 'The Sniper' published in *The New Leader,* 12 January 1923.[3] It was noticed by Edward Garnett who came to the young author's aid. At Garnett's recommendation O'Flaherty's second attempted novel, *Thy Neighbour's Wife*, was accepted by Jonathan Cape. O'Flaherty added a manifesto to the novel in which he said: 'It does not attempt to preach anything. It merely endeavours to be a faithful picture of life as I have seen it'.[4] Edward Garnett now suggested to O'Flaherty that he should write about animals. Later O'Flaherty expressed gratitude to Garnett when he said, 'I owe Edward Garnett all I know about the craft and a great deal of all I know about the art of writing'.[5] Though this may be an exaggeration Garnett did make O'Flaherty realise that to write well required self-discipline and persistent endeavour.

All through the later 1920s and early 1930s O'Flaherty was struggling to evolve some basic values for himself. During this period his literary output was high. He married and became a father. He was restless, moving to Dublin, to rural isolation in Wicklow, to London, to France and visiting Russia. In spite of his literary success he had financial difficulties at times and two nervous breakdowns, caused perhaps by the aftermath of shellshock and his traumatic experiences in the trenches, fictionalised in his war novel *The Return of the Brute*. The high incidence of satire to be found in his work of the late twenties reflects his personal difficulties though his own explanation in his second autobiographical volume, *Shame the Devil*, is: ' . . . what was evil in my nature came from my shame of being humble and innocent; that this shame of humility and innocence from time to time had turned the wine of imagination into vinegar, so that I spat like a horrid cat and snarled instead of singing gently like a lark . . . ' (p. 244).

In 1932 O'Flaherty, now separated from his wife and — after his visit to Russia — disillusioned with Communism, became one of the founder members of the Irish Academy of Letters. During the 1930s three of his novels were filmed, two in the United States and one in France. He continued to travel and wrote his best novel *Famine*, which involved some research. During the war he moved round the Caribbean and South America and finally settled temporarily in Connecticut, where he wrote more stories. After the war he returned to Europe and started to publish in Gaelic. Between 1946 and 1957 he broadcast several stories in Irish and English over Radio Eireann. He continued to move between Ireland,

England and France until 1952 when he started living for the most part in Dublin. Several of his stories have been televised in Ireland and some of his short stories and novels translated into several languages. As a short story writer, particularly, he has a permanent place in Anglo-Irish literature.

This study takes into account one hundred and fifty-six short stories. Thirty-two were collected and entitled *Spring Sowing* (1924); twenty-nine are in the collection *The Tent* (1926); twenty in *The Mountain Tavern* (1929); and twenty in *Two Lovely Beasts* (1948). A selection from the first three volumes was published in London in 1937 entitled *The Short Stories of Liam O'Flaherty* and has since been reprinted in paperback. Six previously uncollected stories were included in a further selection, *The Stories of Liam O'Flaherty* (New York, 1956). One story, 'The Caress', is to be found at the end of O'Flaherty's autobiography *Shame the Devil,* and two others, 'Unclean' and 'It was the Devil's Work, were published with *The Wild Swan* (1932), under that title. The remainder of the stories listed in the appendix to this study have only appeared in periodicals. Other published stories may remain undiscovered for O'Flaherty himself has kept no record of his work. In addition O'Flaherty has two short stories in typescript, 'Bohunk' and 'Wild Stallions'.[6]

The first part of the study analyses the stories from the point of view of chronology and technique, according to narrative treatment and method, showing variation and development. For this purpose the stories are divided into four groups dealing with: animal and nature; instinctive human responses; urbanised man, or man at war; man in community and the longer action stories defined as tales. The strong and weak points of O'Flaherty's style are then analysed, and the different ways in which he adapted language to his artistic intent.

The second part of the study approaches the short story corpus as a whole through the different attitudes and relationships characters have to their environment, in an attempt to define O'Flaherty's subconscious attitudes and preoccupations. O'Flaherty turned back to nature as a starting point from which to show how man deteriorates when he cuts himself off from a natural way of life, for to O'Flaherty if man hides 'in the artificial sewers of cities' he is in danger of losing contact with life and becoming alien to it. D. H. Lawrence, who knew O'Flaherty but who never visited Ireland in spite of his intentions to do so,[7] has expressed his ideal of a unified man in what seems to be a very similar definition to that implied by O'Flaherty. 'It seems to me that when the human being becomes too much divided between his subjective and objective consciousness, at last something splits in him and becomes a social being . . . While a man remains a man, before he falls and becomes a social individual, he innocently feels himself altogether within the great continuum of the

universe. He is not divided nor cut off'.[8] This split man, unable to conform
to what society demands of him, erupts in violence or is obsessed by
fantasies caused by his fears. O'Flaherty has in general been considered a
violent and realistic writer who makes little use of comedy. A breakdown
of humour in his stories reveals that this in fact is not so. Finally the
theme of death is explored and related to the same theme in the novels in
an attempt to see how O'Flaherty views the tension inherent in man's
nature caused by the divine spark within him which desires immortality,
and his animal body which denies it.

The study concludes by summarising the reasons for O'Flaherty's
dramatic and stylistic variety, his artistic achievement as a writer and an
Irishman and discusses why so many Irish writers choose the short story
form.

Edgar Allan Poe, in his Critique of Hawthorne's *Twice Told Tales*,
defined the 'prose tale' as a 'short prose narrative requiring from a
half-hour to one or two hours in its perusal', but definition of the short
story by length is inexact for at what points a story emerges from a sketch
or expands into a novella depends very much on the cultural climate of the
time in which it is written.

Studies of the short story as a genre have been made notably by
H. E. Bates in *The Modern Short Story* (London, 1941), Sean O'Faolain in
The Short Story (London, 1948), and Frank O'Connor in *The Lonely
Voice* (Cleveland, Ohio, 1962). *Studies in Short Fiction* (Newberry, South
Carolina, 1963–), is a journal devoted to the history and form of the short
story. The short story continues to defy precise definition for it may take
the form of a philosophical essay, a reminiscence, a dramatic scene, a
lyrical description, a fantasy, a piece of reportage, a psychological study, a
political diatribe, or even a mixture of these. Some of the other criteria
mentioned by Poe can perhaps be used as a yardstick. A short story – and
the shorter the more this is so – does indeed, like a poem, need to be
artistically and economically composed to achieve both unity of effect,
density of subject matter and artistic intensity, all of which are hallmarks
of the genre.

Poe also believed that a tale should be designed to achieve a single
preconceived effect, a dictum which reflects both the moral ardour and
the surer social values of nineteenth-century New England. Hawthorne, in
his preface to the third edition of *Twice told Tales*, admits that the moral
bones of some stories stick out through the flesh. Psychological realism
and the innuendo of a phrase have progressed since and Hawthorne would
find some elliptical modern authors as strange as the society their work
reflects.

Anglo-Irish literature, starting with George Moore, continuing with
Liam O'Flaherty, Sean O'Faolain, Frank O'Connor and Mary Lavin, to
mention only some of its leading exponents, is rich in the story form and

many good collections of stories by younger writers such as Brian Friel, Benedict Kiely, John McGahern and William Trevor, among others, have been published in the past few years. The modern short story reproduces our flexible, episodic, kaleidoscopic way of life. Its subject matter embodies the changing mood of the writer, who is himself often bound by a number of varied pursuits, and provides the reader with a distillation from the vapour of confusing events and attitudes created by modern communication media. O'Flaherty's stories are a prime example of one writer's variety.

Part I:
Themes, Narrative Structure and Style

1 Animal and Nature Stories

Liam O'Flaherty wrote some twenty-five wildlife and animal stories between 1923 and the late 1940s, and an analysis of them reveals considerable differences in theme and treatment. His first published volume of short stories, *Spring Sowing*, contains nine animal stories. One of the most effective, 'The Cow's Death',[1] tells how a cow, watched by her peasant owners, gives birth to a stillborn calf. The men drag the dead calf across fields and throw it over the cliff onto rocks at the sea's edge. The story describes how the cow, after the humans have left her, becomes more and more distressed until in a frenzy of desire to find her young she breaks through all barriers and discovers the calf's body far below. Unable to reach it she leaps to her destruction just as waves sweep the calf's body from the rocks. The fatalism of the peasant woman, her sympathy for the cow, sets the mood of the story. When the peasant makes the sign of the cross on the cow's side, man and cow are placed symbolically at one; a unity of man and beast which — as O'Flaherty shows in his other stories — is often destroyed by man's insensitivity or cruelty.

By choosing a simple and yet moving situation O'Flaherty has here avoided the danger mentioned by C. E. Montague — a danger which he does not always overcome — he has passed beyond that 'common state of mediocre art in which a naked and uncomfortable theme seems to be trying awkwardly to put on a misfitting overcoat of paint or of language'.[2] The magical interaction of technical effort and imaginative insight has been achieved.

'The Cow's Death' has maternal instinct for its theme. Another *Spring Sowing* story, 'The Blackbird', is a fable in illustration of pride, told with the same extreme simplicity as 'The Cow's Death', the same controlled form rising to an anti-climax when the cat is about to pounce on the singing bird. The description of the blackbird's singing stance reminds one of Chanticleer in Chaucer's 'The Nun's Priest's Tale'. The final lines of the story when the cat growls savagely after the blackbird has escaped and the sparrows twitter in the ivy, form a musical coda to the blackbird's anthem.

O'Flaherty is adept at creating atmosphere and awakening sympathy for the protagonist while suggesting that something more important than a cow's death, or a blackbird's song is really being hinted at; but occasionally as Brandon Saul has pointed out,[3] he allows the feelings of his animal or bird character to become too subtle and this can break the spell of the story.

Such a break does occur in 'His First Flight', a story about a young seagull who is loth to leave the nest. The parents in order to force him to fly abandon him without food high up in the cliff face. Instinctively the young bird searches the empty nest for food. All he can find are dried pieces of spotted eggshell, but this was 'like eating part of himself' which does not sound like bird-thought! 'The Rockfish' is also a fable — on greed. It differs from the three stories previously mentioned in that here the fish meets man as predator. The story is spoilt by a laboured air caused by the too frequent use of 'then', and a rather monotonous sentence pattern.

The remaining animal stories from *Spring Sowing* all concern animal in confrontation with man. O'Flaherty regards animals from different points of view. They are either in their wild state, dissociated from man, as in 'The Blackbird'; struggling against man as predator, as in 'The Rockfish'; or associated with man in his everyday life as in 'The Cow's Death'. Man has therefore two roles as the hunter, and as the tamer, or master, of animals. Man is often shown as selfish, untrustworthy and insensitive in his demands upon animal, taking all he can get and giving little in return, or — in his role as the hunter — allowing his predatory instinct to usurp his finer feelings.

In 'Sport: the Kill' man is brutally obsessive; in 'The Hook' he is treacherous; in both 'The Wild Sow' and 'The Black Bullock' he shows callous neglect. In each of these stories the finer instinctive feelings of the animals contrast with the thoughtless cruelty of man; man who judges himself, by virtue of an intellect which he here fails to use, to be the animals' superior.

In 'Sport: the Kill' the story is told from the rabbit's point of view. With the rabbit the reader creeps down the rocky fissure; smells the dog's fetid breath; hears the boy's hiss and feels the sharp pointed stick inserted and twisted ruthlessly into the skin. When the skin snaps, blind with pain, the rabbit crawls forth into the dog's jaw at the same moment as the boy withdraws the patch of haunch fur impaled on his stick. The slow torture and the inevitability of the whole process is cleverly developed. The reader is caught between the fierce ardour of the hunt, which obsesses the boy and his dog, and the fearful paralysis of the hunted. The agony is protracted first by the boy bruising his hip, then by the dog going off to smell a snail, and then when the stick catches in a cleft. The boy is shown to have no feelings for his dog or for the rabbit. At the end of the story he bashes the dead rabbit's head on a rock, and kicks at the dog.

This man/dog relationship appears again in 'Two Dogs'. The association between man and dog has many human parallels. The dogs are shown as loyal to their master, but the man's love is selfish. He makes use of the dogs for what they may bring him. The final scene takes place below Coillnamhan Fort (O'Flaherty's name for Dun Aengus in his Aran novels and stories), where Feeney is going to fish from the high cliffs. O'Flaherty has remarked that this cliff-top was 'The scene of one of my short stories, the one I love best',[4] and it may well be 'Two Dogs' to which he refers. The action is very clearly visualised with the doubling, leaping and falling of the dogs and the rabbit.

Both these last two stories 'Sport: the Kill' and 'Two Dogs', have the same controlled, simple narrative style. The only descriptive passage, beginning 'then on a summer morning . . .' sets the scene for the climax in 'Two Dogs'. This joyful mood is accentuated before the horror of the climax, and is an ironic anticipation of the mood of the mongrel which, after the greyhound's fall 'began to bark joyfully and ran round trying to catch his tail'. The stressing of joy here is as effective as the digressionary tactics employed in the narration of the rabbit's torture. Such control of mood and structure show O'Flaherty at his best. A good short story suggests rather than states, and these stories pose the question. Is man capable of disinterested love?

'The Black Bullock' and 'The Wild Sow', the two remaining stories from the *Spring Sowing* group, tell how animals, neglected by man, are led into desperate situations and destroy themselves. The animals are acquired for man's profit, they are dependent upon man but neglected by him. The stories satisfy because here again the emotion is controlled, the narrative spare, the details carefully selected.

The six animal stories included in *The Tent* volume deal with similar themes to those in *Spring Sowing*. Five of them are of the same length, less than 1700 words. Only 'The Wild Goat's Kid' is longer. Three stories 'The Jealous Hens', 'The Lost Thrush' and 'The Foolish Butterfly' follow the structural pattern of the *Spring Sowing* group. They open with a 'key paragraph' which takes one into the heart of the situation, and close with a few lines which give it a final twist. 'The Foolish Butterfly' is spoilt by forced imagery. A butterfly's life is undramatic, so O'Flaherty has tried to create tension by means of figurative language. The brief story contains seven similes or metaphors. The butterfly's death by drowning is a symbol of the ephemerality of beauty; but the symbolism is too obvious.

As a developing writer, O'Flaherty is now using more figurative and descriptive language, both of which are stylistic reflections of the author's growing self-confidence. When symbolism appears it is related to an underlying didacticism, which has hitherto remained subordinate. The remaining three stories from *The Tent*, 'The Wounded Cormorant', 'The Conger Eel' and 'A Wild Goat's Kid' show evidence of these features, which achieve a fuller expression within O'Flaherty's human stories.

'The Wounded Cormorant', like 'The Hook', is very clearly visualised. It differs from 'The Hook' and other previous stories, however, by opening and closing with descriptive paragraphs. If these were omitted from the story, as they well could be as far as the action is concerned, we would be left with the immediate opening and closing situations hitherto preferred.

In this story O'Flaherty uses the descriptive approach and conclusion for two reasons. First he is now more sure of himself. As an inexperienced writer he started by paring his natural prolixity but he can now allow himself a small amount of licence, and his descriptions of natural surroundings are, on the whole, excellent. Secondly the cormorant is more of a symbol than a separate entity. The story is an illustration of 'Nature red in tooth and claw', with no mercy for the weak, and the long red strands of seaweed in the opening paragraph point forward to the cormorant's torn and bloody body at the end, lynched and rejected by its fellows.

In 'The Wild Goat's Kid' O'Flaherty has also allowed himself more space in which to create the background. Motherhood is always a tender theme with O'Flaherty and here he has succeeded even better than in 'The Cow's Death' at conveying the fierce possessiveness of the maternal instinct, equivalent in intensity to the mating instinct in the male. Man does not enter this story at all, though the cold ferocity of the dog could be said to parallel that of the boy and his dog in 'Sport: the Kill'; nature sings a chorus, modulated to the dramatic happenings, and the descriptive passages have an orchestral effect as well as strong symbolic undertones.

In 'The Conger Eel' there is a higher incidence of figurative language than in any earlier animal story and for the first time we are shown man neither as predator nor master, but afraid of the eel.

None of the four animal tales in *The Mountain Tavern* measure up to 'The Wild Goat's Kid'. 'Prey', the story of a dying donkey, has as its theme the world's indifference to death. The same theme occurs in a later story 'An Old Woman' in which the dogs follow the woman, as they follow the donkey, scenting her imminent death.

The opening passage of 'The Blackbird's Mate' has a medieval air; its pristine quality reminds one of a poem such as Dunbar's 'Thistle and the Rose'. There is the same clear visualisation of the scene which appears shining and enamelled in its clarity. The blackbird in this story is a symbol.

Even when animals are not deliberately humanised as they are in countless stories, especially those written for children, there is always a temptation for writers of 'true life' animal stories to use the animal as a symbol, or to relate its actions to human ethical concepts, by raising the animal above its instinctive status, and by giving it reactions which it cannot possibly possess. When this temptation is indulged in, the story may acquire a fabulous or allegorical twist. There are, of course, many classical examples of this from Aesop down.

O'Flaherty's better stories suggest more than they state, and he has written well-synthesised fables such as 'The Rockfish' and 'The Jealous Hens'. In 'The Wild Goat's Kid' the white goat is a symbol of love and forthright courage, whereas the black dog stands for hate and sly ferocity, but the didactic principle remains subordinate, and the story is not an allegory because the goat, without being humanised, triumphs as an animal character. In 'The Blackbird's Mate' the case is reversed. The over-stressed symbolic aspect creates a pair of blackbirds with no particular individuality. The story becomes an allegory illustrating the blighting of love and hope. What we remember most clearly after reading it are not the blackbirds but the picture of nature, first as shown in the sensual opening mood of hope and fertility, and then in its wintry guise of sterile despair.

To write animal stories, however, without in any way humanising the animals is not easy, and it becomes even more difficult in an extended work, as Henry Williamson discovered when he was writing and re-writing *Tarka the Otter* (London, 1927), seventeen times. Williamson's aim in his book was to 'cut out untruths and inaccuracies, facile description, inventions not of true imagination',[5] and he succeeded. O'Flaherty did not, however, attempt to keep all his animal stories on the purely mimetic 'true life' plane, though in his earlier stories he set out to do exactly this. What then, led O'Flaherty to use animals as characters? Is it because he loves nature, or has a particular affection for animals?

Another animal story writer, J. W. Fortescue, in the dedication to *The Story of a Red Deer* (London, 1897) says, 'I have ever noticed that they which be fondest of dumb creatures are given to be tenderest to their fellow-men'. Yet the inhabitants of the Aran Islands, O'Flaherty's home, where the struggle for life against savage nature is very intense, have not this sentimental approach to animals. The islanders, as O'Flaherty shows in his stories, think of animals as creatures to be preyed upon in order to sustain life, to be used for what they may produce, or to provide sport which may take a cruel form. J. M. Synge in *The Aran Islands* said 'people are kindly towards each other and to their children, they have no feelings for the sufferings of animals, and little sympathy for pain when the person who feels it is not in danger ... They tie down donkeys' heads to their hoofs to keep them from straying in a way that must cause horrible pain, and sometimes when I go into a cottage I find all the women of the place down on their knees plucking the feathers from live ducks and geese'.[6]

O'Flaherty, in his story 'The Challenge' describes how the tinker's wife continually flogs at the asses with her stick and how their heads are tied together, snouts to the ground. In *Skerrett* (p. 102) there is an account of how Kearney's cow is treated, with scant sympathy, for pain is 'a normal aspect of life'. Is it not therefore strange that O'Flaherty should show such sympathy with animals? The reason would not appear to be from particular affection for animals as such, nor because he is particularly tender to his fellow men.

Henry Williamson and Liam O'Flaherty seem to have been in similar frames of mind when they started writing about animals, the difference being that Williamson withdrew into solitude and learned to love the animal world, whereas O'Flaherty, who had observed this world from childhood, often wrote far from Aran and drew from a wellstocked memory.

Williamson after the 1914–18 war 'found himself out of love with mankind, at odds with his family, weary and nerve-wracked',[7] which is very similar to O'Flaherty's state in 1922. That he was disgusted and disillusioned with mankind at this time appears in his first two satiric novels, and in the penchant for crude violence in his work of the twenties. In *The Return of the Brute* which drew upon his experiences in the trenches — searing experiences which had needed a period of incubation to give them any objectivity — he wrote:

> Gunn, looking at him as he lay on the ground unconscious and caked in slime, like a channel swimmer, had another hallucination. He saw the Corporal's body becoming transformed into that of an animal. At once he hurriedly stepped aside, brushed his eyes with his sleeve and then looked wildly at his comrades. Nobody had noticed him. 'God!' he said to himself, 'what's coming over me?' (p. 90).

Gunn is on the verge of insanity. O'Flaherty himself after being shell shocked spent a period in a mental home.

While Williamson's solitary life brought him to feel more at one with wild things than with human beings, O'Flaherty, after meeting so many different men, and seeing men under stress in such a variety of situations seems to have turned to animals in reaction against men, hoping to find in them the basic realities, the pure passions and the spirit of freedom for which he had sought vainly in man, and which the ideals of religion and Communism also failed to give him.

Writing in 1925 O'Flaherty said:

> I was born on a storm-swept rock and hate the soft growth of sunbaked lands where there is no frost in men's bones. Swift thoughts, and the swift flight of ravenous birds, and the squeal of terror of hunted animals are to me reality. I have seen the leaping salmon fly before the salmon whale, and I have seen the sated buck horn his mate, and the wanderer leave his wife in search of fresh bosoms with the fire of joy in his eye. For me, that man is great who is his own God and the slave man is a harnessed lout who jingles the coppers of his hire in the scales of mediocrity.[8]

This is the passionately rhetorical and idealistic statement of a young man; for true freedom is only attainable when a man has come to terms with himself, and this O'Flaherty had not yet done.

The demoting of man to animal level, and the humanisation of animals are complementary tendencies subconsciously expressing O'Flaherty's personal frustration. Thus, as he progresses as a writer of animal stories the disillusionment with man sometimes enters also into the world of his animal characters, where man and animal meet and conscious symbolic comparisons arise. This is seen in the two remaining stories from *The Mountain Tavern* group, 'The Black Rabbit' and 'The Little White Dog'.[9]

In both these stories the animals are placed by humans in artificial situations. In the first the rabbit is no ordinary rabbit but a vehicle for the housekeeper's jealousy. The first two-thirds of the story are light and ironic. The rabbit, if compared to a dog or a kitten, had nothing uncanny about him, 'but compared to other animals of his own species, he was undoubtedly a sport of nature, a sudden upward curve in the direction of perfection and divine intellect; indeed, he was like the first monkey that became inspired with the vision of humanity. And just as all things that become suddenly different and more beautiful than the common herd inspire hatred and fear in the ignorant, so this beautiful, intelligent black rabbit became the hated enemy of the housekeeper'.

The theme summarises much of what O'Flaherty has hitherto hinted at. Man, if he tames animals for his use or amusement has a responsibility towards them which the housekeeper not only ignores, but deliberately corrupts. By being evil herself she is recognised as such by the cats, with whom she has connived, whose 'glassy eyes stared at her fearlessly', at the end of the story. This story could not be called a 'true life' nature story, nor is it properly a fable, though it has symbolic elements. It is rather a story of the perversion of nature, and man − not animal − is responsible.

In 'The Little White Dog', a fable about courage, animal is again the pawn of man. Both bull and dog remain types. In spite of its brevity the story starts, in the later manner, with a descriptive paragraph, and a redeeming humour, absent in the earlier work, here appears.

The three animal stories in *Two Lovely Beasts* add nothing essentially new in structural approach or treatment. 'The Seal' has the economy of style of the early stories without the stiltedness from which some of them suffer. 'The Seal', 'A Wild Goat's Kid' and 'The Hawk' are all written in praise of courage, in the water, upon earth and in the air. Courage is the quality O'Flaherty most admires.

'The Hawk' is the only story in English O'Flaherty at first agreed to record for broadcasting. It was published in 1956, several years after it had been broadcast in Ireland. This story is a good illustration of most of the tendencies noticed hitherto; with its careful construction, divided into three parts representing a mood or aspect of the action. O'Flaherty here uses symbolism without becoming didactic. The descriptive and narrative parts of the story are well blended and chosen to complement one another. The three parts of the story could be subtitled, the hawk free, the hawk triumphant, and the hawk courageous. Part one shows the hawk in motion. The imagery of this section is bright, swift and fierce. It recalls O'Flaherty's remark already quoted that, 'Swift thoughts and the swift flight of ravenous birds, and the squeal of terror of hunted animals are to me reality'. Part two is full of terms of triumph and exaltation beginning with the opening phrase, 'It was a lordly place'. This mid-section is the weakest part for here O'Flaherty indulges his tendency to over-rationalise animal feelings. The hawk's 'brute soul was exalted by the consciousness that he had achieved the fullness of the purpose for which nature had endowed him'. He rolls as he walks 'in ecstasy, as he recalled his moments of tender possession . . . '; but the story line is strong and this breach of probability not noticeable.

In part three, men come to capture the female bird and the male prepares to attack. 'At this moment of supreme truth, as he stood poised, it was neither pride in his power nor the intoxication of the lust to kill that stiffened his wings and the muscles of his breast. He was drawn to battle by the wild, sad tenderness aroused in him by his mate's screech'. Here the hawk has become a symbol of courage, and the fact that a bird cannot be said to have 'a moment of supreme truth' seems unimportant.

The animal stories are tightly constructed, short and simple. There is little dialogue. The detached narrative method, straight third person, with no intrusion from the author, is effective. All the animal characters are called 'he' or 'she' except 'The Foolish Butterfly' and 'The Wounded Cormorant' which both represent their species, and remain sexless. From the point of view of narrative structure, therefore, these stories are surprisingly coherent, but they show considerable variation. Some of them are straight sketches of animals in action, usually illustrating a quality such as courage, maternal love or loyalty. Some take the form of fables on themes such as indifference, pride, jealousy, greed or meanness, though the moralistic element is in general well subdued. In a few of the later stories the animals are used as symbols and have less individual importance. Unnatural violence only occurs in one story 'Sport: the Kill' where man is the perpetrator, though in 'The Black Rabbit' also, man is the agent of cruelty. Animals play the roles of both heroes and villains, and the latter role they share with man.

Benedict Kiely's opinion that 'O'Flaherty's birds and beasts are the perfect children of the earth and, as a rule, the harmony of their movements on earth is disturbed only by the invasion of man',[10] needs qualifying, for animals are shown preying upon each other in the same way as men prey upon animals. In 'The Hawk' the villain is man, but man preys on the hawk immediately after the hawk has preyed upon the lark.

Another critic's statement that 'the nearer his characters approach to animals the happier he is in dealing with them'[11] also needs qualification in relation to O'Flaherty's human characters, as the admirable animal qualities in these stories far outnumber the despicable. In all the stories the creatures are shown responding with instinctive courage and perseverance in the face of danger. They show selfless attachment and loyalty to their mates and offspring.

A third critic remarked of O'Flaherty: 'He is almost without rival in some of his studies of animal life, and it is perhaps natural that he is most interested in man when man is nearest the animal, as he is, no doubt, in the slums'.[12] Although the comparison is a false one the accusation is worth investigating.

2 Stories of Emotional Response

O'Flaherty takes animals as symbols to illustrate themes, and also writes purely mimetic sketches of animals in action. In the same way there are some stories in which simplified human characters are used as symbols or types to illustrate themes, and others in which the actions of the human characters are mimetically representative.

In his portrayal of animals O'Flaherty necessarily uses a limited emotional range. When he writes about people he also sometimes keeps within a limited emotional range, particularly in stories written before 1930. He does this either by using simple characters, such as peasants or children; or by placing the characters in an overpowering emotional situation or state, where they tend to react instinctively. The actions of people arouse a more personal response than the actions of animals ever can, even when symbolically interpreted, and the reader's critical reaction to such stories is correspondingly a more positive one.

Such stories could be described as dealing with emotional responses. In some of these stories the emotional state of the character is created by the situation described; in others it is the reverse, the situation arises out of the emotional state of the character. Such stories contain no humour, and the characters are always subjectively involved in, rather than objectively detached from, the action, being presented from without in the same way as animal characters.

From the *Spring Sowing* volume there are six stories related to emotional situations, 'Spring Sowing', 'The Landing', 'Beauty', 'Blood Lust', 'The Flight', and 'The Struggle'.

'Spring Sowing' tells how a recently married couple sow their spring seeds for the first time, an undramatic but an emotional situation, an episode in the life of the characters who are typical Irish peasants. They have just enough individuality to sustain interest in them as vehicles through whom the day's sowing is described. The ritual of the sowing is enhanced by symbolic undertones in which the scenery, action and feelings of the couple play a part. Mary, carrying the seeds in her apron, is the woman whose womb will also be fruitful. She walks with 'furrowed' brows seized by a sudden terror as she realises the extent of her double enslavement, to the earth, and to her body. Martin 'absolutely without thought' works furiously for he, as a male, is already proving himself.

As simple peasants, the pair are given neither too much conversation nor profound thought. When Martin's grandfather comes to watch them, he, as the representative of the previous generation, is a reminder of the cyclic nature of all things on earth from the seasons, to seeds, bodies and feelings.

'The Landing' has a plot rising to a climax of suspense. Like 'The Hawk' it falls into three parts, or moods. First there is the introduction in which the two old women sit calmly knitting on the seashore. In the second part of the story the wind rises. The villagers gather on the beach and with the mounting waves the mood of the people also mounts to anger and resentment. In the third part the curragh appears, the women shriek and wail; from the beach comes a babble of voices. This noise and confusion is contrasted with the taut legs and bared teeth of the boatmen as they fight to bring the boat safely in.

If the characters in 'The Landing' could be said to personify defiance and courage, the couple in 'Beauty' illustrate lust, but comparisons are forced and this story fails. O'Flaherty is here not dealing with peasants but with a pair who escape 'flushed' with wine from a dinner party. He ruins the opening paragraph with incongruous imagery and the way in which the man — upon seeing the two trees standing out against the sky — suddenly loses his lust for the woman and replaces it by poetic admiration of the trees, is most improbable.

The theme and narrative structure of 'Beauty' are both weak. The story could have succeeded had it been treated either from a purely physical point of view, impersonally related, or told through the mouth of one character. O'Flaherty has started in the first vein and then switched to the man's point of view when he describes the trees. The trees' branches become hands and cloaks, their knotty trunks all muscles, and to the man's drunken fancy they look like stricken people, but the reader's disbelief remains sceptically unsuspended.

The remaining three stories from *Spring Sowing* ('Blood Lust', 'The Fight', and 'The Struggle') can be considered together. In all three man is reduced to what is wrongly called 'the animal level'; that is, he is shown either deficient in, or temporarily deprived of, reason, and so his emotions are in control: but, since a man's emotions are of a different kind to those of an animal the comparison is fallacious.

These three stories show man driven by hate. A recent critic has stated that 'the main driving force in O'Flaherty's work is a sentiment of hate, so powerful as to tell against ideological coherence',[1] but is this not confusing hatred with rebelliousness, frustration and disgust? O'Flaherty is an idealist 'meditating on the indefinability of the paregoric', as he ironically expresses it.[2] The hatred of the three men in these three stories could not in any case be related to a 'driving force' in O'Flaherty himself for the characters are all in abnormal states. The unnamed 'he' of 'Blood Lust' is of moronic˘ intelligence, or else crazy, and in both the other stories the protagonists are drunk.

'Blood Lust' has no imagery. The style is controlled and stark, the words simple, to conform with the simple thoughts of the fishermen; but the theme does not convince because the man — who behaves like a psychopath — has been given no individuality and fails to awaken our sympathy; the motive for murder — jealousy — seems insufficient. O'Flaherty uses the same jealousy˘ motive in his tragic play *Darkness* (1926).[3]

The feelings described in 'Blood Lust' are of the same order as the neurotic obsessions shown by the characters in so many of O'Flaherty's novels. O'Flaherty himself suffered from hallucinations and emotional brainstorms for some years after being shellshocked. It is this mental state — rather similar to the effect of a depressive drug — O'Flaherty here transposes into the mind of this simple peasant whose idea pushes 'against the rear wall of his forehead', and takes the visionary appearance of a red spot.

'The Fight' is longer than the other two stories and more complex in mood, ranging from ridicule to sympathy by way of laughter. The scene is Mulligan's public house where Black Tom, a peasant, is on a binge after selling his pigs at the fair. O'Flaherty is good at describing the mental processes of the simple man whose frustrated thoughts take visual form, as he showed with Gypo Nolan in *The Informer*.

The hyperbolic dialogue of this melodramatic pub scene is reminiscent of an exaggerated curse attributed to O'Flaherty's father, 'May they spend eternity in sound-proof caves thousands of miles under the crust of the earth with their tongue glued to the roof of their mouths, their ears stuffed with guttapercha and their eyes bandaged with cement'.[4] Black Tom is not able, however, to be rhetorical in anything but tone so he howls instead.

Country pub fights being, after all, common occurrences which show that a man is a man, the barmaid sums it up: 'Poor man, there's no harm in him, only he loses his reason when he has a little drop taken'. When Black Tom gets home he breaks all the crockery and falls asleep on the hearth. The story ends — 'He did that twice every year'. This reflects the barmaid's remark, and brings the story back from the verge of farce, after the description of the fight, to the level of pathos, as we realise how little opportunity this peasant has for variety or excitement; how seldom he can assert himself as an individual.

The *Spring Sowing* emotional-situation stories show C'Flaherty in lyrical, dramatic and melodramatic mood, in various situations of emotional tension caused by love, fear of death, hatred and drunkenness. In *The Tent* there are five more of these stories, the lyrical 'Milking Time' and 'Mother and Son', both on the theme of love; the dramatic 'The Fireman's Death' and 'Trapped' on themes of death and escape from death; and 'The Wing Three-Quarter' on the theme of pugnacity inspired not by alcohol but by fear of ridicule.

Reading lyrical stories such as 'Spring Sowing' or 'Milking Time' it is difficult to agree with H. E. Bates that O'Flaherty hurls untamed words like 'slabs of paint at the page; the world of sea and craggy fields and animal peasants was seen, like Maupassant's, in a vivid glare of light. Emotions here were primitive; passion, greed, physical violence, jealousy, hatred, love, hunger, poverty. Men and women moved with a raw animal fury and lust that was checked only by the inevitable fear of priestly wrath and the terrors of hell'.[5] Such criticism smacks of complacency; a smugness about modern civilisation, the ideals of which are far less secure now than they were when Bates wrote those lines. Since 1941 we realise more clearly that by entirely relinquishing the so-called 'primitive' we lose something, and that the expression 'raw animal fury and lust' is a nonsense.

In fact violent stories such as 'Blood Lust' and 'The Fireman's Death' are far less numerous than those with lyrical, compassionate, ironic or humorous themes. The older O'Flaherty gets the more compassionate he becomes. By the time he wrote the stories in *Two Lovely Beasts* brutal violence has disappeared, and no character is a mere personification of emotion, as could be said, for instance, of the characters in both 'Spring Sowing' and 'Blood Lust'.

The Kitty and Michael of 'Milking Time' are drawn in greater depth than the Mary and Martin of 'Spring Sowing'. The two stories are on similar themes. Both tell of early married love in relation to the husband's first spring sowing of the seed, and the wife's first milking of her new husband's cow; both stories have a sexual undertone, the man's seed and the woman's milk.

'Milking Time', which is much shorter than 'Spring Sowing', has a relatively long descriptive opening passage, and the rest of the story is almost all dialogue. The emotional situation is introduced by two very lyrical opening paragraphs and thereafter conveyed through the mouths of the characters, with one intervention from the narrator. The effect of this is to create real, not type, characters whose speech gives them independent life.

In the opening paragraph O'Flaherty could hardly be said to hurl words like slabs of paint. The alliterating sibilants and repetitions have been carefully chosen to represent the sound of the milk falling into the pail, the smell, and the atmosphere of the summer evening. If this passage is read in the Irish way with very slight aspirations of the plosives *t* and *d*, the sensuousness of the paragraph is further accentuated.

'Mother and Son' shows the same signs of careful workmanship, the same tendency to convey emotion directly through the mouths of the characters, to suggest rather than to state, for more than half this story is dialogue. The story may well be based on a similar situation drawn from O'Flaherty's childhood. He and his mother were very close and in *Shame the Devil* he says of her:

> No sufferings could dull the divine enthusiasm with which life inspired her. She could weep over the beauty of a little flower growing from a speck of dirt on a naked rock as well as for her own sufferings. A lady-bird toiling up a blade of grass brought to her lips a prayer of thanksgiving. A majestic sea-plant, waving in a pool at low tide, excited her imagination to discourse for hours on the wonders of the sea, as she sat with me upon a sunny rock. Then, when my imagination, fed on these fancies, began its own adventures at her knee, recounting what I saw on the crags, the cliffs and by the seashore, how I conversed with eagles, was invited to a mermaid's cave and all the wonders that I saw therein, or how I stole a lark's wings and saw Heaven from the summit of a golden cloud, tears of joy flowed from her eyes and she said God had blessed me with a holy mind, (p. 18).

'Mother and Son' is one of the stories which may have prompted Frank O'Connor's remark: 'O'Flaherty sometimes leaves us with the impression that his stories have either gone on too long or not long enough'.[6] For, by the end of the story, more developed characters are beginning to emerge as their fluctuating emotions are revealed.

Sean O'Faolain said 'that delicate infancy of the heart, with all its wild wonder, and all its wild folly, and all its wild idealism, is the source of O'Flaherty's genius'.[7] Both 'Milking Time' and 'Mother and Son' could be taken to illustrate O'Flaherty's 'infancy of the heart'. The other two emotional-situation stories in *The Tent* could illustrate his 'wild folly' in 'The Fireman's Death', and his 'wild idealism' in 'The Wing Three-Quarter'.

'The Fireman's Death' is based on personal experience, for O'Flaherty himself was once a stoker, and the description he gives of this life in *Two Years* tallies closely with the atmosphere evoked in the story. 'The bloody Irishman from the starboard boiler' may well be O'Flaherty himself. The bare style and symbolic aspects of the character are both early characteristics in this emotional-situation genre.

'The Wing Three-Quarter' tells of a schoolboy in a finals rugger match. He is reputedly a funk but vindicates his courage and becomes the hero of the day. Here, too, O'Flaherty's personal experience as a rugger player stands him in good stead. Regan's reactions under a developing emotional situation are shown and he is clearly defined as a person. Though marred by one or two clichés this story is one of the best examples of O'Flaherty's use of suspense.

In 'Trapped', the last of *The Tent* group, O'Flaherty employed a new narrative technique. The story purports to be biographical, and the author, or omniscient narrator, intrudes in three passages of commentary. The authorial intrusions provide the repetitive refrain, of which O'Flaherty is so fond, and have the effect of distancing Hernon to the dimension of a fly crawling along the crevices of the huge cliffs. This is the tale of a man with a marvellous body and a simple but adequate mind caught in a trap from which only his body can save him. Too much intelligence would in fact be a hindrance. It is a situation upon which, in large part, the survival of the human race must often have depended, especially in places such as Aran. The story has a well-defined form and falls into four parts; before the cliff-fall, Hernon's stupefied reactions until the moon rises, his descent by moonlight, and his swim back. Within these sections Hernon's mood progresses from fearless confidence to terror, through terror to fear of death, through fear of death to thought-free action, through action to relief and pride, and ends with pride tempered by automatic thanks to God. He ends this adventure as fearless as he began it.

From *The Mountain Tavern* volume there are four stories in this category to be considered, 'Birth', 'The Oar', 'The Stream' and 'The Stone'. The first two look back to the earlier stories in theme, and the other two are O'Flaherty's first stories written about old age.

The theme of 'Birth' can be related to that of 'The Cow's Death', but here it is the importance of the calf's birth to the peasants that matters, their emotional expectancy, not the feelings of the cow which are mentioned only in passing. The tone is more discursive than in 'The Cow's Death' and as in the later animal stories there is more lyrical and detailed descriptive background. A sentence such as the following would not have been written by O'Flaherty in an earlier story, for this work is contemporary with 'The Blackbird's Mate'. 'What silence! The daisies had arched their white leaves inwards over their yellow hearts; many leafy ladders, along which the dewdrops slid to the yellow core'. The short practical remarks exchanged by the peasants contrast with the lyricism of the interspersed descriptive passages and also add to the atmosphere.

'The Oar' is on a similar theme to that of 'The Landing'. There is the same suspense, the same clear visualisation of the scene; the same attention to sound pattern, and personification of nature; but the spirit of the two stories is different. 'The Oar' has a fabulous quality which comes from the blending of its realistic setting with its allusively symbolic ending, and the same mixture of realism and impressionism is discernible in the language.

The upheld oar in this story creates the same eeriness as we find in the final passage of Melville's *Moby Dick* where, 'as the last whelmings intermixingly poured themselves over the sunken head of the Indian at the mainmast, leaving only a few inches of erect spar yet visible . . . at that instant, a red arm and a hammer hovered backwards uplifted in the open air, in the act of nailing the flag faster and yet faster to the subsided spar'. In fact, O'Flaherty is probably more directly beholden for this uncanny rendering of the external to Joseph Conrad, of whose work he was a critical admirer, and of whom he had written in 1925: 'Reading Conrad is like reading a fairytale for grown-up people. Somehow, using ordinary incidents and ordinary people as his materials, he weaves a cloak of romance out of space'.[8]

In 'The Stream' and 'The Stone' O'Flaherty first writes about old age, a theme he was to return to in 'Lovers', 'The Old Woman', 'Life' and 'Galway Bay'. Both these stories give double impressions, the first is a progressive picture of life as seen through the mind of the aged character, and the second a cyclical impression showing their life as a point in an ever-recurring life-cycle.

In 'The Stone' the unnamed protagonist is a type-figure for senile old age. In his mind past and present mingle and create a kaleidoscopic, visionary world. The story is built round this mirage and the emotional reaction to which it gives rise. At first the old man thinks he is — as in the past — going off to fish. This fantasy becomes confused with mental associations as he arrives at an old bench, where he remembers resting after bringing in his first catch. The second section of the story shows the old man noticing the stone near the bench. He becomes obsessed by the desire to lift the stone once more, as he had in his youth. He ends by falling dead over the stone. He is found by the villagers who, in the only dialogue passage, act as a chorus, 'there is nothing in all creation that isn't more lasting than man'. The youths who now come up will one day in their turn become old men in a never-ending cycle of life and death. They subdue the earth, of which the stone is a symbol, and they will in their turn be subdued by it.

'The Stream' has the same cyclic pattern of youth, old age and death but O'Flaherty has here had difficulty in controlling his narrative point of view. This fault and an inconsistency in the underlying theme, flaw the structure of the story. It is the tale within a tale, narrated without the symbolic undertone of the opening section, that makes the story inconsistent. The account of the old woman's youth, purporting to come from a mad mind, is too coherently and objectively related. It is not a vision but an extremely realistic account of the happening. The reader could, however, accept it, were he not at the end of the story asked to return to the spirit of the symbolic opening passage and listen again to the old woman as she utters her second incantation (the refrain in this story), which is a variation on the theme of the first.

'Lovers' is an uncollected story first published in 1931. The story concerns the meeting of two old people Michael Doyle and Mary Kane who had been lovers in their youth; it is told in dialogue except for the opening section which brings out the helpless stupidity of old Michael. Mary's happy youthful memories contrast brutally with actuality, for Michael is now in his second childhood and Mary, unhappily married and then left a childless widow, has only 'a sad memory of a love that was strangled in its cradle'. There is no symbolism in the story which is consistently related from the simple characters' points of view, nudged gently by the recorder in the prose passages.

The three emotional-situation stories in *Two Lovely Beasts* are longer than the earlier stories, show more tranquillity and compassion, and less blatancy in the description of physical detail. They are 'The Old Woman', 'Life' and 'The Parting'.

'The Old Woman' of the first story is physically just as repulsive as the old people in 'Lovers', 'The Stone' or 'The Stream', but her outward appearance is shown to be unimportant. This story conveys profundity of thought by means of simple statements obliquely suggesting an unobtrusive allegorical element. This is something O'Flaherty attempted but failed to achieve in 'Beauty' and 'The Stream'.

The deeper meaning is conveyed by the reactions of the three characters who represent three generations, Nellie, Julia and the old Maggie. Slinking in the background is a yellow dog — the harbinger of death and symbol of evil. The dog, like the dog and the crows in 'Prey', follows Maggie and sniffs at her heels hungrily. Maggie — otherwise gentle — strikes at the dog and curses it.

The main body of the story is told in dialogue between Julia and Maggie. Constantly repeated is the refrain, from Julia, 'There are many ugly things in God's world. It's only kindness that saves us from damnation'; and Maggie's 'There are only lovely things in God's world'. The purity of Maggie's thoughts is contrasted with the filth of her body, whereas Julia's house and body are scrupulously clean but her mind is tainted by fear of ugliness and sin. As in 'The Hawk' the dramatic impact of the story and our sympathy for old Maggie mask the underlying symbolism. The story's refrain reflects the attitude of O'Flaherty himself. As a younger man he delighted in showing 'the ugly things in God's world'. In his later stories ugliness, when it appears, is tempered with compassion and is viewed in perspective, as if the author, no longer so emotionally involved, had achieved a more balanced and tolerant viewpoint.

'Life' like 'The Old Woman' again refers to the cyclic pattern of human life, represented here by the baby, the mother and the grandfather. The baby — symbol of life's renewal — brings new hope into the household, even though he is the last of fifteen children and his mother has long lost the dewy-eyed vision of life that we find in 'Spring Sowing' or 'Milking

Time'. 'Everything is more lasting than man' says the grandfather, echoing the formula uttered in 'The Stone'. This old man is as childlike as Michael in 'Lovers'. He is led from the room, as a neighbour remarks 'The longest journey from the womb to the grave is only a short one after all', which is the theme of the story. This story contains the same high proportion of dialogue which has been noticed as a later development in O'Flaherty's stories.

In these stories introducing old people O'Flaherty has chosen emotional situations which show man's consciousness of time, his awareness and acceptance of death. This awareness sets man apart from animal. It is no coincidence that the most aware of the old characters, the woman in 'Lovers' and the protagonist in 'The Old Woman', are the most effective. The only characters in all the stories considered in this chapter who could be called 'animal-like' are those who are either insane, drunk, senile or still infants.

Two other stories of this type, 'Desire' and 'The Mirror' were first collected in the New York (1956) edition of O'Flaherty's stories. 'Desire', a symbolic little story of man in miniature, with its threefold repetition of the sun as 'the eye of God', is spoilt by the same fault that occurs in some of the animal stories, for O'Flaherty has over-rationalised the baby's reactions.

In 'The Mirror' the refrain takes the form of rather ineffectual ejaculations. The last quarter of the story starting with the first 'Aie! Aie!' is improbable, for O'Flaherty's female psychology is questionable. Does an innocent girl, however modest, when she sees her naked body the first time feel so filled with fear and shame that she staggers from side to side 'owing to the drunken tumult of her blood'? A narcissistic reaction of admiration and curiosity is more likely. O'Flaherty has here imagined the male reaction and placed it in the mind of the girl who is physically affected by the sight exactly as most men would be. Neither is it very probable that a girl would dream about 'love's awe-inspiring fruit, the labour of pregnancy' until she were actually pregnant: before that she is more likely to dream about her ideal future lover. There is too much of O'Flaherty himself in both the baby and the young girl of these two stories.

'The Parting', from *Two Lovely Beasts*, is a very mature story, based on O'Flaherty's personal range of emotional experience, and entirely convincing. This story connects with the earlier 'The Inquisition'. Thirteen year old Michael Joyce is going off to the mainland to join a seminary. The emotions of the boy are entered into much more deeply than those of any other character in this group of stories, but the boy remains a type figure. H. H. Murray thinks this story is reminiscent of Joyce's 'Eveline',[9] but Eveline is more deeply drawn, and whereas she longs to escape from the situation in which she is entrapped to Frank's arms, Michael has a childish longing to remain in his present situation, to feel his mother's 'loving arms about him'.

The character of Michael is well drawn. The difficulty he has in mastering his emotions sharpens his senses and with his usual acuity O'Flaherty describes the sights and sounds at the quayside which affect the boy — impressions which O'Flaherty must have himself experienced when in his youth he went to watch cattle being loaded.

The situation of the young bullock is used as a parallel to that of the boy. Like Michael the bullock is headstrong, but being an animal it cannot control its feelings so it attempts to escape and is mastered by force. The animal's behaviour is also implicitly contrasted with that of the human characters. Its uncontrollable fear is found pitiful both by Michael and Mrs Joyce, but when the father loses control of himself on the quay the rest of the family are either angry or ashamed.

Those critics who believe that O'Flaherty is most interested the nearer his characters approach to animals, in whatever way this may be interpreted, would do well to study this story. The emotional feelings of the boy contrast with his self-controlled exterior throughout the story.

As Martin represents one possible future open to an Aran peasant and Michael another, Barbara Joyce represents a third choice, that of emigration. The final lines of the story express Michael's double separation, physical and spiritual. As a priest Michael will become estranged from his home environment just as much as Barbara with her 'little round hat, surmounted by brightly coloured artificial flowers.'

As a young man O'Flaherty could not have written this story with its complex range of emotions, and its unobtrusive social commentary.

Having cut a linear swath through O'Flaherty's emotional-situation stories, it should be possible to see some development in his treatment and narrative structure. The violent emotional situations often found in the earlier stories gradually disappear, so does the lyricism present in 'Spring Sowing', 'Milking Time' and 'Birth'. All the later stories of this type depend on the emotional states to be found in old age or extreme youth, and the characters are now shown in greater depth, though they occasionally, as in 'Life', remain type figures. Their character is revealed obliquely by a varied narrative viewpoint, rather than being directly described. This indicates both greater skill and more human awareness on the part of the author. We see old Maggie through the eyes of both Julia and Nellie, we are told about her by the narrator, and she also speaks for herself. This tendency also, of course, conforms with the higher dialogue content in some of the later stories. In the later stories there is more compassion, a limited capacity for reflection rather than merely instinctive reaction and a spirit of acceptance or toleration rather than revolt.

Do these stories show that O'Flaherty is interested in man 'nearest the animal'? This is only true if by 'animal' is meant man, acting instinctively rather than thoughtfully, under the stress of abnormal emotion, in a dangerous situation, as an immature being in whom halfformed ideas cannot yet be rationalised, or man by nature simple and incapable of deep thought. All the people in these stories are simple peasants except the characters in 'Beauty', the least successful story in the group, and the protagonists of 'The Fireman's Death' and 'The Wing Three-Quarter' whose minds are simplified by pain and fear.

How O'Flaherty reacts to 'man nearest the animal', in the sense of becoming depraved, when man becomes divorced from nature and enters the town, will be investigated in the next group of stories to be considered.

3 Urban and War Themes

O'Flaherty has written a group of stories dealing with men living in towns, or urbanised in outlook, and four stories about man at war. All these stories show man divorced from nature whether by environment, choice, or circumstances. As with the stories in Chapter 2 in none of this group does the action take place over a period of more than twenty-four hours. The stories vary between 1250 and 5000 words in length, and only two were written after 1932. In one story the character creates the situation, but in all the others the characters find themselves in a particular situation which gives rise to the story, either directly as a result of the situation, or from the reaction the situation awakens in the characters' minds. All these stories arouse a reflective rather than an emotional response in the readers. Eight stories contain satire, sometimes combined with ridicule.

The characters of these stories are either subjectively involved in or objectively detached from the action according to the handling of the narrative view-point. It follows, therefore, that the narrative technique is more varied than in the stories considered previously. The multiple and converging narrative view-point has either a kaleidoscopic or a three-dimensional effect upon the characters. In place of the occasional fable-type story examined in the previous chapters we here find a 'moral' element appearing in social criticism of the contemporary Irish scene.

Urbanised man — that is man oriented towards town rather than country life, whether or not he lives in a town — as shown in these stories, is not capable of disinterested love, but is usually a bewildered, decadent or brutalised creature.[1]

These stories contain much despair and any humour is at man's expense. Characters die violently or unnaturally and there is no impression of cyclic renewal. The characters, though drawn from a wide range of backgrounds, are all imbued with various forms of self-interest based on graft, lust or fear, and only one has the smallest inkling of the meaning of love.

O'Flaherty has written only two short stories about man in the slums, in spite of John Eglington's remark quoted at the end of Chapter 1; but it seems he has deliberately chosen to represent urbanised man from a biased viewpoint. It should be possible to discover his purpose in doing so.

'The Tramp' is the longest story of those now under discussion. It is narrated from a multiple point of view. The story opens with a description of the yard of the workhouse hospital and two of the paupers. Onto the scene comes the tramp. 'He appeared silently at the entrance of the shed and paused there for a moment while his tiny blue eyes darted around piercingly yet softly, just like a graceful wild animal might look through a clump of trees in a forest'. Here the country faces the town. O'Flaherty add to this description of the tramp an account of how his physique attracts yet repels the paupers Deignan and Finnerty.

Deignan's state of mind sounds very like that of O'Flaherty himself expressed in *Two Years*:

> ignorant, without belief, without will to forge the scattered and diverse fragments of my material intellect into such homogeneous substance as would give me power over my fellows, I was beginning to see that I must remain a wreck; that it was not the war which had made me a wreck, but nature, which had destined me for other things. Greater or less? That mattered nothing. The important thing was to know and to accept (p. 349).

Deignan in this story neither knows nor accepts. Finnerty, the other pauper, says he has been ruined by drink and women — both temptations fully experimented with by O'Flaherty himself.

The tramp is still in touch with nature, but the other two men think only of their own desires, both are outcasts from society. When the tramp sees the sun he exclaims, 'Doesn't it make ye want to jump and shout'. 'I'm afraid I'd rather see a good dinner in front of me', replies Finnerty. The tramp, by opting out of society, has overthrown all responsibility. He says, 'That's my religion and it's a good one. Live like the birds, free'.

Satisfaction, according to this story, cannot come from fulfilling your own base desires as Finnerty does, nor from a fearful urge to be respectable, which hamstrings Deignan, nor from abdicating all responsibility and existing, as does the tramp; though of the three the tramp's road is the best. The tramp is the freest human being because he is still in touch with nature, and untrammelled by man-made conventions. The tramp alone shows generosity of spirit.

Except for the opening passage the story is almost all dialogue. By showing the multiple view-point of his three characters dramatically O'Flaherty has brought them closer to the reader and created a mosaic of their personalities and experiences.

'The Doctor's Visit' is reminiscent of Chekov's 'Ward Six'. The view-point is shared between the omniscient narrator and the protagonist, Maurice Dowling. When we listen to the narrator it is evident that Dowling suffers from illusions and obsessions. We are shown the other patients objectively, but Dowling is presented subjectively, and thinks himself to be perfectly sane. The story turns on the ambiguity of the double view-point. It succeeds because the view-point is controlled, conveying well the extreme self-absorption of the insane.

In 1925 E. J. O'Brien wrote, 'The sense of action in the changing concept of the short story rests no longer in the external sphere but in the subconsciousness'.[2] 'The Doctor's Visit' fulfills this requirement. The dramatic moment is withheld to the last. In fact the sense of action lies within the subconscious thoughts of the characters in all but one of the stories in this group.

In 'Josephine' the dénouement of the story hangs on a fact only revealed after the situation of the characters has been explored. One is here reminded of Katherine Mansfield rather than Chekov, for it attempts above all to be a story of atmosphere, created from the conflicting mental states of the two characters Josephine and George O'Neill.

Josephine is an over-refined intellectual and George represents the racy aspect of 'culture'. Both are not only alienated from the natural beauty of their surroundings, but alien to each other. Having presented his two characters objectively through a narrator whose neutrality is sometimes doubtful, O'Flaherty now brings the reader nearer these people, towards whom some prejudice has been awakened in the reader's mind, as he moves into dialogue and the subjective view-point of each.

There is a fivefold narrative point of view in this story, that of the narrator, those of the two characters in their inner thoughts, and those of the two characters as they are expressed to each other. This multiple and shifting view-point creates the kaleidoscopic effect which causes the evanescent quality of the story.

Throughout the story O'Flaherty suggests rather than states; the characters, equally self-centred, play with each other. The 'apple' in George's throat, mentioned twice as being in frantic movement, suggests Eve the temptress. Marriage is treated as a social convenience by the woman – something to avoid by the man. Josephine is the daughter of a man of 'taste and regularity'; George the son of the principal shopkeeper of Kilmurrage, yet their social advantages have done them nothing but harm. Their conversation is deliberately genteel. – Josephine calls George a 'cad', while George thinks of Josephine as 'passée'. Behind this veneer of worldliness, however, they react instinctively, for when George leaves Josephine 'as he walked, he felt a ticklish feeling in his thighs and down the backs of his calves as if he were walking in a field with his back to a bull'.

O'Flaherty has explored the Dublin slums in *The Informer*. He enters them in both *The Assassin* and *Insurrection*, but apart from the uncollected first person impressionistic sketch 'A Public-House at Night' he has written only two short stories set in the slums, 'Unclean' and 'Wolf

Lanigan's Death'. Evidently it is not necessary to enter the slums in order to find depraved man.

'Wolf Lanigan's Death' is the only story in this group in which the sense of action does not lie within the conscious or subconscious thoughts of the characters. Its narrative view-point is that of the omniscient narrator, and only the exterior actions and behaviour of the characters are shown. Wolf Lanigan as a character has much in common with the characters of the emotional-situation stories, for he is simplified both by stupidity and the fear of death. The story tells how Wolf Lanigan, a wanted murderer, escapes, takes refuge with his mistress Rosie, falls into a drunken and exhausted sleep, and is shot by her.

The story falls neatly into three parts. The first and last parts are narrated in prose, the central part in the form of a dramatic scene. This story is reminiscent of *The Informer*, the difference being that whereas the novel is a melodrama of conscience, Wolf, being exteriorised, remains a type-figure and this limits the story's effectiveness.

Of *The Informer* O'Flaherty wrote,

> it should be a sort of high-blown detective story and its style based on the technique of the cinema. It should have all the appearance of a realistic novel and yet the material should have hardly any connection with real life. I would treat my readers as a mob orator treats his audience and toy with their emotions, making them finally pity a character whom they began by considering a monster.[3]

In fact the deeply drawn Gypo Nolan creates such an illusion of reality that the reader can sympathise with him from the start. In a short story this is not as easy to achieve and Wolf Lanigan's only redeeming feature is that he has, according to his lights, shown kindness to Rosie. He is deliberately bestial. The atmosphere of the story is one of degradation, fear and despair.

Wolf passes through mean streets and up stairs to the sordid room he shares with Rosie. This is similar to the scene in *The Informer* where Gypo takes refuge in the bedroom shared by old Louise Cummins and the prostitute Katie who betrays him. Of Katie O'Flaherty says, 'She loved him in her own amazing way. The last remains of her womanhood loved him as she might have loved a mate. But those shreds of love lived charily among the rank weeds of vice that flourished around them'. Rosie, in this story, is not as far gone in vice as Katie. The words 'pale', 'white', 'lifeless' and 'glassy' constantly repeated in describing her, convey her soiled innocence and the hypnotic quality of her actions.

After the murder, the extinguishing of the light in the room and the shattering of the lamp's chimney, which has earlier been described as already broken, are connected to the adjectives used to describe Rosie, and also symbolise her insanity. Like *The Informer* this story is highly realistic and yet Wolf and Rosie move like flat characters on a frieze. Rosie is little more than a ghost and Wolf, whose forehead 'sloped straight back from his eyes', is subhuman. Unrelieved by any humour or the faintest gleam of affection this violent story loses the impact it might otherwise have achieved, for it is well composed and well written in a mood of cold anger. The story contradicts O'Flaherty's remark in *Shame the Devil*. 'I do love humanity. And I claim that it is to my training as a soldier I owe the flowering of that love. Without it and without having taken part in the great holocaust of the war, I might have grown into a barren scholar, or a warped aesthete, a pretty pedlar of emasculated thought . . . ' (p. 239).

Before turning to the other slum story, 'Unclean', there are four war stories to consider, 'The Sniper', 'Civil War', 'The Mountain Tavern' about the Irish civil war, and 'The Alien Skull' about the 1914—18 war. All four stories show complete actions rather than episodes, economically told and under 2000 words in length. All show man in war stifling his finer feelings.

In William Troy's opinion 'of the Dublin group *The Informer*, *The Assassin* and two earlier stories "The Sniper" and "Civil War"', are based on real or imagined circumstances . . . As a whole they constitute the most remarkable record of that period which we are likely to receive; the most complete because derived largely from personal observation and participation; the most reliable because written without any other bias than that of artistic selection'.[4] This statement might apply to Ernie O'Malley's *On Another Man's Wound*, written, of course, after Troy had made this statement, but it hardly seems valid in regard to O'Flaherty's work. When O'Flaherty wrote about war he drew upon material of which he had personal experience, but his reason for writing is to damn warfare in general as inhuman and debasing. The historic aspect and factual accuracy of the work is secondary. In *The Martyr* he showed the absurd side of civil war, and only in *Insurrection*, written much later, are the heroic as well as the debasing possibilities of war explored.

'The Sniper', with its surprise ending based on coincidence is in the older tradition of Maupassant and O'Henry. It must have been written very shortly after the Four Courts Rebellion in which O'Flaherty took part on behalf of the Republicans. The sniper is given no name and remains a type figure illustrating all those caught up by warfare and forced to shoot the enemy, who turns out here to be a blood brother.

O'Flaherty's abruptness and economy of style in his early work, is ideal for this story where the effectiveness depends upon a controlled emotional response. That he finds war foolishly destructive and dehumanising is most clearly shown in *The Return of the Brute*, a savage satire set in the mud of World War I and written almost entirely in dialogue to give it more dramatic effect. 'The Sniper' is narrated from a limited view-point. It is a good example of what Sean O'Faolain has called the eel-trap of immediate convergence on the moment.[5]

The sniper's actions are based on fear, on his instinct of self-preservation. There is little imagery and the few realistic details are well chosen. The variation of the 'camera-angle' across to the opposite roof, down to the street, back to the sniper, together with changes in the sniper's mood, carry the story swiftly forward.

O'Flaherty's second war story, 'Civil War' is also omnisciently related and economic, but it contains more description than 'The Sniper'. On the roof of a slum-street public house two men are trapped, waiting for death, trapped in the same way as the sniper, but with less chance of escape. The second paragraph contains a carefully linked series of repetitive words, 'roof', 'multitude', 'slept' and 'Republicans', designed to set the flat tone of disillusionment in which the story is written. The action turns on the conflict of personality between the two trapped men, an idealist and a realist, an abbreviated echo of similar confrontations developed to greater depth in novels such as *The Martyr*, *Land* and *Insurrection*. Apart from the descriptive introduction and some introspective passages about Dolan's suffering, the story moves fast, at times with the staccato abruptness of 'The Sniper' and we are given no hint where the author's sympathy lies. The theme of the story is the pitilessness of war, to Dolan a wilderness where he is cut off from life. It seems you can only be a fearless soldier if you stifle your better feelings by an effort of will, or else lack such feelings; otherwise you go mad as Gunn does in *The Return of the Brute*.

Stifle the feelings long enough and they become warped. This is shown in 'The Alien Skull'. In this story Private Mulhall has been chosen as a scout to enter the enemy lines during the night. He is a hardened soldier of 'ferocious courage' whose feelings have been cauterised by three years at the front without leave. Life means little to him. When he jumps on top of a man in the enemy trenches he is slowly won over by the innocuous youth he there discovers:

> They sat in silence for a whole minute, looking at one another in a state of ecstasy. They loved one another for that minute, as saints love God or as lovers love, in the first discovery of their exalted passion. They were carried up from the silent frightful corpse-strewn battle-field into some God-filled place, into that dream state where life almost reaches the secret of eternal beauty.

This sort of thing is quite unsuited to a battlefield . . . Passing from the exaltation of love to the exaltation of furious despair Mulhall kills the enemy soldier and is then himself shot on his way back. The story — and the title is ironic — is a condemnation of man brutalised by war. Here, rather than in the slums, man comes nearest to being an animal. Mulhall is well realised. He is a squat man, thin and hard with eyes like a ferret. His reputation for courage he has earned only at the expense of a warped personality. O'Flaherty's opinion of the 1914–18 war is recorded in *Two*

Years as, 'the victory of a mob over another mob, equally senseless. That barren and inglorious war, whose record is mud and noise and obscene poison . . . ' (p. 74).

In 'The Sniper', 'Civil War' and 'The Alien Skull' we see war through the eyes of the soldier. 'The Mountain Tavern' differs from the other three stories not only by being written largely in dialogue but because it also gives the civilian point of view. The story is set in a framework of snowbound countryside described in two lyrical opening paragraphs which evoke well the still, pure remoteness of the wintry mountain atmosphere. In these paragraphs there are echoes of Joyce's last paragraph of 'The Dead', but whereas Joyce uses the churchyard to represent isolation, O'Flaherty compares the silence to that found in an empty church. Both writers use the word 'universe', both use alliteration and repetition.[6]

This nature framework is in deliberate contrast to the rest of the story, which is about the impurity of man. This is directly conveyed in the opening line of the third paragraph: 'There came the smell of human breathing from the east'. An unpleasant smell to taint the air which has 'the sweetness of ripe fruit'. But the Republican soldiers, like the other characters are oblivious of the beauty of their surroundings. The occupants of the ruined tavern curse the soldiers and have no pity for the dying man. In a country setting this is all the more shocking. The falling snow at the end of the story is a symbol of nature's imperviousness to the inhumanity of man to man.

'Unclean', O'Flaherty's other slum story, is one of the longest in this group and the latest by date of publication. Like 'Wolf Lanigan's Death' and the four war stories it has a completed action. The story, which in 1932 would have been considered obscene, is omnisciently related, though speech is put into the mouths of both characters, and Lydon, the protagonist, indulges in some interior monologue. Lydon, a respectable but pathetic figure is sinned against rather than sinning. Like Mr Gilhooley in the novel of that name he lacks love but does not know what the word means.

When Lydon meets the harlot her eyes are described as having 'that curious combination of innocence and wickedness, which is a characteristic of the sensual woman, the born harlot, the woman who gives herself freely without love'. One doubts here whether any woman is born to be a harlot, any more than any man is born, like Lydon, to have a frigid wife! Lydon's lust is aroused by this woman and his subconscious grudge against his wife, once he is drunk, is vented on the harlot. Rhys Davies wrote of this story: '"Unclean" is sour and sordid: like all Mr O'Flaherty's work in this genre it is too bald and definite in its squalor to become literature: it has too much story, in the sense that the *News of the World* on Sundays has too much story. Here the flood of poetry, the sense of wonder and delight, that is in Mr O'Flaherty is withheld: his mind has seen a story, he must get it down quickly on paper. But his blood has not been touched'.[7]

On the contrary when O'Flaherty writes in a brutal vein he is expressing his own frustration and anger against man's imperfections related to his potential. For this purpose he usually chooses an unbalanced protagonist. Lydon has the remains of a social conscience, but he is in thrall to circumstances from which he has insufficient guts to escape. As captive indeed to his wife as a tame ferret, he flushes out the rabbits in their pitiful slum burrows, rabbits which become vicious under attack and the biter gets bit.

The irony in this story implies a criticism of loveless man, part of a more extensive criticism of society, which is fully expressed in *The Puritan*, published in the same year as 'Unclean'. In this novel Ferriter — the name is perhaps significant — who has murdered Teresa Burke as a 'sacrifice of blood' is, towards the end of the book, sitting in a bar talking to a harlot. He tells her: 'You have killed something also, something that you were taught to believe should not be killed . . . But here there is no joy. So we both suffer, you and I. We have killed something, each of us, so we are sad and lonely and afraid. Don't you understand?' (p. 262).

Two other stories published in *The Tent* also imply social criticism, 'Blackmail' and 'The Tyrant'. Both are anecdotes in which there is little action, the situation arising from the thoughts or speech of the characters. Sheridan of 'The Tyrant' is a similar type to Kenneally in 'Blackmail', equally ambitious, dishonest and ruthless but more prosperous and sophisticated. Most of 'The Tyrant' is related through the mind of Mrs Sheridan. Sheridan remains a flat figure, illustrative of the story's dominant theme. Helen Sheridan, 'a flabby woman of forty', is in a state of interior revolt against the sycophancy and hypocrisy of her husband who tyrannises her and uses her as an instrument of his ambition. Like many of O'Flaherty's characters who wish to revolt but are powerless to do so for some reason, she takes refuge in fantasy. Attacked by her husband she has hysterics, then a hallucination in which the cold air is personified. Here, as in 'The Mountain Tavern', nature is used as a symbol of purity and the nature passage of her hallucination, linked to the opening paragraph of the story, creates a symbolic framework.

There are, however, some weaknesses in 'The Tyrant'. Too little is shown of the husband's point of view, so he remains a melodramatically vicious figure. Helen's cloud of thoughts, her desire to float away, her personification of the air, sometimes appear improbable because the symbolism is not consistently realised. Neither is she seen consistently as a person. Her face is described as beautiful, mild and white and later as 'flabby, down-trodden'. The twin themes of the story are first that of an unscrupulous man who is trying to gain power in the Irish government, and secondly the desire of his wife to attain spiritual independence. But

Helen's muddled and mystical feelings appear in their own way as illusory as the ambitions of her husband.

'The Sensualist' is a theme story as its title implies, with illustrative characters. The protagonist, Corcoran, is drunk with lust and conceit. His moment of comic self-revelation in front of the mirror is less effective because of the narrative technique. Had O'Flaherty used Corcoran as narrator for most of the story he could have given him greater depth. As it is the self-revelation is as superficial as Corcoran's character. The story is also too long for its hackneyed theme and could be classified as an emotional-situation story except that Mrs Mallon is throughout in control of her faculties. The characters Sheridan, Kenneally and Corcoran in the last three stories considered, are all lawyers. Evidently O'Flaherty has a grudge against the legal profession.

'The Terrorist' is another unsatisfactory story. Here again the pro-tagonist remains a type figure. This is the only story of those under consideration in this chapter where the character creates the situation, which exists largely in his imagination. 'The Terrorist' is reminiscent of *The Assassin* in the same way as 'Wolf Lanigan's Death' is reminiscent of *The Informer*. Louis Quigley is obsessed by 'the drones soured by their own luxury', represented by the well-clad people in the more expensive seats of the theatre where he intends to hurl his bomb. O'Flaherty likes creating obsessed characters. In the emotional-situation stories many simple characters were shown to be obsessed by one overpowering emotion. In these stories man is obsessed by the desire for power in 'The Tyrant', temporarily obsessed by sexual lust in 'Unclean' and 'The Sensualist', or the lust to kill in 'Civil War' and 'The Alien Skull'.

Quigley is as mad as Dowling in 'The Doctor's Visit' but the reader is told far less about him, and he remains the mouthpiece of his idea. 'Before he hurled the bomb he would utter aloud his prophecy. It would go forth to all the world as a clarion call. The tocsin would be sounded that night. "The blare of trumpets at dawn on the banks of the Po, as the squadrons of Hasdrubal's Nubian horse ... ." Prophets immolate themselves'. Presumably Quigley is an educated, or perhaps self-educated man. In *The Assassin* O'Flaherty uses the same comparison: 'The sound of Tumulty's steps made McDara start with pride and he saw again, on the banks of the Po, Hasdrubal's horsemen, caparisoned, with thundering hoofs', (p. 95). As McDara's thought this is, however, completely out of character.

This story should have been related selectively through Quigley's mind, but the only passages thus related stress Quigley's abnormality, and when he does take over the narrative the language becomes rhetorical, literary and exaggerated. The story is unconvincing because the theme is expressed through the mad Quigley's obsession, and the reader's attention is divided between the madness of Quigley's impressions, the method of the narrator's disillusioned but florid commentary, and the ironically expressed truths underlying both. The result is phantasmagoric. The story is intended to describe the mind of a man driven mad by the discrepancy between his ideals and reality, and I have lingered on it, in spite of its artistic inadequacy, because this discrepancy is often what motivated O'Flaherty himself as a writer.[8] If the protagonist is to be a vehicle for satiric commentary, if his imagination is to create a situation as a character he must be more thoroughly revealed, something which O'Flaherty achieves with McDara and Ferriter in *The Assassin* and *The Puritan*.

In *The Mountain Tavern* there are two stories of urbanised man 'The Sinner' and 'The Fall of Joseph Timmins'. The latter connects with 'Unclean' as the protagonist again has a barren unloving wife. But this wife, instead of being a virago and cuckolding her husband, is piously frigid. She has 'sunken undeveloped breasts, shaped like a flat board against the bedclothes'. On their wedding night she turned all the holy pictures to the wall and sprinkled them with holy water. She is now a confirmed invalid. Joseph Timmins has lecherous thoughts about a maid, whom by the end of the story he has got as far as embracing when his nephew enters the room and catches him in the act. As Joseph has a reputation for morality and self-control, to the nephew he appears a hypocrite, and this is his 'fall', a fall of reputation. But to the reader the development of Joseph's thoughts which is very well managed, has revealed a lonely, frustrated man. This story is much more subtle than 'Unclean' because Joseph has been revealed three-dimensionally, by the narrator, by the other characters and by himself. The same ironic implications are conveyed as in 'Unclean'.

'The Sinner' tells of the early married troubles of Buster and Julia Rogers. The narrative point of view is at times weak, there are clichés and two weak authorial intrusions. Julia, in the same way as the protagonist of 'The Mirror' is a whimsical figure, too obviously the author's puppet. Her behaviour is improbable as, during the story, she runs through the gamut of a whole range of emotions.

Michael H. Murray has said of O'Flaherty, 'Whenever he rejects the straight narrative told for its own sake for the short story of philosophical statement, artless grace gives way to inappropriate imagery, careless structure and tedious repetition'.[9] Although the 'whenever' makes this too sweeping a statement, it does apply to half of this story. The other half is successful. The best passages are the dialogue between Sally the maid and Julia, and the farcical episode when the well-bred Julia masters her husband by beating him with an ashplant.

The only sin, according to O'Flaherty, is through lack of love not to realise oneself fully as a human being. This self-abuse can take the form of self-indulgence, as with Buster, or self-protective puritanism, as with Julia, and both are equally degrading.

Both the remaining stories to be considered here, 'Charity' and 'The

Inquisition' were published in *The Tent*. The former is also about a character who has not yet realised himself, and is a good sketch of a drunkard. Except for short descriptions at the beginning and the end it is written entirely in dialogue.

O'Flaherty most often shows priests who are grasping and hypocritical, but the Father Waters of this story shows no signs of this. Reddon's argument is that though a drunkard, he is still a gentleman. As a drunkard he steals, as a gentleman he refuses charity. According to his muddled thinking he has come to the priest because 'Your business is to deal with drunkards and scoundrels and thieves . . . If there are no poor and sick, what use are you? You belong to me because I am a drunkard'.

As he is about to leave, the priest, pitying his abnormality, gives him money. It is now the priest's turn to be reduced to hopeless tears as he thinks. 'What am I to do? He'll come again in a few days and the same thing will happen'.

Michael H. Murray has called this story and 'The Inquisition' together with 'Offerings' and 'The Outcast' explicitly drawn diatribes against the Catholic clergy and says O'Flaherty's aim in both is 'an exposition of "truth" and he relegates his narrative to a mere vehicle designed to deliver the message'.[10] The theme of 'Charity' is, however, stated by its ironical title. This priest is in fact the only character among all those being considered in this chapter, who is shown to have any idea of the meaning of love. Why is the priest crying at the end of the story? For the man Reddon might have been, or once was? For the gulf between the ideal of charity and its practice? For Reddon's suffering which he is powerless to alleviate? Or because the priest is sorry for himself?

'The Inquisition' connects with the later published 'The Parting', considered in Chapter 2. The protagonist is probably based on O'Flaherty himself, for in *Shame the Devil* (pp. 20–1) he gives a description of how, aged thirteen, he was sent to the Holy Ghost Fathers as a postulant, but when the time came to take the soutane he refused to do so. Cleary in this story is sixteen and could easily be the Michael Joyce of 'The Parting' three years later. He is a postulant in a religious order who rebels against the restrictions imposed on his mental liberty. The sin for which Cleary is made to feel guilty is buying forbidden cigarettes. The story relates the development of Cleary's mental state until by the end he has decided to free his soul from 'these terrible exponents of dogmas that were now its enemies', before all the love in his soul has been killed.

Michael Sheehy has remarked on the similarity between the state of mind of Cleary in 'The Inquisition' and Stephen Dedalus in *A Portrait of the Artist as a Young Man*;[11] though the sixteen year old Stephen is a much more self-conscious and aware person than Cleary. Cleary's aspiration is, however, not far from the thought expressed by Stephen. 'His soul had arisen from the grave of boyhood, spurning her grave clothes.

Yes! Yes! Yes! He could create proudly out of the freedom and power of his soul, as the great artificer whose name he bore, a living thing, new and soaring and beautiful, impalpable, imperishable'.[12]

Cleary's hatred is hatred of everything he now knows to be false, not a hatred of everything he hopes to discover. His new cosmos must be built on light, love and peace. This is an implied criticism of the Christian seminary whose teaching has inspired him with none of these things. Leading up to Cleary's vision of his new cosmos are passages in the story referring to darkness, terror and hatred. Fr Harty is an embodiment of the terrible dogmas that made men do such cruel things.

'The Inquisition' was chosen for special mention and printed by E. J. O'Brien in his volume *The Best Short Stories of 1926* (London, 1927), which he dedicated to Liam O'Flaherty. In the preface to this volume O'Brien wrote, 'The first test of a short story, therefore, in any qualitative analysis is the test of how vitally compelling the writer makes his selected facts or incidents. This test may be conveniently called the test of substance'. He adds that a second test is also necessary, the test of form.

The substance of this story is too well integrated, the character of Cleary too realistic and compelling for the story to become merely an explicitly drawn diatribe against the Catholic clergy, as Mr Murray believes. It does, however, contain a strong denunciation of that travesty of Christian love created by fanaticism, of which the priests themselves are also victims. At the priest's insistence Cleary betrays his comrades and with this action despises himself and the avenging God, for whom Fr Harty has set himself up as mouthpiece. Cleary now realises that love based on fear is impure and he decides to gain his physical as well as his mental freedom. The structure of the story is built up by its controlled view-point, which moves easily between Cleary's own and that of the narrator, so that Cleary's thoughts and sensations are expressed both subjectively and objectively. There is also a dialogue between Cleary and the priest resulting in a third view of Cleary when his speech is contrasted with his thoughts.

The story begins on a note of dread and ends on a note of exaltation. There is narrative irony in this for both states are false. The story ends in mid-air for the physical action of Cleary is less important than his mental state.

As only two stories with urbanised characters were written after 1932 there is less evidence of change in narrative structure in this group. Treatment of the themes is, however, revealing.

Roland Barthes, the French critic, has said:

Literature, since it consists at one and the same time of the insistent offering of a meaning, and the persistent elusiveness of that meaning, is definitely no more than a language, that is, a system of signs; its being lies not in the message but in the system. This being so, the critic is not called upon to reconstitute the message of the work, but only its system . . . [13]

O'Flaherty's system in this group of stories — as mentioned at the beginning of this chapter — is to use the anecdote rather than the completed action plot. It is only in his later work that plots become predominant. Six stories are not anecdotes but the others all have 'open' endings upon which the reader can put his own interpretation, or they are part of an action which initiates or reveals a state of mind.

Only three stories 'The Sensualist', 'The Terrorist' and 'The Sniper' have dominating themes so that the characters remain illustrative types. This is appropriate in 'The Sniper' where the character stands for a universal soldier, and the situation is strong enough to bear the theme; but 'The Sensualist' is a weak story because both theme and characterisation are hackneyed. In 'The Terrorist' the character creates the situation but he is unconvincing, here the theme is a part of the character (Quigley's obsession), so the story fails. The characters of 'Wolf Lanigan's Death' are also illustrative but here again, as in 'The Sniper', the strong story-situation carries them with it.

In all the other stories the motivation is revealed by the unfolding plot and the characters are representational, though — as has been remarked in respect of some stories — they are not always sufficently revealed, usually because of a badly handled narrative point of view.

In 'The Inquisition', 'The Tramp', 'Josephine' and 'The Tyrant' the moral or didactic element takes the form of satire against the church and social ambition, but only in 'The Tyrant' is the didacticism tiresome. There is satire combined with comedy or melodrama in 'The Sensualist', 'The Sinner' and 'The Fall of Joseph Timmins', which are all concerned with aspects of sexual lust.

Nature keeps well in the background in all stories except 'The Mountain Tavern'. Nature is mentioned in passing in 'Josephine' and 'The Tramp' and used as an image of escape in 'The Tyrant'.

The thoughts expressed by the characters are never very profound, nor are the qualities most of them display attractive. We are shown plenty of hypocrisy, conceit, indecision, dishonesty, selfishness, greed or lust, cunning and self-aggrandisement, cruelty and terror. We see no normal family life and all the couples portrayed are trying to exploit each other in one way or another.

Urbanised man in these stories is shown as highly self-centred, while man at war is warped. It is evident from these stories that O'Flaherty is disillusioned with the urbanised Irishman. Sean O'Faolain, in a gentler way than O'Flaherty, expressed his opinion of his fellow-countrymen when he said:

It suddenly broke in on me that Ireland had not adjusted herself to the life about her in the least little bit. Irishmen in general were still thinking about themselves, or rather, in their usual way, double-thinking or squint-thinking ... to dodge more awkward social, moral and political problems than any country might, with considerable courage, hope to solve in a century of ruthless thinking ... But when it comes to writing about people who, like the Irish of our day, combine beautiful, palpitating tea-rose souls with hard, coolly calculating heads, there does not seem to be any way at all of writing about them except satirically or angrily.[14]

Nevertheless O'Flaherty's primary purpose in writing these stories was not criticism of the Irish but criticism of man in general. There is, too, an underlying vein of self-criticism, because O'Flaherty is often himself more involved with his characters than he should be — hence, the occasionally intrusive author. He is far from being an impassive writer.

This personal involvement is expressed by O'Flaherty in *Two Years* where, following upon an arrestingly visual description of a dosshouse where he is spending the night he asks himself:

Are these my own, normal eyes, that see these men, distorted from the shapes and portraits of kindly beings into dark, rabid ghouls? Or has some ghoul made my own soul darker than the soul of a most brutal murderer, or that an epilepsy of my sight fashions darkness, sin, and bestial ugliness on every face I see?

... And then a counter exaltation raised me up, and I saw a beautiful purpose in this vision of human ugliness, such as da Vinci saw, following the carts of doomed men to the gibbets, or Goya gaping at the dead that hung rotting in the noose. And I said almost aloud: 'Have you forgotten so soon? Henceforth this is your great curse as well as your great happiness, to see the souls of men naked and even the most foul a brother to your soul, which contains it. Bow down, even like the simple peasant who kisses the bountiful corngiving earth. For the most criminal of these gives you a rich gift, the substance of beauty.[15]

By presenting urbanised man from a biased view-point, by showing the bestial effects of war on man, O'Flaherty has not only shown the dangers to man's humanity inherent in these ways of life but he has attempted to create a sordid beauty. It can be inferred that O'Flaherty fears within himself a loss of the power to love, and that he has in these stories used the weapons of satire and horror to force both himself and his readers into greater self-awareness.

Man's behaviour in these stories cannot be called 'nearest the animal', he is far too self-conscious for that, but they do stress the dehumanising effect that war and town life may have.

4 Man in Community: The Teller and the Tale

The rest of O'Flaherty's stories which amount to more than half of those he wrote, are on rural themes, or about man oriented towards the country, and most of the characters are peasants. Men are shown working with rather than against each other, so often a group of characters is involved and we see the more complicated reactions of men to community life. In some of the later stories, however, a confrontation occurs between traditional and new ways of life – rural and urban man meet.

The general tone of these stories is one of affectionate or ironic good humour. The restless ferocity of the novels makes only occasional appearance. One story, 'The Ditch', contains violence, and two stories, 'Offerings' and 'Poor People', are satirical. There are many humorous sketches written in a pure spirit of fun, such as 'Selling Pigs' and 'The Stolen Ass'.

From a narrative point of view there is considerable variation. All the narrative techniques mentioned hitherto are used, but in addition more first person narration and editorial intrusion appears and some stories are tales, that is stories with developed plots in which the time sequence is either retrospective or progressive over a protracted period.

This chapter will consider these stories from a narrative point of view through, (a) editorial intrusion and first person narrative; (b) the structure of the tale and (c) the treatment of later stories written in dialogue dealing with the confrontation of new ideas, or new versus old ways of life.

Editorial intrusion occurs in 'Trapped' and 'The Sinner'. In the former the intrusions are effective and in the latter they are unnecessary. First person intrusion is an early characteristic in O'Flaherty's work and may point to (a) the difficulty he had in remaining impersonal or controlling his point of view, and (b) to a subconscious imitation of the oral story-teller, to whom O'Flaherty must often have listened in his youth.

These intrusions usually consist in short phrases or sentences. Such intrusions occur in four early uncollected stories: 'A Grave Reason' which ends 'So do we'; 'The Cake' where the narrator intervenes with a personal reminiscence about the protagonist; 'Idle Gossip' where the interjection

'Why, I don't know' appears; and 'Limpets' where the narrator makes a first person remark in parenthesis.

There is also a group of early tales in which the narrator intervenes by associating himself with the peasants so that phrases appear such as 'our western land', 'live among us', 'our village', 'our district', 'our part of the country', and there are some first person singular interventions from the narrator. In a tale these interventions are more effective than in the stories. They give the illusion of written-down oral narration, for the omniscient old bard was personally present, and also bring the narrator close to his characters. Tales in which such interventions occur are 'The Mermaid', 'The Old Hunter' (where the intruding narrator takes over the end of the story), 'Red Barbara' and 'The Caress'. In 'Stoney Batter' there are also eye-witness narrative intrusions.

O'Flaherty used the 'I protagonist'[1] technique in two early stories 'A Tin Can' and 'Swimming' which both purport to be autobiographical anecdotes from his childhood and the early tale 'Irish Pride'. He used the 'I witness' narrator technique twice, in the personal impressionistic sketch 'A Public House at Night', and in 'A Fanatic', one of his latest tales. As these two stories were written about thirty years apart it is interesting to note that the 'I' of the early story is more emotional but less compassionate than the 'I' of 'The Fanatic'. The characters in the early story are given no direct speech whereas in 'The Fanatic' the narrator and protagonist converse at length. Both stories are set in dingy taverns, both have the same air of nightmarish unreality, yet in the early story the narrator states 'let that horrid fellow dream his mad, ferocious dreams . . . ,' and remains personally untouched by what he sees; but in the late tale the narrator ends 'now it was through pity that I shuddered, not at all through fear'.

The four tales in which a first person narrator is used are 'The Black Mare', 'The Old Hunter', 'Irish Pride' and 'Proclamation'. 'The Black Mare' is the most traditionally oral of all O'Flaherty's stories.[2] The protagonist/narrator addresses himself to the interlocutor in person, calling him 'Stranger, who has been in many lands across the sea'. The story of this exceptional mare is in the Gaelic tradition of the wondertale. There is a high incidence of imagery, some of it a typical Christian/pagan mixture. The story-teller uses proverbs twice, 'talk of beauty today, talk of death tomorrow', and 'the laugh is the herald of the sigh' introducing anticipation – an oral tradition – for in the end the beautiful horse is destroyed. The speech rhythms and tendency to hyperbole are also those of the spoken tongue in for example, 'back over the strand again we went, the black mare and I, like lightning flying from the thunder, and the wave that rose when we passed the rock in the west had not broken on the strand when we turned again at the sand bank'. The story-teller, Dan of the Fury, is recounting in retrospect this tale of his youth. Not only does he recapture the scene of the horse race visually, but with a gesture he indicates the scene giving an illusion of actual presence when he says 'you see that strand . . . '. We have to imagine the movement of the sweeping arm which he here must make.

Professor Delargy has said that 'the film is the modern folktale'.[3] Both A. E. Coppard and Elizabeth Bowen compared the short story to the film,[4] for visual images now take first place over the speaking voice. O'Flaherty has a vivid visual imagination, yet he comes from an oral community. Perhaps it was the difficulty of conveying gesture and facial expression in print that led O'Flaherty in his early work to pay more attention to colour and sound; to forsake the traditional method of *oratio recta* for one of narrative description. It was only as he gained confidence and personal detachment as an author, that he increasingly wrote tales, at first with intrusions from the narrator and later without. At the same time his later stories present his characters more dramatically by means of dialogue.

In the first person tale, 'The Old Hunter', there is structural evidence of O'Flaherty writing down a story in the modern concept — dialogue plus descriptive visual summary, which also serves the purpose of comment or conveys the passage of time, and then lapsing into the older tradition in which you listen and watch the story-teller's face.

'The Old Hunter' starts with an omniscient narrator and dialogue. In generalised commentary there is the first introduction of an oral tone when the present tense is used and we follow behind Mullen and the horse until they arrive at the smelly drain. Then in the second half of the story the narrator suddenly intrudes personally with 'in the following April another extraordinary thing happened to the horse. I must say that he had improved considerably during the winter'. At the end of the story the narrator again appears with 'and then two months ago I met Mr Mullen . . . .' It appears from this ending that the story was in the first place supposedly related by Mullen to the narrator, and is here retold by the author/narrator who has intervened in person. The intervention effects a pause in the tale as the point of view shifts.

The tale 'Proclamation' has a first person narrator introducing a first person statement. It is the only story of this type O'Flaherty wrote. The narrator introduces the protagonist's written statement, which he supposedly reads aloud, as an extraordinary document which 'in my opinion, tells the story of the murder with remarkable clarity'. In his letter of proclamation the protagonist, John Considine, Brigade Commandant in the civil war, attempts to explain how he fell 'through the callous ingratitude of people in high position'. The letter is full of narrative irony. It is written in rambling style and then drops into dialogue. The casual tone of the letter contrasts with the unpleasant story it relates.

'Proclamation' shows deliberate confusion of narrative techniques and styles. The letter opens with an attempt at stilted formality explained by 'the public official connected with education' who the writer says has helped him; but abbreviations, colloquialisms and exclamations increase until the epistolary style is abandoned in favour of dramatic dialogue, almost as if Considine were illiterate and dictating to a scribe. The confused styles effectively add authenticity to the narration and increase the narrative irony.

O'Flaherty wrote no first person novels and to judge from these few stories the use of the first person was a narrative technique which he found too limiting.

O'Flaherty has written nineteen tales, only four of which 'Accident', 'The Flute Player', 'Grey Seagull' and 'Proclamation' are not about peasants. Yeats once told the young James Joyce: 'The whole ugliness of the modern world has come from the spread of towns and their ways of thought, and to bring back beauty we must marry the spirit and nature again'. This opinion is echoed by O'Flaherty in *Shame the Devil*.[5] In his rural tales he creates characters in whom the spirit is married to nature. He is concerned with the forces at work which are attempting to effect, or in some cases have already effected, the spirit's divorce.

There is one tale, 'The Black Mare' in the *Spring Sowing* volume, two in *The Tent*, 'The Old Hunter' and 'Stoney Batter', four in *The Mountain Tavern* 'The Fairy Goose', 'The Child of God', 'The Painted Woman' and 'Red Barbara', and seven other uncollected tales 'Patsa or the belly of Gold', 'Irish Pride', 'Proclamation', 'It was the Devil's Work' 'The Mermaid', 'The Caress' and 'Accident' all written by 1935. Post-war tales are 'Two Lovely Beasts', 'The Flute Player', 'Grey Seagull' and 'The New Suit' (in *Two Lovely Beasts*), and 'The Fanatic' (*The Pedlar's Revenge*).

In 'Stoney Batter' O'Flaherty has written a complex tale of community life in a village with some social commentary but this remains implicit because of the narrative technique. As a child the narrator knew Stoney and can therefore describe how his reputation and status deteriorated over the years. The narrator's point of view is limited, however, for he remarks 'as far as I know', 'I don't remember', 'I remember the day well', or 'here it is best to skip over a period of eight months as I have no definite knowledge of what happened myself'. Avoiding thus the possibility of an objective judgement the didactic element of the story is weakened; irony arises from the narrator's limited viewpoint, and his personal identification with the villagers creates authenticity.

When this limited narrator presumes to omniscience, as in the scene after nightfall between Louise and Stoney, when he could not possibly have been present, the story takes on a fictitious air, and — as in all personally related stories — the reader subconsciously allows for the narrator's subjectivity, for facts based on hearsay rather than knowledge. This too has the effect of removing the implied social commentary into the background.

Beneath the humorous vein in this story nevertheless lies the conclusion that if an individual loses his self-respect and is abandoned by his family, if he refuses to maintain the 'exemplary' standards of his community, he will be thrown out, even though guiltless, even though as a younger man he was 'hero in our village and over the whole parish', for traditional peasant society is fickle to the non-conformist.

A personal narrator who is one of the people is also used in 'Red Barbara' as the spokesman of the people's ideas. The action of this tale stretches over several years. The narrator remains throughout detached from the externalised characters Barbara and Joseph, of whom he says, 'it seemed that she had somehow asserted mastery over him'. He is sufficiently detached to present the points of view of both characters yet by being one of the people he conveys implied sympathy with their traditions.

'Red Barbara' hovers between its realistic and its symbolic content for the characters are illustrative types. Red Barbara stands for earthy fertility, and Joseph for the man of creative mind but impotent body. Throughout the story the accepted norms of the villagers are stressed by the narrator. There is very little dialogue so the characters remain distant, revealed only by their background and actions which are all to some extent symbolic. O'Flaherty is here aiming at a poetic and dramatic rather than a psychological reality, and the type characters illustrate the conflicting issues of tradition and change in Aran peasant society. The symbolic effect is stressed by the use of rhetorical phrases such as 'And lo! He whose fair hair curled in a straight line on his forehead like a ram, had no issue'. But the cultivated flower to which Joseph is also compared gradually becomes wild and goes to seed. This is conveyed by the progression of the seasons. After Joseph's death weeds quickly choke his carefully cultivated garden.

The traditionalist villagers reject Joseph's ideals on 'how life might be improved and how a new race of men could be produced by making the world beautiful'. To them beauty is a part of strength not gentleness, life is a struggle against death, a vital, fertile body is more important than a vital, fertile mind, and 'it was not pleasant, but it was the custom among the people' for the wife to wait outside the tavern while the husband got drunk.

The community of islanders remains shadowy. Referred to throughout as 'the people', they act as a chorus, and it is significantly 'a woman of the people once more' that Barbara becomes at the end of the story. Although O'Flaherty was more aesthetically than morally concerned when he wrote this carefully constructed tale, Joseph, in the same way as Skerrett, represents the would-be reformer, or the outsider like Fergus in *The Black Soul*. He is the individual struggling against the entrenched habits of a closed community. The civilised versus the primitive. This tale is also representative of the equivocal attitude O'Flaherty himself has towards

Aran. O'Flaherty was the same age as Joseph when he wrote this tale and was as much of an outsider to the community of his childhood as Joseph is.

O'Flaherty's split feelings for Aran appear even more clearly in 'The Child of God' which is related with neutral omniscience except for one passage where we enter Peter's mind. There is a long introductory passage full of circumstantial detail about the characters and background of the O'Toole family. The protagonist has much in common with O'Flaherty himself. Like Peter O'Toole O'Flaherty was born when his parents were both over forty and grew up very close to his mother, as he shows us in *Shame the Devil*. Like O'Flaherty's father, Peter's father was also a Fenian. Like O'Flaherty Peter is sent to a seminary, is expelled, later disappears abroad and returns to Aran unexpectedly. Like O'Flaherty Peter shocks his family by his atheism and his nude paintings, equivalent to O'Flaherty's early unpublished stories about 'society women', though it is not recorded that he ever showed these to his family. This story is important for an understanding of the tensions within O'Flaherty and shows how he regards the peasants with a mixture of distaste and affection.

In this tale the attitude of the O'Toole parents towards their prodigal son is significant.

> The two of them felt in their minds that this strange being, who had been their son, was so utterly remote from them that they were terrified of hearing anything of his past. It is impossible to explain the instinct of peasants, their aversion for anything unlike themselves and their intuition for sensing the presence in strangers of forces which are alien to their own nature.

Peter's mixed feelings are expressed in these two passages: 'And now, when the joy of meeting had passed, the horror had come into his mind. He found himself looking at them with strange curiosity. He saw, for the first time, that their bodies were uncouth. Their faces had that ignorant fear in them, the ignorant fear of the animal looking at a strange thing'. But later, looking at the peasants, Peter finds they have 'strange, beautiful faces, all sombre and dignified; mysterious faces of people who live by the sea away from civilisation; age-old people, inarticulate, pitiless, yet as gentle as children'.

Like O'Flaherty, as we see in *Shame the Devil*, Peter has a gaiety 'born of his "creative mania"' which makes him impervious to emotional ties and he cannot succumb to the wishes of those he loves. Leaving, he realises that his mother believes 'for ever and for ever, even through eternity, where damned souls cry out in anguish, he would be lost to her. Lost for ever'. It is therefore more than a physical parting. This is exactly the situation of O'Flaherty himself as he tells us when describing his visit to his mother's grave (*Shame the Devil*, Chapter 2) and accuses himself of having broken her heart.

The superstitious conservatism and the lovable qualities of the peasants are well conveyed in this tale; also the reactions of violence which arise from fear in the peasants, and from frustration in Peter. Peter's horror at the peasants' ignorant fear turns to aggression. 'He must attack them, all of it. Why had he been drawn back? To attack it, them, everything', which is just what O'Flaherty does in his early novels *The Black Soul* and *Thy Neighbour's Wife* and later in *Skerrett*. His parents and the people fear 'the dominant strange force he represents', a fear which not even family love can overcome. The Church — as in almost all of O'Flaherty's work — acts as an agent of fear, so that when the O'Toole house is stoned and Peter's father rushes out and fearfully flings himself on his knees before the priest, the priest angrily banishes Peter from the parish. Yet in Peter's mother, at the end of the tale, love triumphs. She cannot bring herself to curse her son, and her curses give way to prayer — something which would have been more fitting in the priest.

Events in 'The Fairy Goose' occupy an indeterminate period of time. As in 'Red Barbara' the characters are externalised and remain types. This tale is omnisciently related though some incidents are left to the reader's interpretation. Mrs Wiggins 'possibly seeking to gain popular support, either went into a faint or feigned one'; the priest 'either became ashamed of having beaten the old woman or he felt the situation was altogether ridiculous'. The narrator, by remaining impersonal, by impassively presenting the reactions of both villagers and priest, allows the irony of the situation to speak for itself.

Frank O'Connor has summed up this tale as 'the story of a feeble little goose whom the superstition of her owner turns into the divinity of an Irish village . . . In essence, it is the whole history of religion . . . but because he is feeling rather than thinking, O'Flaherty never permits the shadow of a sneer to disturb the gravity of the theme'.[6]

O'Flaherty maintains such a straight face that the story is at the same time ludicrous and profound. When the goose becomes sacred 'all the human beings in the village paid more respect to it than they did to one another', and neighbouring folk come as 'pilgrims secretly from afar'. But the mass feelings of the villagers towards the goose and its owner change dramatically from respect to hatred after the priest's visit, because the priest has made them fear.

When the departing priest says 'fear God and love your neighbour', he has touched upon a theme which underlies all O'Flaherty's work, for fear and love cancel each other out. Therefore the story ends symbolically, 'these women maintain that the only time in the history of their generation that there was peace and harmony in the village was during the time when the fairy goose was loved by the people'.

A close-knit community must be based on love, and that the object of all the love in this story is a goose is a damning criticism of orthodox Christianity whose tenets have been twisted from a religion based on love to one based on fear. The same incompatibility of love and fear is shown when Red Barbara lies under her husband 'in terror, supine and trembling' because she does not understand him, and 'soon after her fear turned to hatred'. In 'The Fairy Goose', after the goose's death 'it is certain that from that day the natives of that village are quarrelsome drunkards, who fear God but do not love one another'. The implication is that this fear too may turn to hatred — as it does in 'The Child of God' — unless the villagers find another object upon which to lavish their love. It would seem therefore, that O'Flaherty thought deeply before writing this tale and it is only apparently based on feeling because the thought has been successfully expressed in the form of a moral fable.

The superstitious fear of the peasants is again the subject of 'It was the Devil's Work', another tale with type characters and a neutrally omnisciently narrator through whose detachment the satire takes effect; but this tale differs from the others so far considered by being written in dialogue except for short passages of summary and the narrator's conclusion.

Rhys Davies described this tale as having O'Flaherty's 'usual bucolic vigour and hard laugh'.[7] The peasants in it are horrified at the birth of a two-headed calf, and one of them says 'A man might as well pay his money to the village sorceress as to the priest, for all the protection he gets against misfortune'. The simple credulity and dread of natural phenomena to which they attach supernatural significance could — with minor alterations — be the reaction of primitive peasants anywhere. Their religious beliefs and pagan superstitions are inextricably mingled. The whole story is a diatribe against ignorance couched, however, in humorous terms, and upon the way the Church has played on the people's fears encouraging them to be superstitious.

'The Caress', O'Flaherty's next tale by date of publication, contains references to 'our village' and 'our island women', so that the narrator is here again one of the people. This tale also has a high dialogue content and a repetitive element which is a feature of so many of the stories. Showing no particular innovation in narrative technique 'The Caress' is important, however, for the light it throws upon O'Flaherty himself. The tale occurs at the end of *Shame the Devil*, forming the penultimate chapter. Just before he starts to write it O'Flaherty reflects as follows:

> I still have a grievance, whereas I should be free from all malice . . . It was and is really malice, to make them responsible for some imaginary wrong that has been inflicted on me by society. Imaginary, I say imaginary and stress the word, because wrong cannot be inflicted on one as an artist, there being no universal criterion of good and evil by

which the artist can separate those experiences that are positive from those that are negative (p. 249).

How true it is what Dostoieffsky [sic] said, that the more a man concerns himself with generalizations about love for all humanity and setting aright whatever he finds wrong in the construction of human society, the less love he has to waste on his friends and dependants and those with whom he comes directly in contact during his daily life . . . I have gone mooching in search of truth, while shutting my eyes to it wherever I met it . . . The word malodorous no longer stank in my mind, (p. 251).

and after completing the story he ended *Shame the Devil* with 'I have said goodbye to my despair, since it cannot stay the swooping of the carrion crows'.

'The Caress' therefore expresses a new intention on O'Flaherty's part to avoid the bitterness which comes from the tension of personal frustration, to attempt to convey no message in the form of satire. In all the stories he subsequently wrote there is this spirit of detachment and good-humoured tolerance. The change of intention O'Flaherty here decides upon has been critically described by Roland Barthes:

> On peut faire de la littérature une valeur *assertive*, soit dans la réplétion, en l'accordant aux valeurs conservatrices de la société, soit dans la tension, en en faisant l'instrument d'un combat de libération; à l'inverse, on peut accorder à la littérature une valeur essentiellement interrogative; . . . Cette interrogation, ce n'est pas; *quel est le sens du monde?* ni même peut-être; *le monde a-t-il un sens?* mais seulement, *voici le monde, y a-t-il du sens en lui?*[8]

By passing from a state of assertion to one of interrogation, O'Flaherty also passed from the method of telling to the method of showing, and hence increasingly to the dialogue method of presentation — 'here is the world' — without editorial intrusion. The reader is in future always left to draw his own conclusions from the contrasting attitudes presented by the characters, a method only occasionally used before *Shame The Devil* was written. The same spirit of detachment is discernible in his three latest novels *Famine, Land* and *Insurrection*, but not in *Hollywood Cemetery* where the personal disillusionment experienced in the filming of *The Informer* caused a return of frustration.

'The Caress' is therefore a tale of pure entertainment. It reverts to a theme already used in an early sketch 'Match-making' but here greatly expanded. There is considerable variation of mood and tempo in this tale, some excellent dialogue and lyrical prose passages. The aging suitor Delaney, significantly described as 'malodorous' and 'unseemly like a rampant goat, which at the fall of autumn goes abroad upon the crags', is vanquished by drink and worsted by the young and optimistic. By the end of the story his drunken body is laden 'like a corpse' on the horse's back. He — by illustrating the destruction of the evil principle — is emblematic of O'Flaherty himself.

From this detached intention, apparent in O'Flaherty's later tales and stories, there arises not only a more oblique revelation of character by the multiple selective narrative viewpoint, but also a less definite idea of what the author intends his reader's reaction to be. A moral conclusion is implicit in the tale of Stoney Batter, but when we come to 'Two Lovely Beasts' the moral conclusion is ambiguous, for O'Flaherty has here, as Stephen Dedalus recommends, refined himself out of existence.

O'Flaherty however, disliked shopkeepers. In *A Tourist's Guide to Ireland*, speaking of the gombeen man, O'Flaherty remarked, 'it is the decent human being who is most easily and surely broken by an overwhelming oppression . . . It is the cunning type of peasant who rises out of this hellish life'.[9] In 'The Red Petticoat' he tells how a cunning peasant gets the better of a cunning shopkeeper. In 'Mackerel for Sale' he shows the returned emigrant, Bartly Tight furiously inveighing against the decadence and apathy of the villagers who, he says, are in the power of priests, gombeen men, shopkeepers, police and lawyers. In 'Two Lovely Beasts' there is no hint of approval or condemnation from the narrator, and both sides of the situation are presented through the characters.

The time is the 1939—45 war, the action takes place over more than a year, and the tale, told largely in dialogue, is of how Colm Derrane, 'the cunning type of peasant', succeeded in raising himself from his hereditary penury to become a shopkeeper, but at great physical and social cost to himself and his family. According to Derrane, as he constantly repeats, all his family need is courage. He shows the same ruthless and cunning courage as we find in 'The Seal', equal to the foolhardy physical courage shown in 'Grey Seagull', or the proud moral courage of Miss Newell in 'The Eviction', and courage with O'Flaherty covers a multitude of sins. Gorum, the village leader, represents the community's point of view. 'That's how we live here in our village by helping one another . . . We only manage to live by sticking together . . . Whoever tries to stand alone and work only for his own profit becomes an enemy of all'. This is what happens to the Derranes. In the end they leave the village in their new jaunting car to live in a town as shopkeepers where people will not know they were once poor. Gorum, who utters a prophetic refrain of disaster at intervals in the tale, shouts a farewell, voicing the vituperative impotence of the oppressed.

Because the points of view are expressed directly through the mouths of the characters we are left with several questions. Can a man from such a background rise above it without losing some of his humanity; and if he does is he to be condemned for his selfishness or praised for his courage? Is it wrong to be ambitious and ashamed of poverty, for what after all is progress? The future life of the Derranes is unimportant. The tale is about their break from community life, a break more difficult to achieve than by the more usual means of emigration.

In these tales, because of the longer time sequence and varied scene, O'Flaherty is able to present a progressive type of action with changing or developing attitudes. The result is a more complex plot structure than that found in the stories.

In *A Tourist's Guide to Ireland* O'Flaherty made a number of serious and mocking remarks about the Irish peasantry. Serious is his opinion that, 'while I do not ascribe to our peasants in their present state any excellent qualities of civilisation and culture, I see in them the germ of future greatness'; mocking is his comment, 'just as the child is a menace to the household, so is the peasant a menace to society and good government'.[10] In O'Flaherty's rural community stories and tales he illustrates the pressures from without which are breaking up Irish peasant society. These may be economic, causing dispersion of the family, as he shows in 'The Letter' and 'Going into Exile'; or there may be exploitation of the peasant from within the community by the gombeen man or publican, as shown in 'The Red Petticoat' and 'Mackerel for Sale'. He also shows the intransigence of superstitious ignorance aroused in the peasant against those who seek to alter, or escape from the traditional way of life in 'Red Barbara' and 'Two Lovely Beasts'; and the role of the Church in hindering rather than fostering the peasants' education in 'The Fairy Goose' or 'It was the Devil's Work'. Yet the peasant is shown to be possessed of courage and loyalty and has a great potential for development, and this is evident from the themes chosen for O'Flaherty's late peasant stories such as 'The Blow', 'The Post Office', 'The Pedlar's Revenge' and those published in *Two Lovely Beasts*. Of this volume of stories George Brandon Saul remarked: 'Nor does *Two Lovely Beasts* contain much of the wildness common to his earlier work. Indeed, it has less emotion than emotion recollected in tranquillity ... O'Flaherty seems mainly interested in offering a group of characters without much special significance in themselves ... And their presentation is curiously casual, for the narrative rarely carries the reader to any point of particular significance'.[11] All these late stories have a social interrogative value.

From the point of view of narrative structure the significance of these late stories is that, if we exclude the three animal stories and the two descriptive pieces 'Light' and 'The Tide', we are left with eleven stories and four tales in the *Two Lovely Beasts* volume, ten of which are written almost entirely in dialogue. To these ten we can also add 'The Post Office' and 'The Pedlar's Revenge' published elsewhere. Before 1930 O'Flaherty wrote only six dialogue stories, 'The Tramp', 'Josephine', 'Selling Pigs', 'The Stolen Ass', 'Match-making' and 'Mackerel for Sale'.

Many of the characters in the late stories are old people, and many are victims of circumstances. Their reactions to frustration vary; they can take refuge in fantasy-relationships as do Nuala in 'The Wedding' and Jones in 'The Flute Player'; they can react with courage and dignity to blindness in 'The Beggars', to old age in 'Galway Bay' or social downfall in 'The Eviction'; or they can become perverted and bitter as in 'The Lament' and 'The Pedlar's Revenge'. What is common to almost all these stories is that the characters take charge through the dialogue method of narration, or through the narrative or dialogue flashbacks which help to reveal their state of mind.

These stories appear casual and rarely carry the reader to a significant conclusion because the author or narrator remains completely detached and the characters themselves have become more important than the action; something which points to a greater sense of humanity in O'Flaherty himself.

Two earlier stories in which individuals attempt and fail to stimulate the peasants were 'Red Barbara' and 'Mackerel for Sale', but in four late dialogue stories O'Flaherty shows the open confrontation of the old order with the new.

In 'The Eviction', a story spoilt by over-melodramatic treatment, we see the Anglo-Irish Newell, once 'the most notorious rackrenter in the whole of the west' being evicted from Barra Castle. The two flashbacks in the story are related by characters and the omniscient narrator intervenes only briefly at intervals to describe the scene. Major Newell is a paralysed old man, and his sister — as brave in her own way as the elderly rider in 'Grey Seagull' — is very British in her mixture of sentimentality and arrogance; but for her loyalty to her brother, and her dignity in the face of humiliating circumstances she deserves admiration.

The Irish attitude is divided. There is the group of old servants who have worked at Barra Castle since their childhood. 'None of them had received any wages for the past ten years, since the collapse of the Newell family fortunes. Yet they stayed on through long habit and a sense of loyalty'. There is Hurley, a local solicitor, and Geraghty of the Civic Guard who says of the Newells, 'You can't help feeling sorry for them'; and there is Festus Lynch, now the strongest man in the country, who has waited forty-six years to claim his revenge against the Newells. When Hurley suggests Lynch should 'let bygones be bygones' Lynch becomes hysterical and tells the story of his Mother's eviction by Newell. Lynch's hatred may be justified but nevertheless, says Hurley, 'to see a kind man turned into a savage by bitterness' is shocking, and it is also cowardly to kick the fallen.

The sense of interrogation left by this story is that perhaps the dignity of *noblesse oblige* shown by Miss Newell — an authority based on unshakable self-confidence — is something which is lacking in the new Ireland. None of the Irish characters seem confident, least of all Lynch who would otherwise show more magnanimity. A new order ruled by Lynch and based on revenge will be no more successful than the old oppressive rule of Newell.

The same lack of self-confidence is evident in Sheila of 'The Lament'. In this story the action is unimportant and provides a background to the dialogue between Sheila and the Stranger. The fault of the story is that the characters are too obviously vehicles for social comment. Sheila's father the boatman represents the old order, and Sheila the new. But Sheila is confused and bitter. She is dissatisfied with her father's world, disillusioned with the new Ireland, yet too inhibited by traditional attitudes to accept the 'pagan' ideas of the Stranger. She says, 'What's the good of new houses when the spirit of the people is broken . . . they live on the dole and, what's more, they don't believe any more in the old fairy tales'. The Stranger expresses the girl's predicament and also O'Flaherty's favourite theme, when he says,

> The iron heel of superstition is pressed down upon their heads. All this damn fool nonsense about paganism, for instance, and Catholic action. Hatred! that's all you people preach. Why not preach love for a change and see what will happen? Why not believe people are good instead of believing they are possessed by the devil?

The Stranger represents O'Flaherty's ideal Irishman, open, fearless, active and energetic — hence his ironic title. The contradictions in the mind of Sheila and her physical frustration are very well conveyed. She represents the Irishman or woman who is disillusioned with Ireland's so-called divine mission, and takes refuge in fantasy and sterile regret. The fact that she is physically attracted to the Stranger and yet flinches when he touches her is also symbolic of Ireland at large.

In 'Galway Bay' the indefatigable old man who still has all his teeth, whose eyes — like those of a captive hawk — are being captured by death while still in their prime, represents the old order, withered but intact, now something of a laughing stock and an attraction for tourists. The successful blending of this abstract concept with the physical description, character and anecdote about the old man's behaviour on the Aran/ Galway boat, is a mark of O'Flaherty's personal detachment and maturity as an artist.

The old man represents all that O'Flaherty admired in his father's generation and which has already been supplanted to a certain extent by spurious values. He is proud, fearless, witty, outspoken, uncompromising and shrewd. He bides by the life he knows and no other. His pugnacity and bad temper add poignancy to his thought, 'let me die on my feet in the sunlight. Don't let me become a mockery for the wicked and the senseless. Leave me with my strength until I die'. With this old man will die part of the courage, goodness and sensitivity O'Flaherty finds to be the positive qualities of the peasants and which must be weighed in the scale against their negative qualities shown in other stories.

When the old man makes the sign of the cross over the animals we are reminded of the same gesture in 'The Cow's Death', for this old man and his 'cow are one. Being in his dotage he is not bound by conventional behaviour and his childlike impetuosity alternates with the wisdom of old age. When the boat reaches Galway 'at the water's edge lay the tall grey houses of the old Spanish town and beyond, the new town rose, bright and arrogant, like the new breed that was conquering the old'. The old man walking up the street now appears as he is, not as he would like to be, his bombast gone, and 'the cow was almost as thin and decrepit as himself'.

'The Post Office', in which the world comes to a remote western Ireland village, is a dramatic mixture of irony and comedy, with its rapidly shifting and subtle dialogue representing juxtaposed trains of thought. There is — as in 'The Lament' — a touch of satire against the new speakers of Irish when the 'poor creatures' who are the peasants, listen to the tourist who speaks the local dialect perfectly and say to themselves in wonder, 'In the world today good Irish like his is only spoken by poor people and a few Government officials. This man is not poor and he looks too decent to be a Government official . . .'

This story is in the form of a colourful dramatic scene set in the Post Office, and the short narrative comments are all in the form of stage directions. Both villagers and tourists are slightly larger than life to bring out the backwardness of this 'obscure and miserable village' and the superficial sophistication of the tourists with their flashy dress and knowledge of foreign languages.

The village with its name Praiseach, meaning 'confusion, disorder and shapelessness', is a microcosm of backward rural Ireland with its people's long folk memory and developed community sense. The postmaster Martin Conlon is also confusion itself, trying but failing to cope with modern changes. He bears some resemblance to Pat Coleman, the Kilmurrage postmaster in *Thy Neighbour's Wife*. His dignity and professional status are challenged by 'the smiling rogue' of a 'foreigner' from Dublin who wants to send a telegram to Los Angeles. The Spanish girl's ironic recitation of Lorca's poetry, which is to form her telegraphed impression of Praiseach, is in curious contrast to the shouts of applause with which it is greeted by the villagers. In fact each time in this story that the villagers shout, applaud or roar with laughter they are providing an ironic refrain, for the laughter is at their own expense.

Lorca's attitude to the primitive Andalusians is not dissimilar to O'Flaherty's attitude towards Aran and western Ireland. There is subtlety in the poetic quotation. O'Flaherty, like Lorca, is on the side of the peasants against the dehumanising effects of civilisation, so many facets of which appal him, but the peasants also stand for a way of life which faces the threat of destruction — hence the first word of the Spanish telegram 'Muerto', with which the story ends. It is significant that the characters in the post office are all old people waiting to draw their pensions and the only young characters are the three strangers. This deliberate accentuation of the generation gap is not accidental.

With the theme of this last story O'Flaherty has come a long way from the simply constructed peasant stories collected in *Spring Sowing* thirty years before. Now the foretaste of the physical disintegration of the old society shown in an early story such as 'Going into Exile' has become a cultural certainty, so that — apart from their literary value — his peasant stories form a valuable record of Irish social change.

5 The Control of Style and Language

From his letters to Edward Garnett two contradictory factors emerge which may explain the variety to be found in the quality and tone of O'Flaherty's literary style.

In several letters O'Flaherty refers to particular effects he is trying, or has tried, to create, thus showing that at times he wrote with extreme care. He tells Garnett 'The Cow's Death' has 'That feeling of coldness' for which he is striving.[1] A month later he again mentions 'The Cow's Death' and remarks to Garnett, 'you taught me to write that one'.[2]

Like many a young writer O'Flaherty was at first irritated at the discipline Garnett suggested he should impose upon himself, the lack of which appears in the formlessness of his first novel *Thy Neighbour's Wife* with its many unwarranted authorial interpolations. We see from an outburst to Edward Garnett that O'Flaherty fought against conscious control over his style. 'Damn it man, I have no style, I don't want any style, I refuse to have a style. I have no time for style. I think style is artificial and vulgar'.[3] Later he tells Garnett, 'I don't think I exert any judgement whatsoever in my writing at the moment of writing but seem to be impelled by the Aran Islanders themselves who cry out dumbly to me to give expression to them'.[4]

On the other hand in 1924 O'Flaherty wrote Garnett a long letter detailing his plan for *The Informer* explaining how he intends to vary the style. It is at first to be 'brutal . . . without finesse, without deviation, without any sweetness, short and curt like a police report'. Later in the book the style would change 'almost imperceptibly' to suit the development of Nolan's character until, when he is shown as a soul in torment the style is 'definitely sympathetic, lengthens itself out, softens, strikes a note of joy in the eternity of nature'. At the end of the book when Nolan makes an attempt to escape 'here the style completely changes and becomes like a wild storm, cascading, abandoned, poetic'.[5]

At times O'Flaherty wrote as a very careful craftsman; at other times he dashed off short stories as pot boilers.[6] He tells Garnett that to draw attention to *The Informer* he has written ten stories in three weeks.[7] The effects of care and carelessness are both evident in the stylistic unevenness of O'Flaherty's short stories.

By creating 'that feeling of coldness' which O'Flaherty mentions in 'The Cow's Death' he has achieved emotional restraint, and the effectiveness of the story lies in the detached simplicity with which it is presented. As a young writer O'Flaherty instinctively realised that to write well he must keep himself out of his work, but he always had difficulty in doing this, and when some form of personal affirmation intrudes his style often breaks down. By expressing satisfaction with the effect he achieved in 'The Cow's Death' O'Flaherty has given us a yardstick by which we can measure the degree of detachment or 'coldness' he achieved, or failed to achieve, in his other short stories. Richard Church, in an extremely perceptive review of *Spring Sowing* remarked:

> I receive at present the impression that he is disciplining himself mercilessly, excising his own temperament to the point of self-discouragement. There is a phrase recurring frequently in the book which betrays him. After some meticulous description, he will round it all off with a weary gesture by the phrase, 'or something', as though he is chafing against his self-imposed task . . . [8]

O'Flaherty aimed at a detached literary personality which must not be so detached that it becomes cold, in the sense of lacking feeling, but must be sufficiently detached to allow the situation to speak for itself. He succeeds in this aim when he gives us a clear exposition of an objectively seen situation, as in 'The Cow's Death'; and fails when he gives us a blurred because subjectively-coloured situation, in which he intrudes his own emotional response to a social situation as in 'The Outcast', or imposes it in a character who is too different from himself to embody it, as occurs in 'The Mirror'.

At his most effective O'Flaherty always uses a mingling of the visual and aural response in his work. This applies both to imagery and choice of words. He is also fond of repetition for immediate emphasis, or in the form of a repetitive refrain.

O'Flaherty defined art as 'not based on a theory, nor on any preconceived dogma but it springs out of life and is brought to life by a vision in the mind of the artist, which, in itself, comes into the mind from a wild fever in the bowels and is inexplicable.'[9] When O'Flaherty's vision remains untransformed, if he allows his subjective feelings to intervene inappropriately, the writing deteriorates, however genuine the inspiration behind the work. This lack of control or detachment can appear in the narrative structure in the form of unwarranted authorial intrusion; it can appear in the tone of his work as waggish satire, to be found in *A Cure for Unemployment, A Tourist's Guide to Ireland*, or in the 'Great Chair! Great Priest!' at the beginning of 'The Outcast'; it can also appear as a certain flamboyancy noticeable in 'The Mirror', 'Beauty', 'The Terrorist' and 'The Ecstasy of Angus'; or it can cause stylistic lapses.

Very often O'Flaherty released his personal emotion in the form of controlled satire, laughter or violence. He remains most effectively detached in his animal stories, and in some of the later dialogue stories in which the characters are allowed to speak for themselves.

That personal involvement can result in inappropriate imagery is illustrated in 'The Landing' where there are two curious similes: 'There was a sudden ferocity in her words that was strangely akin to the rapid charges of the wind coming up from the sea about them, cold, contemptuous and biting like bullets flying across a battlefield fired by unknown men against others whom they have never met, the fierce and destructive movement of maddened nature, blind, and rejoicing in madness'.[10] The comparison of the sea to bullets is an attempt to relate O'Flaherty's own intimate experience of the sea to his experience on the battlefield, for though not many of his readers will be intimate with the sea, many — for this story was written in 1924 — are likely to have known the battlefield. Elsewhere in the story the fishermen's wives are compared to 'the wives of ancient warriors who watched on the ramparts of stone forts while their men fought in front with stone battleaxes against the enemy'. No doubt O'Flaherty here has the Aran forts in mind and the second historically inaccurate use of 'stone' is intended to stress the hard faces of the women. Both these comparisons, however, jar the reader in the context when the enemy is the sea, well-known to these islanders.

In 'Beauty' the breathing of the couple 'sounded like the thudding of two propellers heard distantly from the bowels of a ship'. This simile again relates to a personal memory from the period O'Flaherty spent as a stoker, but its decorum in the context is questionable.

O'Flaherty's subconscious mental preoccupations can, of course, produce effective images as in 'The Sinner' in which Julia beating her husband is compared to a peasant woman beetling clothes at a well. Here, the incongruity of the comparison is amusing and not inappropriate to the theme of the story.

In general the two principal reasons for stylistic breakdown in O'Flaherty's work are technical failure and personal involvement. Technical weakness, due perhaps to O'Flaherty's mood when he wrote, leading to inadequacy of artistic judgement, is responsible for the lack of control over narrative point of view, unnecessary repetition, clichés and other stylistic faults. An unresolved personal involvement causing a lack of detachment can lead emotionally to faulty imagery or floridity of style, and intellectually to obtrusive satire. One suspects that O'Flaherty sometimes uses his writing as a personal outlet and when he does so falls into the trap so neatly defined by Mark Schorer. 'To say what one means in art is never easy, and the more intimately one is implicated in one's material, the more difficult it is. If, besides, one commits fiction to a therapeutic function which is to be operative not on the audience but on the author . . . the difficulty is vast . . . Technique which objectifies, is under no other circumstances so imperative.[11]

Writers usually share with painters the gift of visual imagination. It helps them to remember and 'fix' scenes and faces, or to recreate a scene visually, drawing upon a vivid visual memory. There are numerous passages of description in O'Flaherty's peasant stories which testify to his powerful visual imagination. This is particularly evident in his nature descriptions as in: 'When the foam bubbles are flying in the wind above the cliff-tops on an April day and the gay sun, shining through the rain, is mirrored in their watering globes, they are more beautiful than rare pearls', ('The Mermaid'). Some of his descriptions of characters are so clearly visualised that one suspects they are based on memories of people he has known in his youth: here is the old carpenter from 'A Tin Can' — 'his reddish beard thick with white shavings, his pale face puffed, his loose grey frieze trousers, with the large, black, square patch on the seat, bundled about his waist like a sack'.

That the visual is important to O'Flaherty is also shown in his deliberate use of colour, as in 'The Oar' where the bream have 'gauzy red lips', 'the enchanted light' is described as red over a black sea. 'The hairy yellow anchor rope' refers back to the 'clustering yellow weed' of the previous page. White, black, red and yellow is the lurid colour scheme of the story.[12]

In 'The Blackbird' the light breeze makes 'little whitish ridges' through the dark fur on the cat's back. The dun body of the blackbird, the blackened moss which the cat smells and the pointed grey stones create a deliberately drab colour scheme in keeping with the half-light in which the action takes place.

Another example of O'Flaherty's use of colour is the opening paragraphs of 'Mackerel for Sale'. In the first two paragraphs 'white' occurs six times, 'black' four times, 'yellow' twice, and 'grey' three times. This colour scheme is emphasised not only by the repetition of the same words, but by the use of adjectives such as 'pale', 'spotless', 'silent', 'torrid' and 'sallow', and clinched by the alliteration contained in the last line 'gleaming granite boulders, strewn sparsely, white in the sun'. In 'The Cow's Death' there is an effective visual simile. The breath of the cow 'came in long pale columns, like sunbeams coming through the windows of a darkened church', illustrating the force of the cow's laboured breaths ejected in the form of columns rather than clouds of vapour, and pointing to the underlying mystery of birth and death. This would have strong religious associations for O'Flaherty, however he might attempt to sto shrug off his orthodox Catholic affiliations.

The small actions of O'Flaherty's characters are often important as a pointer to their inner states of mind, especially in his early work where he uses little dialogue, but also in a late story such as 'The Fanatic'. We have an example of this in 'Going into Exile',[13] in which neither parent can quite comprehend the reality of their children's departure. Their inability to express themselves verbally creates an effect of mute suffering. Unspoken feelings which pass between the father and his son and daughter are suggested by physical gestures. Father and son walk about outside and 'yawn without need pretending to be taking the air'. The daughter crushes a handkerchief between her hands, then she finds her father's eyes upon her, his thumbs stuck in his belt.

In many stories O'Flaherty shows his strong visual inclination by the variation of camera angle and distance in his descriptive writing. 'Wolf Lanigan's Death' opens with a long shot of the horse-drawn barge coming slowly down the canal. 'There was no moon, but now and again glaring lights from the tramcars that rattled over the Bridge lit up the dark waters of the Canal, the grey bulk of the barge, the taut rope, the narrow gravel path and the two lean horses walking slowly in single file with their heads drooping'. The aural effect of this passage lies in the rhythm of the prose, suggesting the plodding movement of the horses. When Wolf Lanigan leaps ashore and runs up the alleyway we are given a close-up of what he finds in the shed seen by the light of his torch. After crossing a maze of dark streets he arrives at the corner of a street and we get a perspective view: 'at the end of the street a blaze of light struck him, running low to the ground in parallel lines until it ended in a dark lane at the far end'.

The same method is used in other stories such as 'The Sniper', 'Civil War' and 'The Touch'. In 'The Touch' the story opens with a distant view of the galloping mare seen in terms of white and red. We are gradually brought closer and given a minute description of the rider, Kate Hernon; then the camera's eye moves away again to the grey sand 'dotted with little cocks of the red weed, all the way up the strand from where the waves were breaking'.

In his early work where the dialogue content is small, and in the animal stories, sound also plays an important part and often, like the use of colour, it is used to create atmosphere. In O'Flaherty's later work much of this aural description is replaced by dialogue. An example of the use of sound in O'Flaherty's early genre can be found in 'The Letter'. The story opens with a lyrical passage of description in which the words have been carefully chosen to create both a visual and aural response:

It was a summer afternoon. The clear blue sky was dotted with fluttering larks. The wind was still, as if it listened to their gentle singing. From the shining earth a faint smoke arose, like incense, shaken from invisible thuribles in a rhapsody of joy by hosts of unseen spirits . . . . Everything listened to the singing larks in brooding thoughtlessness. Yea, even the horned snails lay stretched out on grey stones with their houses on their backs.

The passage breathes an air of peacefully rapturous indolence, yet by the end of the story the family, instead of being in harmony with their surroundings, are estranged from them. They weep while the larks sing. Their daughter has not only been torn from her social background, but she will in her new life now become a social outcast. The transition of feeling is stressed by the imagery and vocabulary. In the opening passage the grass blades make gentle sounds 'like the sighs of a maiden in love'. The two girls who bring the letter are images of purity with their 'dainty white pinafores', 'bobbing golden heads', but the continued triumphant singing of larks as the story ends is contrasted with the frenzied despairing wail and harsh sound of the broken human beings.

In another story 'Trapped', sound — it being night — plays a more important part than sight. When the cliff collapses 'the silence was broken by a slight snapping sound like the end of a dog's yawn'. The wings and screams of the birds provide a musical accompaniment to the situation. When in the end Hernon utters a wild yell of relief the sound re-echoes in the sea caves so that the birds rush out screaming and 'the air was full of terrifying sound'.

The importance given to sound in O'Flaherty's early work indicates that he often intends his stories to be heard with the inner ear, but sometimes he also wishes to appeal to the outer ear and some of his work begs to be read aloud. This impression was confirmed when I asked O'Flaherty why he had not written more poetry and he replied 'What is poetry?' and recited the opening paragraph of 'The Oar' as follows:

Beneath tall cliffs,
two anchored curraghs swung,
their light prows bobbing on the gentle waves.
Their tarred sides shone in the moonlight,
In each, three stooping figures sat on narrow seats,
their arms resting on the frail sides,
their red-backed hands fingering long lines,
that swam, white, through the deep dark water.

This is a visual passage written, not only to impress the inner ear, but with oral intent as the heavy punctuation shows.[14]

O'Flaherty uses punctuation to control the tempo as well as the meaning of his words, and attention to his use of punctuation will often give us a clue as to how he intends a passage to be read. Each of the two following excerpts, which contain a sentence without a verb, illustrate this point: 'A sheep rose, cleared her nostrils and began to browse without moving. The queer sound of grass being chopped!' ('The Birth'). 'The Sun rose into the heaven. There was a fierce heat. Not a breath of wind'. ('The

Reaping Race')'.

In the same way that O'Flaherty creates visual effects by means of varied devices such as the use of colour, description of physical action, control of camera angle and distance, and visual imagery, so, when creating sound effects, he uses the appeal to the inner ear by means of imagery, vocabulary, punctuation and the description of sounds. By writing a passage of lyric description such as the opening lines of 'The Oar' he is organising the language, in the same way as a poet does, and thus drawing attention to its sound, an effect which is heightened when the passage is read aloud. Another example would be the opening paragraph of 'Milking Time', the effect of which is only fully apparent when read aloud, using an Irish accent.

In his later stories O'Flaherty passed from the method of telling to the method of showing and the musical or 'sung' narrative present in some of his early work is replaced by the dramatised spoken word. A look through the stories in the *Two Lovely Beasts* volume shows that, subtle though the characterisation often is, there is nothing here to compare in restrained emotional intensity with early stories such as 'The Oar' and 'The Landing'. If the opening paragraph of 'The Oar' is read alongside the opening paragraph of 'The Lament' or 'The Mirror' it will be seen that, though in both of these later stories O'Flaherty is also setting the scene for the story which follows, the prose pales by comparison to the effectiveness of that used in the earlier story.

On the other hand the lyrical impulse still occasionally emerges in the later stories , either in dialogue as when the blind man of 'The Beggars' listens to the music and hilarious shouts on the racecourse and murmurs . . . 'Black, hungry winter is no more and the son of man is dancing on the grass'; or more often it is present in a descriptive story such as 'The Mirror'.

This brings us to the consideration of another typical characteristic of O'Flaherty's style, his use of repetition.

It should be said at once that some of O'Flaherty's repetition is unconscious and due to carelessness. In 'The Sinner', for example, evidence of stylistic weakness occurs not only in the use of clichés such as 'sorely tempted', 'boon companion', 'a transport of passion' or 'wreathed with smiles', but there is also a threefold repetition of 'because' just before Julia jumps out of bed and rings for Sally. In 'The Landing' carelessness occurs in the weak image: 'It was a spring evening and the air was warm and fresh as if it had just been sprinkled with eau de cologne or something', and the word 'something' is repeated a line farther on.

In general, however, it is easy to distinguish between haphazard repetition which contributes nothing and may sound clumsy, and the deliberate repetition used for emphasis, for its euphonic value, or to reproduce speech patterns.

Deliberate repetition to create emphasis, when it is used in a passage of narrative, can take the form of a keyword as with the word 'crooning' at the beginning of 'Milking Time', used in connection with the woman herself, her voice, her lips, her words and her dreaming thoughts. This is not only an associative word symbolic of the woman's future state as a mother, but it also acts as a musical refrain to colour the mood at the beginning of the story.[15]

Repetition may sometimes take the form of linked associative words which carry the emotive content. This is illustrated in 'Blood Lust', towards the end of the story; 'His lower lip began to tremble. His right knee began to tremble. Then the trembling spread all over his body. He felt a desire to yell but he repressed the desire'. Later in the same paragraph other repetitive word pairs occur such as 'forward', 'idea' and 'fear' as the climax is built up by a chain of sensations associated with movements.

In the following passage from 'The Oar' O'Flaherty uses repetition in the way Coleridge uses it in *The Rime of the Ancient Mariner*:

> Suddenly it became more silent. As when lead melts and flows in a silver stream, all smooth, so the wavelets melted into the sea's bosom. Now a motionless black floor supported the motionless coracles. Now there was no moon. Now a black mass filled the sky. From afar a bellowing noise came and then a wave shimmered over a smooth rock quite near. Tchee . . . ee . . . ee, it said.

It is obvious that O'Flaherty is here again drawing attention to the sound effects of the words and using punctuation, repetition and alliteration to do so.

Repetition is also used at the end of 'The Oar' to mark the rhythm of the plunging oars, 'Again the lightning flashed. Again they saw the oar, now hurled aloft sideways. There was no hand grasping its handle. Again darkness came'. The three terse dialogue passages which mark the turning points in this story have also been carefully chosen: 'In the name of God, cut. Cut. Oars out. Cut': 'Strengthen your right hands and keep your faces to the sea. Keep her out': and 'Sense comes before courage. Three widows are enough. Row, you devils. Row'. The story ends with 'We saw an oar by the Serpent's Reef, raised up to heaven with a hand grasping it. It followed us and no hand was grasping it'. All these spoken remarks contain repetition, here a realistic reproduction of speech for the speaker is under emotional stress.

There are many examples of spoken repetition in O'Flaherty's dialogue when the character unconsciously repeats himself, as we often do in speech. An example can be taken from 'The Eviction' when Lynch is looking at Colonel Newell's portrait: ' "I wanted above all", he shouted passionately, "to get that grinning, bloody face into my power. I'll soon take that grin off it. We'll soon see who will be the last to grin. I'll soon fix that face. It won't be grinning long. Upon my oath, that face will soon look different" '. Repetition under stress of excitement also occurs in Aunt Penelope's speech when she is urging Grey Seagull on to win the race, ('Grey Seagull').

The other form of repetition used by O'Flaherty is contained in the form of phrases sometimes identical and sometimes repeated with variation which have the effect of a refrain, either uttered by the same voice, by different single voices or in the form of a chorus. Analysis of O'Flaherty's use of this device shows that although in general it is a rhetorical way of inducing or suggesting emotion, often it also acts as a leitmotiv pointing to the underlying archetypal theme of a story. Repetition is then being used to illustrate the traditional or collective significance behind the story.

Repetition of this type occurs in five of O'Flaherty's earlier stories, 'The Landing', 'Going into Exile', 'The Stream', 'The Mountain Tavern' and 'Red Barbara'; and in six later stories 'Life', 'The Challenge', 'The Wedding', 'The Old Woman', 'The Beggars' and 'The Mirror'. Although 'The Mountain Tavern' is about war, the characters in all these stories are peasants and the settings are rural.

In 'Red Barbara' the repetitive phrases form a chorus which is voiced by the narrator in the form of comments about the villagers' reactions in phrases such as 'the people also grumbled', 'the people marvelled', 'the people learned', 'the people began to whisper', 'the people laughed' and so on. The people's behaviour shows the traditional reactions to an outsider who has come into their peasant community, and this is the theme of the story. Unvoiced and impersonal, 'the people' stand for exclusive tribal man.

In 'The Mountain Tavern' the repetition is contained in symbolic recurring references to the falling snow. O'Flaherty here uses the traditional symbol of snow to represent abstract purity, as a double motif to point the contrast between enduring Nature versus transitory man, and the essential purity of man which he vitiates by doing evil.

The falling snow, though appearing as a description of nature and creating a nature-frame round the story, is therefore introduced with far more subtle intention than just the production of aesthetic effect. Not only does the word 'snow' occur twenty-eight times in this story, but it is repetitively associated in various phrases with derivatives of the verb 'to fall'. In the first paragraph we read: ' . . . There was absolutely nothing, nothing at all, but the falling flakes of white snow, undeflected, falling silently on fallen snow'; falling snow is mentioned five times more in the body of the story such as in 'the snow fell, fell now, in the fading light, mournfully, blotting out the sins of the world'; and it occurs again in the final paragraph: ' . . . Night fell and snow fell, fell like soft soothing white flower petals on the black ruin and on the black spot where the corpse had lain'. 'The Mountain Tavern' and 'Red Barbara' are, however, the only short stories in which O'Flaherty contains the repetition within descriptive narrative.

In 'The Mirror' the repetition takes the form of a series of ejaculations which occur seven times: 'Great God!' 'Good Lord!' (twice), and 'Aie! Aie!' (four times), used as a rhetorical device to draw attention to the emotions or physical sensations felt by the girl. But the presence of the narrator is so strong in this story that the ejaculations, which purport to come from the girl, are inconsistent, the last two being particularly intrusive, for no simple peasant girl thinks of herself in terms of a 'Miraculous chalice of life' or 'a radiant virgin wantoning . . . ' These are the author's description of her naked body mirrored in the pool.

All eight of the remaining stories contain spoken repetition carrying a traditional or collective connotation. In 'The Landing' Mary Mullen says: 'Drowned, drowned they will be', and works herself into a frenzy of fear and lamentation. Twice later she shrieks the same phrase again. The description of her outlined against the sea typifies the situation of many another Aran woman before and after her, widowed and rendered childless by the sea.

In 'Going into Exile' towards the end of the story the keening begins: 'A dismal cry arose from the women gathered in the kitchen, "Far over the sea they will be carried", began woman after woman and they all rocked themselves and hid their heads in their aprons.' Here again these women are not lamenting only these exiles, but all exiles — in fact, the state of being exiled.

This kind of repetition amounting to an archetypal refrain connected to birth, marriage and death also occurs in 'Life', 'The Wedding' and 'The Old Woman'. In 'Life' there is a repeated lament, 'everything is more lasting than man', uttered by the grandfather when he sees his new grandson; varied to 'the longest journey from the womb to the grave is only a short one after all' spoken by a neighbour; and terminated by the grandmother in her lamentation for the newly dead: 'Och! Ochon! . . . Och! Ochon! My love! it was you that was lovely on the day of our marriage . . . '. This lament is counterpointed by a minor theme which, in the same way as the keening, expresses the superstitions of the peasants towards the evil eye, whether it takes the form of death or possible mishap. This is expressed in the form of repetitive and precautionary blessings, 'May God bless you', 'May God preserve the little one', and 'Oh! my darling, you're the love of my heart', applied to the baby but related to the same terms used of the old man in his wife's final lament.

In 'The Wedding' repetition on a theme of marriage is provided by 'unhappy is the bride the rain falls on', spoken by Nuala; 'happy is the bride the sun shines on', sung by the children; and at the end of the story 'an aged woman stood on the threshold of the house, rent her hair and began to chant the wedding lamentation in a shrill voice. She was the bride's mother'.

In 'The Old Woman' there is no keening, but her repeated, 'There are no ugly things in God's world' in response to Julia's 'What horrid things there are in God's world', expresses Maggie's longing for an ideal state and her determination to deny evil.

The orally expressed repetitive phrases in these stories emerge in the form of a keen, an expression of faith, a denial or a wish, as in 'The Beggars' where the blind man repeats, 'I wish you all a happy death. None of you know the hour . . . '. Repetition occurs in 'The Stream' in the form of the hag's incantation, 'Flow on, white water . . . Let nothing that is young be merry, while you flow . . . '. In O'Flaherty's parody of a flyting match, 'The Challenge', a refrain is used deliberately, following the Irish oral pattern.

All these refrain-like repetitions vindicate the positive forces of life in reaction to the fear of death or weakness, sadness or evil, but they also express an elemental sorrow, a struggle against disillusionment and disbelief in a life which man can, at best, enjoy for so short a time. It is interesting in this connection to recall Synge's comments when describing a burying and wake in Inishmaan where, he says, one is forced to believe in a sympathy between man and nature,

> this grief of the keen is no personal complaint for the death of one woman . . . but seems to contain the whole passionate rage that lurks somewhere in every native of the island. In this cry of pain the inner consciousness of the people seems to lay itself bare for an instant, and to reveal the mood of beings who feel their isolation in the face of a universe that wars on them with winds and seas.[16]

Were all O'Flaherty's refrains to voice the feelings, or describe the behaviour, of his peasant characters, we might presume that by using them he is merely being faithful to the traditional habits of life and speech of his people. But the fact that he also uses descriptive narrative repetition in 'Red Barbara' and 'The Mountain Tavern' points to a subconscious as well as a deliberate reason for his using this literary device.

It has already been suggested that the influence of O'Flaherty's early life in a traditional community may be traced through narrative structures, such as editorial intrusion, especially in his early work. It is also suggested that this liking for repetition, which he shows at all stages of his literary development, has been subconsciously affected both by Gaelic speech, and by the story-telling he heard as a child. For a characteristic of the folk-tale is to use formulaic repeated phrases to create a special rhetorical effect. Tom O'Flaherty mentions that in his youth the Aran islanders had stories for each season, and describes how the villagers used to gather every evening in the O'Flaherty home and pass the time telling stories and discussing various subjects, often well into the night.[17]

Vivian Mercier has discussed the closeness of the Irish short story to oral tradition.[18] He favours the view that oral literature has had a direct influence, but he does not find O'Flaherty to be, on the whole, a very oral writer.

It is true that O'Flaherty's stories are an art form intended for the printed page, but his frequent descriptive aural as well as visual effects, his use of punctuation, repetition of words and phrases, all point to the fact that, in some of his stories at least, he expects his reader to listen and not only to visualise his stories, and that his aural and visual imagination were both active when he wrote them. It is probable that O'Flaherty's attention to the aural has been affected by, and perhaps also inherited from the oral culture into which he was born.

Part II:
The Protest of Vitality

6 Man as Part of Nature

Vivian Mercier, in his introduction to the 1956 New York edition of some O'Flaherty short stories, says he believes O'Flaherty's true subject to be the relationship between man and nature but 'even the solace which nature offers to man is unflattering because it leaves him helpless', and he adds that 'over and over again in O'Flaherty's stories the point is made that nature is both friend and enemy; even in the animal stories nature is at war with herself'.

In conversation with Mr O'Flaherty he told me this introduction annoyed him and put a false interpretation on his work. It therefore seems important to see what other conclusion can be arrived at of the relationship between man and nature, which undoubtedly emerges as a central preoccupation in O'Flaherty's work. Nature here stands for the physical aspect of the world of which man's nature or physical make-up is an integral part.

To O'Flaherty nature is not something to be philosophically analysed. Instinctively he turns to nature as a source of spiritual richness and strength to salve unsatisfactory personal experiences, whether social, religious or political. In *Shame the Devil* he tells himself, 'Renew your friendship with nature. In this lies your chance of regaining peace' (p. 217). O'Flaherty's love of nature stems in part from his early environment, so that nature is emotionally connected with Aran and comes to be connected with the spirit of Ireland. As Crosbie expresses it in *The Martyr*: 'All round the sordid town there lay a darling loveliness, that sad Irish loveliness which makes the heart sick with a mystical lust for union with the holy motherland . . . ' (p. 60).

Apart from the physical environment of his formative years and the influence of his mother, who O'Flaherty tells us in *Shame the Devil* was a great nature lover, another traditional factor probably colours O'Flaherty's attitude towards nature; this is the traces that still remain in Aran of the pre-Christian Celtic cult which worshipped Dagda, god of good with the sun-like face, and treated nature as an absolute. This nature worship also appears in Irish folktales, many of which O'Flaherty would have heard as a child. Alfred Nutt, attempting to define the special charm of the Gaelic folktale finds one of its characteristics, common of course to many other national folktales, to be a prevalent animism, 'the acceptance of life common to, not alone man and animals, but all manifestions of force. In so far as a distinction is made between the life of man and that of nature at large, it is in favour of the latter, to which more potent energy is inscribed'. The Gaelic folktale also reveals an 'elaborate system of custom and ritual based upon the idea that between men and the remainder of the universe there is no difference of kind. A concept of the cosmos is thus arrived at which, more than any religious creed, fulfills the test of catholicity'.[1] One could quote many examples from short stories, such as 'The Salted Goat', 'The Black Mare', or 'The Fairy Goose', and the Aran novels, where the speech or action of the Catholic peasants show familiarity with this hereditary animism. It also appears in O'Flaherty's imagery as when in *Mr. Gilhooley* the sun is compared to the monstrance raised aloft by the priest in Benediction or the opening lines of 'The Blackbird's Mate' where the sunbeams are compared to the laughter of a happy God.

Opposed to this animistic view of nature, however, was the biblical view of nature, as interpreted by the Catholic Church, which O'Flaherty must have received in his formal education. In this view man is a special creature added to nature by an act of God, and though he is part of nature his divine soul is the more important part of him. This metaphysical dualism of body and soul has the effect of demoting nature and those instincts and passions of man which he holds in common with animals. It must also be remembered that in O'Flaherty's youth Catholic children were taught that Darwin's theory of evolution was heretical.

The importance given by O'Flaherty to nature is not pagan in a religious sense, except in as far as it reflects the traditional behaviour of the peasants, but rather an attempt to redress the unity between man and nature which had been weakened or overthrown by Christian interpretation particularly by the contemporary doctrinal tendencies of the Roman Catholic Church whereby the supernatural replaced the natural instead of reinforcing it, as O'Flaherty illustrates in 'The Inquisition'. The influence of industrialisation and scientific discovery has also tended to separate man from nature, in that it breeds a sophisticated person, as O'Flaherty shows us in 'The Tyrant'. Although he uses instinctive rather than rational channels of approach O'Flaherty's basic tenet is similar to Teilhard de Chardin's conclusion written in the early 1930s that 'the *only truly natural and real human unity* is the spirit of the earth'.[2] Both writers were, for different reasons, unpopular with the Catholic hierarchy, though what Teilhard de Chardin calls his 'profound tendencies towards pantheism' (op. cit., p. 91) need not be contradictory to Christianity as he attempts to show.[3]

If O'Flaherty is indeed attempting to restore man to his natural birthright a wrong nuance is given by the statement that O'Flaherty was 'the celebrant of timeless mysteries — mysteries rooted in Nature and in that portion of Nature embodied in the life of man'.[4] For O'Flaherty man *is* nature, there is no dichotomy between body and soul, and nature does not destroy man in death except in the physical sense. O'Flaherty appears to believe that perhaps the whole world as known by the human consciousness is related to the world of physical fact in some fashion analogous to the soma and the psyche in the individual man. William Troy, who finds O'Flaherty's work nearer to the early Gaelic folk literature than to any of his contemporaries, is right when he says: 'Neither intellectual refinement nor the impediment of culture and religion operate to confuse the complete identification with nature which is the predominant feature of his work'.[5]

This identity of man with nature means that O'Flaherty's concept of nature cannot be put into a neatly logical formula. Though the use of nature in O'Flaherty's work is so intimately connected with his deepest feelings and beliefs, he has never made a statement of these beliefs, nor would he wish to do so. It would be a mistake to read into his work a philosophical theory of nature or a natural theology. He says 'a poet must understand the truth before he can create poetry, but he must forget it before he can release the energy necessary to sing his song',[6] and to him there is no difference in kind between poetry and the inspired writing of prose. He would, however, be the first to admit that not all he wrote is inspired. O'Flaherty took a number of years to stabilise his ideas and resolve the contradictions inherent in his traditional Aran culture and his Catholic upbringing confronted by other equally irreconcilable elements in the modern world. His views, however, whether he ever formulated them clearly or not, even to himself, ultimately emerge as sympathetic to a concept of the universe as an organism in harmonious development of which man is an integral part. His work charts the stormy passage he made before reaching an at least partial personal resolution of his problems, and such can be inferred from his rebelliousness as a young man.

In August and September 1924 O'Flaherty was behind the publication of the only two issues of a magazine *Tomorrow*. The aim of this paper was to give voice to the non-conformists and radicals opposed to the existing literary order, and O'Flaherty told Edward Garnett in a letter, 'of course I use it merely as a platform for myself'.[7] The editorial policy of *Tomorrow* was that 'no man can create . . . who does not believe, with all his blood and nerve, that man's soul is immortal, for the evidence lies plain to all men that where that belief has declined, men have turned from creation to photography'.[8] This immortality of the soul is humanist rather than Christian in concept, for in an ariticle by 'Sachka' it is stated 'the words we use have been fashioned and turned through myriads of minds like pebbles on a long sea shore. In each thought and shade of feeling are the shades of the dead'.

The August issue of *Tomorrow* caused an outcry, however. Not only did Margaret Barrington's story 'Colour' tell of a white girl physically attracted to a negro, but Lennox Robinson's story 'The Madonna of Slieve Dun', about a girl who dreamt she had been chosen to give birth to Christ, was condemned as blasphemous. After this O'Flaherty, Austin Clarke and F. R. Higgins in turn wrote letters to *The Irish Statesman* recommending revolt not passivity — which is a central principle with O'Flaherty to this day.[9]

From O'Flaherty's contributions to *The Humanist* in 1926 and 1927 we may infer that he also concurred with the aims of this magazine the first editorial of which stated that 'the hope of the world is in religion, but by this we do not mean creedalistic religion'.[10] It is significant that 'The Fairy Goose', about religion as a manifestation of nature, was specially written for *The Humanist*, and that 'Birth', which celebrates the communion of man, beast and nature, was also first published in the same periodical.

O'Flaherty believes that Christianity as interpreted by the orthodox has produced a truncated man, so O'Flaherty had to create a new whole man for himself and within himself. This new man's nature was to be fully integrated in nature. It was the struggle to do this which urged him on. In this struggle, forsaking Catholicism he turned back to physical nature from which he drew sustenance, beauty and peace. The contradictions he found in nature enabled him to resolve some of the contradictions in man. It follows therefore, that if for O'Flaherty man is an integral part of nature it would be false to consider his use of nature without including man's part in it.[11]

The most extended nature/man relationships are to be found in O'Flaherty's novels. Some examples from them will illuminate the treatment of the same relationship in the short stories as a whole, for as Maurice Shadbolt, the New Zealand writer, has pointed out, 'it is no use going to a particular short story in the hope of ascertaining a writer's individual vision as one might go to a particular novel . . . . A story writer's vision may only be seen in the accumulation of his works . . . [12]

Both O'Flaherty's earliest novels, *Thy Neighbour's Wife* and *The Black Soul* are set on the island of Inverara (Aran) in the early 1920s. O'Flaherty attached great importance to these two books. Of the first he told Garnett 'They go into rhapsodies about my short stories but they refuse to discuss *Thy Neighbour's Wife*'; and of *The Black Soul* he said, 'If there is anything in me it's going into it, so you can see my bare soul and measure its worth when you read'.[13] In *Thy Neighbour's Wife*, which attempts to define religion, the pagan and Christian elements of the island culture are brought into contrast. In Chapter 2, for example, where the Midsummer Festivals of St John's Eve are described, we are reminded that these are related to the pagan bonfire feast to the druidic god Crom Dubh. In Chapter V when Father McMahon falls off his bicycle onto the beach, the old woman comes and chants the spell of Crom over the curate, pouring sand from a periwinkle shell over his forehead, while a fisherman also brings holy water from his curragh. McMahon's crooked casuistry in his self-communings in Chapter VI acts as an exposition of the hypocrisy or unconsciously bifurcated allegiances of the other islanders. The pagan/Christian contrast is returned to in Chapter VIII where the annual race meeting celebrates the first recorded race which, according to local folklore, took place on the islands in A.D. 457 between St Patrick and a Druid; and when the half-drunk curate sets out in an oarless curragh — as the holy men of old had done for a penance — there is an exciting account of the struggle between man and the elements in the storm during which all McMahon's pretences drop and he is reduced to 'a mere atom'.

The Black Soul, divided into four sections corresponding to the seasons, is about a human soul related to nature's rhythm. Each section of the book opens with a powerful description of the seasonal landscape or seascape, and the mood of each season is related closely to the mood of the characters. In his hopeless winter mood Fergus O'Connor, who reflects much of O'Flaherty's own character and background, describes his memories of the battlefield, his two years' post-war wandering, and imagines returning to Dublin 'burrowing in the bowels of philosophy, trying to find consolation one day in religion, next day in anarchism, next day in Communism, and reflecting everything as empty, false and valueless' (p. 33). Fergus, like O'Flaherty himself at the time, is still suffering from the after-effects of shellshock. 'The sea and the wind were mad and he felt that he too was mad with them. They were committing suicide in their madness. So would he, but as soon as the thought came it terrified him' (pp. 40–1). Later, lying beside Mary 'like wild nature outside, lying bare in its winter sleep, his soul rested. So they waited, resting, he, she and nature, as if they were waiting in silence together for the beginning of life' (p. 74). This shows man feeling himself to be a part of nature. Later Fergus comes to feel kinship with the fish prowling in the depths — a kinship which, to judge from his animal stories O'Flaherty himself must also have felt.

After this, except for *The Wilderness*, *Skerrett*, *Famine* and *Land* — the last three set in the past — O'Flaherty's novels have a largely, if not entirely, urbanised setting. *The Informer, Mr. Gilhooley* and *The Assassin* roughly correspond datewise with the most violently realistic period in the short-story writing, and to a period of considerable personal disillusionment, financial strain and bad health. *The Informer* was badly received even though it won the James Black Tait Memorial Prize (1926). 'Y.O.' reviewing the book in *The Irish Statesman* called the characters monstrosities from the abyss, who react like blind infuriated animals.[14] A reviewer of *Mr. Gilhooley* called the book 'a matter of unrelieved gloom to every character in it'.[15] Gilhooley is described in the novel as 'a distant, slender root, withering in barren soil, yearning for the mother sap' (p. 183). The protagonists of all three novels, Nolan, Gilhooley and McDara, are tormented individuals, like McMahon and O'Connor in the two earlier books, but these three are captive to town life and estranged from their right relationship with nature.

In *The Assassin*, McDara — a thinly-disguised author figure who is obsessed by the futility of endeavour — compares himself to Nietzsche's image of a pine tree hanging over a cliff and longs for the wild scenery of his youth where

> wild earth and sea and man and animal, became, in his imagination, a single gesture of furious longing and revolt, a sudden, powerful heaving up towards the expression of something eternal and majestic. As if all life and movement had united in one effort to abolish death and weakness and create an unchanging eternity of force

and McDara comes to feel in himself 'the embodiment of the whole power of the universe',[16] because in a moment's imaginary splendour he has reunited himself to nature, the source of energy.

In *The Informer* a rare description of nature projects the decadent town atmosphere onto the bonds of humanity. 'It was a hard, mountainous wind, a lean, sulky, snowy wind, that rushed through the sleeping city savagely... The clouds arose, their hanging rumps cut away by the new-born wind. They hung high up in the heavens, gashed and torn, with a sour expression on their grey, slattern bodies'.[17] The adjectives in this passage and the personification of the clouds make this comparison effective.

During the same period that O'Flaherty wrote these three novels about tormented man in a town he wrote a fourth novel *The Wilderness* with a contemporary rural setting. This book was not published because, according to Mr O'Flaherty, it was never finished. It does not, however, read like an unfinished novel and it was serialised during 1927 in *The Humanist*:[18] it throws additional light on O'Flaherty's treatment of the man/nature relationship as a whole.

The Wilderness is set in an Irish valley 'where men are few and solitude makes living things brood awfully upon the majesty of the unknown universe'. The principal character is Lawless, a mystic visionary, at times reminiscent of Christ, at times a disciple of Nietzsche, who is looking for God and represents the religious principle. His face bears 'the ecstatic tender look of one who is in harmony with Nature'. He lives in a hut with goats. He asks himself, 'Can all this beauty have no meaning?... I must transcend all fear and love all things. Then all things shall be made manifest'. In the end he conquers his fear of death but his desire to love all things comes to include love for another man's wife.

A second character, old Patrick Macanasa, has a face which bears 'the strange expression of melancholy wisdom that old ravens have'. He represents the earth principle, a decaying figure descended from Gaelic chiefs, long dispossessed of their hereditary rights. He is malicious and mean; his only passion a peasant's clodlike love of the land. This love is 'cold because it lies so deep, deep in his nature that even when a manifestation of it reaches his consciousness it comes with a dull flicker of pure joy that almost immediately is overcome with fear and perishes in a brooding hatred of something unknown. He is happy only when he is rooting in the earth or tending his flocks'.

Both these men possess passion of a different kind for the world of nature, the one ecstatic integrated with nature, the other possessive buried deep in his own, human nature.

A third figure, Dr Stevens, is a man whose passion in life is an intense curiosity, the love of knowledge for its own sake. He is a free-thinker and represents the scientific principle; an atheistic philosopher more interested in life than in heaven, for 'the mental attitude of reverence, which is a necessary quality of belief, was impossible for him'. There is as much spiritual antagonism between Stevens and Lawless as there is social antagonism and incomprehension between Macanasa and Lawless. The love of all three men is imperfect for Lawless attempts to love like a god and ends by loving himself as a godlike figure, Macanasa is fearful and so incapable of spiritual love, and Stevens loves only ideas not mankind. The three men also represent beauty, evil and truth imperfectly represented as abstractions in human terms: and they stand for the threefold qualities of mysticism, violence and creativity found in nature herself which are complementary but which war continually in nature as in man. The love of the woman for Lawless is based only on physical attraction and the love of the Parish Priest for his religion is a cold doctrinal love in which fear and love are shown to be antagonistic. The thesis behind the novel is a complicated one, as a social criticism of the Irish situation is also involved. Philosophically this is the most ambitious novel O'Flaherty ever attempted.

Lawless tries to detach himself too much from the world and teeters on the verge of insanity. In his final ecstasy he has a vision of beauty in which he expresses the union of immortal man and nature; 'Whither yet souls? Through the sea, where the great eels wind among the swaying weeds, round and round the surface of the earth ... Come souls and share this lovely majesty'. Stevens, to whom the world is a mockery, invents a patent lozenge which ensures amorous power while life lasts. This, he says, is the next best thing to the immortal love sought by Lawless. Macanasa intrigues to gain possession of the land. Each kind of love has an element of this ideal in it but all are sterile because they are basically selfish.

Beneath the mad fantasies of Lawless lies much of O'Flaherty's personal disgust. This is particularly evident in the long dialogue between Lawless and the Parish Priest. The Priest accuses Lawless of being a pantheist and Lawless replies in words reminiscent of the eschatological discourse from St Matthew XXIV. 'I am not anything for which man has yet found a name. For man is only just beginning to strive towards a new manhood. And everything that he has inherited is rapidly becoming confused, language, thought and religion. Before a birth there comes a terrible cataclysm'. He tells Macanasa 'you were offered the universe and you could only see the acorn in the earth's mud'.

Nature is more than a background to the story. It provides the ground theme. The pragmatic Stevens tells Lawless; 'When fanatics worship your bones and wage wars over your mythical tombs.[19] That won't be your triumph, though, for nature will have swallowed you back into her womb and will smile at man as before, jeering at his vain efforts to unravel her secrets . . . What good is the submission of the individual to this universal need of man to learn more and more, so that some day man will be so strong that nature will bow before him'. Lawless's faith in the immortality of man is, however, unshaken by Stevens' argument. He says 'Science has broken her puny javelin on the rock of my belief. I stand defiant and free. Unconquerable'. This freedom claimed by Lawless is the freedom from fear and hatred, without which love cannot exist. He accepts death as a sacrifice of the body to enable the soul to become one with the eternal beauty of nature, with the universe with which in his ecstasies he has felt united.

In *The Wilderness* O'Flaherty sets out to illustrate that though man is incapable of rising above his human limitations, there is beauty and necessity in his revolt or struggle to integrate himself. In *Land*, perhaps O'Flaherty's weakest novel but the one in which his theories on the meaning of life are most clearly expressed, we find Raoul's statement. 'The soldier, the poet and the monk represent what is finest in man. They represent man's will to power, to beauty and to immortality. They alone among men are capable of complete love because they love the unattainable. Their love is never tarnished by possession' (p. 53). In his last novel *Insurrection*, the peasant character of *The Wilderness* (Macanasa) becomes the soldier Madden; the scientific freethinker becomes the monklike but pragmatic Kinsella who has once dreamed of becoming a famous chemist; and the mystical Lawless becomes the poet Stapleton.

In *Insurrection* the three characters are united in achieving the common aim of Irish independence, whereas in *The Wilderness*, set after the civil war, the three characters are not only antagonistic but incompatible, which is, of course, socially significant. The ideal man, integrated with nature should possess some of the qualities from each of the three principles, however these may be expressed. This ideal state corresponds to

G. B. Shaw's 'godhead in which all life is human and all humanity is divine; three in one and one in three . . . in short, the dream of a madman'.[20]

The conflict within man's nature and its reflection in the world of nature at large is also illustrated in O'Flaherty's only allegory, a 10,000 word novella entitled *The Ecstasy of Angus*, set in the mythical land of Banba. In this long short story Angus, the legendary god of love of the Fir Bolg people, who are supposed to have settled Aran, has overcome Crom the god of death. The men created in Angus's image go to the fairyland of Youth when they die. Angus is so creative, however, that he approaches Mananaan the god of the elements, who lives in a cave at Arranmore, to ask for more territory withdrawn from the sea upon which living things may continue to multiply in peace. Mananaan refuses to help and the angry elements unleash a great storm.

A beautiful earth fairy Fand, now comes to Angus in his distress and tempts him to break his vow of chastity, in return for which he has the power to create men and women in his image. Though Angus cannot conquer the elements Fand persuades him that in return for fleshly delights he will be reborn to an immense joy in the senses which will help him to forget his limitations. Fand tantalises Angus in nature's contradictory way, blowing first hot and then cold to test his adoration of her and pique his desire. Angus, though enthralled by her, realises that 'the brute fury with which you have infected me is the curse of my infidelity already destroying my godly innocence' (pp. 26—7).

Awakening after his mating with Fand Angus finds he has lost his youth and beauty, killed the gods and sown enmity in nature. Confronted by the newsprung Tree of Knowledge he finds it guarded by the warlike Genius of Unrest.

> His face struck terror into Angus. Passions unknown among the gods, or among the mortal beings he had created with his breath, were imaged in this spirit's eyes. And yet, although the eyes looked evil and terrifying, they were fascinating, like the eyes of a snake before it leaps and shoots the venom of its tongue. They held the glorious melancholy of incurable unhappiness, the lust of conquest and the pride of genius (p. 39).

He tells Angus that Fand shall bring forth a godless son

> born in your image but of the earth's substance. And his seed shall conquer the universe through the dual agency of this tree's knowledge and my genius. I shall enter unto him at birth and impregnate his mind with my quality, which shall give him no peace, until the cycle of his life has been completed and he hands on his task to his successors (p. 41).

By this mating of the ideal and the physical O'Flaherty proclaims the inescapable tension within man's nature, at once a part of nature yet resisting nature, leading to man's ambivalent potential for love/hate, gentleness/brutality, which appear so often in his characters.

Angus is not comforted by the assurance of the Genius of Unrest that his son will inherit his love but, dying, bequeaths a curse to his natural son that he shall always remain in thrall to the powers of his mother, who will 'for ever inspire him with the same maddening lust and shall in the same way for ever rob him of his strength, his youth and his wisdom, and cheat him for a few short moments with delicious ecstasy, only to make the ensuing despair more death-giving', (p. 24). I have quoted from his allegory at length because I believe it is the nearest O'Flaherty has ever come to an explicit statement of his belief in man as an integral part of nature.

Human love, will always be as apparently unstable as nature herself, even though it partakes of the divine. Man's capacity for divine love is, on the other hand the only thing which raises him above his natural state.[21] The similarity between this allegory and the creation myth in Genesis is obvious, but the differences are more important. This son of the god of love and mother earth, this man, is identical with Francis Thompson's

> Great arm-fellow of God!
> To the ancestral clod
> Kin,
> and to cherubin; ('Any Saint')

but his *inborn* nature is to blame for his duality. Adam's fall took place after his creation but the fall of Angus takes place at man's conception, and man is given no domination over nature but is a part of it, as changeable as nature and as subject to the elements.

Man is therefore an integral part of nature raised above it not by his capacity for thought which is tied to his physical limitations, but by his sense of worship, or comprehension of beauty. Man's capacity for thought, associated with the Genius of Unrest in the allegory, is according to O'Flaherty a curse rather than a blessing, and it is no coincidence that so many of O'Flaherty's most successful short stories deal with animals or very simple human beings.

O'Flaherty uses nature sometimes in several ways simultaneously; as a setting for his stories, as a symbolic framework within which the action takes place, as a metaphor for the expression of character or incident, or personified as part of the action. We also saw that nature only enters into two of the urbanised stories, 'The Mountain Tavern' and the 'The Tyrant', in each case to accentuate man's separation from and/or longing for nature.

In 'The Wild Goat's Kid' nature sings an audible chorus, modulated to the dramatic happenings and at the same time the characters are a part of nature. When the kid is born the white goat was 'gloating over the exquisite thing that had been created within her by the miraculous power of life'. The dog arrives and attacks the goat, hoping to get at the newborn kid hidden in the rocks. The goat repels him but then night falls and 'The sharp rushing wind and the thunder of the sea only made the silent loneliness of the night more menacing to the white goat, as she stood bravely on the limestone crag defending her newborn young.' But, after the goat has killed the dog: 'Night passed into a glorious dawn that came over a rippling sea from the east. A wild, sweet dawn, scented with dew and the many perfumes of the germinating earth'.

'The Touch' is one of the stories in which nature forms a symbolic framework.[22] As with the falling snow in 'The Mountain Tavern', driving hail introduces and ends 'The Touch'. The story opens: 'A white mare galloped west along the strand against the fierce spring wind. Her tail was stretched out straight and motionless. Her nostrils were blood red. Flecks of foam dropped from her jaws with each outrush of her breath. Hailstones, carried slantwise at a great speed by the wind's power, struck with a loud noise against the canvas of her straddle'. On her back is Kate Hernon carrying food to the men on the beach for 'the local people had been gathering seaweed from the surf since before dawn over at the far end of the strand. Now the grey sand was dotted with little cocks of the red weed, all the way up the strand from where the waves were breaking'.

The exuberance of the girl's spirits is in keeping with the weather. Kate, watching Brian loading the seaweed, 'became intoxicated with passion . . . Although another heavy shower of hail was now falling and beating sharply against her cheek, she was unconscious of the impact'.

At the end of the story when Brian and Kate's passion has been thwarted by the latter's father, we see her sitting by a fence sheltering against the hailstones. Her sadness is too deep for tears, 'she just sat looking across the narrow road in silence at the cold white stones that were beating fiercely against the cold black stones'. As with the singing larks in 'The Letter', though here in a different key, the wintry weather starts by being a symbol of joyful energy in the girl and ends by becoming a symbol of the hardness ahead of her as she realises 'that this first touch of love would be the last touch and that she was henceforth sold to a man whose touch would be a torture to her flesh'.

In 'Going into Exile' nature is used to reflect the inner feelings and sensations of the human characters. While the farewell dance goes on, outside the cabin

a starry June sky was visible and, beneath the sky, shadowy grey crags and misty, whitish fields lay motionless, still and sombre. There was a deep, calm silence outside the cabin and within the cabin, in spite of the music and dancing in the kitchen, a starry June sky was visible and, beneath the sky, Patrick Feeney's eldest son Michael sat on the bed with three other young men, there was a haunting melancholy in the air.

The passage, with its deliberate repetition, and rather odd punctuation brings the sky right into the room.

When Feeney and Michael go outside to talk 'they stood silent and sombre, like nature about them, hugging their woe'. At dawn 'people looked out and saw the morning light sneaking over the crags silently'. At the end of the story 'the hot June day was silent. Listening foolishly for an answering cry, the mother imagined she could hear the crags simmering under the hot rays of the sun'.

In 'Poor People' too, men are a part of nature. The story opens with a description of the harsh surroundings which gives us a foretaste of doom. This aspect of nature is directly connected to the destiny of the people who struggle to gain a living under 'the great whip of poverty' and the 'great lash of hunger'. When the sun rises, though the birds' singing is described as sweet music, the red seaweed shimmers on the beach 'like freshly spilt blood on which the sun is shining, against the dark blue background of the freezing sea'. The little red veins on the back of the woman's hand, the red body of the horse, and the 'salt lump' which rises in the man's throat, are directly related to this nature description.

When the child dies and the keening starts it is described as 'a long, broken sound, wallowing with the sorrow of souls', to parallel the 'long broken sound wallowing on the white sand of the beach' in the opening paragraph. The body of the child will go under the ground and become part of the 'form of the earth' on top of which the red seaweed will be spread.

In 'Red Barbara' nature is used as a metaphor for both character and incident. Joseph creates a cultivated type of garden to reflect his cultivated mind. He talks to the awestruck villagers 'about the elements, about God, about animals, birds and fishes; ideas which had never before been heard in the village'. Barbara moves 'like a young tree swaying in the wind'. She is very much a creature of the earth. When she goes to the old midwife she is told to sit each day by the sea beside a dark pool where the mermaids are said to live and may be heard singing on stormy nights to entice the drowning seafarers to their cave. 'There the sea air is so strong that it enters the blood with the force of an intoxicating drug . . . '

But this action proves as fruitless as the intellectual Joseph's attempt to regain strength by lying naked in the sun. Barbara's ex-husband, and the man she marries after Joseph's death are both wild creatures of the sea — to whom alone she can be fruitfully wed.

'The Ditch' opens with a description of the protagonist Michael Cassidy, the farm labourer, which relates him immediately through its imagery to the world of nature. He is part of animal and plant life, and like other forms of growth a product of the earth. His face is 'like an ape'. His nostrils are 'like the mouths of little bells'. His cheeks are 'dark brown, like that of the uprooted earth when it is parched by the sun'. He is toilworn, each mark on his face a furrow of pain. He is so tired now that he is remote and alien from the surroundings through which he passes on his way to the farm. He does not notice the 'rich smell of exuberant growth', or 'the grinning sinister' colours of the hedges, nor hear the sounds of beasts and people. The scene has now been set by means of natural description; hints dropped about the apelike appearance of the man and the colour of the hedges; we know we are not going to hear a pleasant story.

When Cassidy is asked for help by the heavily pregnant Maggie, at first 'the impulse to murder darkened his face; the brute instinct which urges all animals to slay the useless and sick of their kind. It passed rapidly, in a moment. It was followed by another impulse. He thought of the law and he grew afraid'.

When they go to the tinkers' ditch the place is described as dusky silent and sinister. When Michael returns to the ditch later he finds Maggie asleep. The bats buzz, small animals make other noises, and he is terrified. Later when Maggie has given birth in the yellow moonlight her face looks 'yellow, wan, tired and sinister', and a page later Cassidy becomes aware of her 'sinister mad eyes'. He covers the baby, called 'the thing', with a sack, and goes off to drown it.

Most people would find this story repulsive. Neither of the characters rises much above animal level, though the man shows some thwarted attempts to do so, but each time he is repelled by the woman. Both are captive to fear, and as animals in captivity sometimes do, they destroy their own offspring. The title of the story is symbolic of their low moral state.

In 'The Landing' and 'The Oar' the sea is personified and becomes one of the characters. 'Don't tempt the sea with your words. Don't talk of drowning', cries Bridget in 'The Oar'. The sea 'began to swell and break its back . . . it began to growl and toss about as if monstrous teeth were being ground'.

In 'The Oar' the people and the sea become frenzied together. It should be noted that in Ireland the word 'mad' has the same double meaning as it also has in the United States, but which it no longer has in British English. 'Mad' here means both 'insane' and 'angry'. A few paragraphs later the image of madness is again used but this time unambiguously when the waves are compared to 'visions that crowd on a disordered mind, each standing apart from the other in crazy independence'. The sea is a killer but 'in the moment of delirium when their boat bore down on death they no longer feared death', for they have become one with nature's rhythm.

'The struggle to recover the sense of relation to nature and to God, the recognition that even the most primitive feelings should be part of our heritage, seem to me to be the explanation and justification of the life of D. H. Lawrence, and the excuse for his aberrations'.[23] This is T. S. Eliot's opinion of D. H. Lawrence, but it could also be applied to Liam O'Flaherty. O'Flaherty would probably agree with Lawrence that 'you can have life two ways. Either everything is created from the mind, downwards; or else everything proceeds from the creative quick, outwards into exfoliation and blossom . . . the actual living quick itself is alone the creative reality'.[24]

Human life if lived in 'friendship' with nature is as naturally cyclic as all living things and death is only tragic if associated with defeat or disease of the spirit. Death to Maggie in 'The Old Woman' is part of 'the lovely things in God's world'. She remains undefeated, as does the Hawk killed fighting to save his mate, or the old man in 'Galway Bay' whose fierceness declines with the setting sun, and who prays 'let me die on my feet in the sunlight'.

One of the best illustrations of O'Flaherty's nature concept linked to man's dual nature is shown in an early story 'The Mermaid'.

In this story Michael McNamara, the young hero, epitomises human physical perfection: 'To strength and comeliness, the two most-coveted virtues in our Western land, Nature had added countless others no less desirable. So that it seemed a young god had come to live among us'. He also seemed to be 'master of all crafts by the grace of Nature'. He falls in love with a girl whose 'beauty is too perfect to endure', and after an ecstatic month of marriage she dies. At first Michael falls into despair bordering on madness, and if not restrained he would – like the cow in 'The Cow's Death' – have flung himself bodily into his wife's grave. When his reason returns, however, his love turns to that higher form of love which distinguishes man from other creatures. Inspired by this love he thinks he hears her calling him. He forgets all sorrow and sets off in a boat to seek her. 'As the wave carried his boat at headlong speed towards the cliff, he saw her, with her arms stretched out, beckoning to him'. The 'ecstasy of eternal love' into which he swoons as his arms close about her wraith is equal to a poetic inspiration, or to a divine vision which lifts man outside himself, though – as this story shows – both the origin of this feeling and the form it takes, are based on the physical.

Tensions arise in man when his often misdirected ideals, born of knowledge and his potential for divine love are thwarted by the circumstances of his life. In O'Flaherty's characters such tensions may cause violence, and obsession, which will be considered in the next chapter.

7 Violence and Obsession

The violent actions and emotions which so many of O'Flaherty's characters show, the obsessions from which so many of them suffer, are expressions, either direct or transferred, of inner tension. An analysis of the methods of expressing tension through violence, or relieving it through an obsession, would, however, be too complicated if we considered both simultaneously, even when, as in 'Blood Lust' — the character has an obsession and also reacts violently.

It is clear from a reading of *Two Years* that the young Liam O'Flaherty was a quick-tempered, truculent person given to sudden explosions of anger, and also that conflict and contrasting emotions are for him part of beauty. In this book he says:—

> When I am under the influence of any of the great and beautiful emotions, sorrow, joy, love, hatred, or creative passion, then I move through crowded streets like a glutton at a feast, and revel in the presence and in the contact of countless images of myself. Then I see beauty in every face, and every moving body is wild with teeming images of adventurous drama and the clashing sounds of traffic are the hurly-burly of a giant tournament, where man, through his great genius, surmounts the limits of his earthly sphere, by filling the universe with his boundless energy. Then I suck strength from every alien muscle and sinew as I pass and my imagination reaches godly heights, loaded to bursting point from the store of tales and fancies that each face offers to my eyes . . . (pp. 49—50).

But these participating moods of energetic elation alternate in cyclic fashion with moods of withdrawal and despair connected with neurotic obsessions. The two alternating phases of O'Flaherty's personality create a divided self which is reflected in his violent and obsessed characters.

O'Flaherty himself dates this 'dual personality' of his from childhood. Early in *Shame the Devil* he recounts how the 'angel of revolt' entered into him when, at the age of nine, to frighten his mother, he told her a lurid story of a labourer murdering his wife in his potato garden and dancing on her body to make it fit the furrow. His mother at first believed him until she rushed out and found the wife in question 'knitting peacefully on the doorstep'. She then burst into tears and made the boy pray.

> I wept with her while we were on our knees, but I afterwards walked along the clifftops and shouted in the face of the strong wind that came up from the radiant sea. And from that day I had my dreams. I became a dual personality. The one wept with my mother and felt ashamed of his secret mind. The other exulted in his mind and began to dream of greatness (p. 19).

Later in the book he says 'all passion is beautiful whether it is hatred or love' (p. 184). For O'Flaherty violence is the necessary complement to gentleness. These apparent opposites, omnipresent in nature, are a natural part of life. He also believes violence to be a necessary part of art. In a 1925 book review he wrote:

> But in order to be a work of genius, a novel must offer something more than a perfect style . . . It must be a relentless picture of life, as lashing in its cruelty as the whip of Christ when there are money-changers to be beaten from the Temple, as remorseless as the questions of a jealous lover. It must have the power to invoke great beauty or great horror in the same breath as it calls forth laughter from the lips.[1]

To this temperamental predilection for violence, hatred or horror and artistic conviction of its validity, were added various sociological factors which accentuated this inborn tendency and aesthetic belief, so that for O'Flaherty violence also became a channel through which he could attack society and release aggression born of frustration.

At the age of twenty-one O'Flaherty said he was already an outcast from the mode of living of his ancestors, 'through the world knowledge that had made me discontented with the narrow scope of their experience . . . ' (*Two Years* p. 76). His revolutionary adventures in 1922 completed his ostracism. 'Ever since then I have remained, in the eyes of the vast majority of Irishmen and women, a public menace to faith, morals and property, a Communist, and atheist, a scoundrel of the worst type, a man whom thousands would burn at the stake if they had the courage' (*Shame the Devil* p. 22). The very exaggeration of his statement expresses hurt.

No doubt this bitterness was increased by the instability of temperament O'Flaherty finds typical of an Aran islander when he says in *Skerrett* (pp. 55–6):

> The surrounding sea, constantly stirred into fury by storms that cut off communications with the mainland, always maintains in the minds of the inhabitants a restless anxiety, which has a strong bearing on character, sharpening the wits and heightening the energy, but at the same time producing a violent instability of temperament.

To this inheritance can be added the aggressive spirit which is not only an evident part of O'Flaherty's character, but which he considers typical of his contemporaries. In *The Puritan*, speaking of Ferriter's sister Agnes he says: 'She had furthermore the aggressiveness that is typical of our generation, no doubt a product of the violent upheaval caused by the revolution, the anger of a class that has been enslaved for centuries and is eager to parade its freedom in a harsh manner' (pp. 136–7).

In the 1920s O'Flaherty's novels were not well received, and though he became well-known as a short story writer, it was into his novels that he had poured his heart. In 1932 when *The Puritan* was banned in Ireland W. B. Yeats wrote praising the book and added, 'I am myself, however, most concerned with the fact that the ban may have a very bad effect on O'Flaherty himself. Some years ago he wrote a novel of perhaps equal power, *The Informer*, and followed it with *Mr. Gilhooley*, a book more unequal, I think, but magnificent at moments. He found himself generally attacked and for some years produced nothing but open or disguised politics'.[2] O'Flaherty's 'disguised politics' include, of course, his satirical stories against the new political upstarts in Irish society, such as 'Blackmail' and 'The Tyrant', the novels *The Assassin* and *The House of Gold* where violence and politics or social criticism go hand-in-hand, the satires *A Tourist's Guide to Ireland* and *A Cure for Unemployment*, and the satiric novel *The Return of the Brute*, all three virulent works.

Sean O'Faolain, describing his first meeting with Liam O'Flaherty remarks, 'all the turbulence, energy, eagerness, swagger, noisiness were on the surface like sweat. They come from the nervosity inside which exudes them like sweat', and adds that his fury is 'at a life that cannot contain its own beauty less wastefully, that seems to destroy and hate its own fineness, and Life, of course to him means Ireland'. According to Sean O'Faolain the violence of O'Flaherty's characters is like 'the scream of a safety valve'.[3] This violence can either be the fury of suppressed energy as in the violent stories of the *Spring Sowing* volume; or it can convey social criticism in violent action or violent language. This is discernible in the violent current running through *The Tent* and *The Mountain Tavern* story collections.

Benedict Kiely remarked that O'Flaherty 'whether he knows it or not, has always had a certain amount of trouble with Dark Daniel intruding himself where, artistically, he isn't wanted',[4] and he finds pride at the root of this sense of social exclusiveness which may express itself as a neurosis, or find outward expression in brutality or other forms of aggression. 'Dark Daniel' here stands for O'Flaherty's personal sense of alienation as it appears in the hero of his play *Darkness* or in the Stranger of *The Black Soul*.

At the end of *Shame the Devil* O'Flaherty admits that he suffers from pride and arrogance which has made him malign. He compares this part of his nature to the eye of a snake and realises that it is an inescapable part of him. 'Even on a desert island it would be there, now distant, now by my side, having sport with me. Such being the case, I must face it boldly and try to put it in harness', (p. 250). The pride he here mentions is in effect his artistic egoism which must be controlled or sublimated into impersonal forms.

If it is agreed that O'Flaherty's personal violence can be attributed to a complicated mélange of personal and social factors it would be a misconception to attribute the violent strain in his work simply to bestiality or the desire to shock. O'Flaherty's characters are often subjected to the same paradox expressed in *Shame the Devil* when he states, 'I have shamed the devil into obedience by an exhibition of inverted pride greater than Lucifer's' (p. 284). This 'inverted pride', the sometimes whimsical revelation of his own worst features, is the method O'Flaherty also uses with his brutal human characters, and this brutality may take the form of physical violence or mental torture, self-inflicted or imposed on others.

To sum up, in his earliest work O'Flaherty uses violence to relieve personal tension caused by unexpended energy. To this is later added violence which sometimes expresses his disgust against society. To these two reasons must be added a third, O'Flaherty's belief in the cathartic effect of violence as a valid aesthetic experience. It is in this aspect that violence is closely related to the man/nature relationship. For O'Flaherty the real horror is not violence, which is always an expression of passion, however thwarted or misdirected this may be, but a satiated indifference or an apathy which does not exist in nature.

> It is an indifference born of a continual satisfaction of the passions, or worse still, of a self-satisfaction that quenches the fire of the soul. Here is the earth in all its nakedness, without flowers or trees or birds to make it tame and friendly. There is the sea, sombre and dangerous in the light of evening. There is the air, grown cold, to give you an indication of the storms that buffet man. But all that is good if you accept it as good (*Shame the Devil*, p. 217).

These various kinds of violence appear as dark and often interwoven threads running through the emotional colour scheme of O'Flaherty's short stories.

Physical violence appears in no story written after 1932, but does occur in thirteen earlier stories. In the *Spring Sowing* stories 'Blood Lust', 'The Struggle' and 'The Fight', as already noted in Chapter 2, the protagonists are motivated by hate and all are in abnormal states of mind, which makes such naked emotion excusable to the reader. The protagonist of 'Blood Lust' is obsessed by an insane jealousy of his brother; in 'The Struggle' the protagonist is drunk. In both these stories the sea is calm and nature seems asleep, dissociated from the antic violence of the men. In 'The Fight' the protagonist's drunkenness releases his frustrations which take physical form. In each of these stories the principal character has a possibly imaginary grudge against the man he attacks, for the real cause of the violence lies far deeper and is connected with his inability to fulfill himself. In physical violence O'Flaherty gives fictional form to overwhelming sensations of unresolved physical tension from which he suffered himself as a young man.

The physical violence of the war stories on the other hand, has its mainspring in another kind of physical tension, the mastering of fear. In O'Flaherty's war stories the men are not in the heat of battle, but exposed to a situation in which their response as individuals is what counts. When in 'The Sniper' the protagonist has killed his enemy the battle fury aroused in him by his instinct of self-preservation is dissipated and in a moment 'the cloud of fear scattered from his mind and he laughed'. In 'Civil War' Murphy has overcome his fear of death and replaced it by a 'desperate hatred' for the enemy. The way he continues to fight after being wounded shows him to be possessed by a hatred stronger than himself. Dolan, however, cannot overcome his fear, he feels 'hatred of the people who slept; hatred of the soldiers who were setting the distant street on fire . . . But he didn't want to die. The fear of death made his teeth chatter', and he also fears Murphy. When the enemy arrive and kill Dolan in cold blood, to the violence born of hatred and fear is added the violence born of cruelty, also indirectly related to fear.

In 'The Alien Skull' Mulhall's long experience in the trenches has taught him to overcome fear by hatred. It has become a reflex action in his mental processes. For him the enemy is no longer fully human. This hatred is based partly on Mulhall's instinct of self-preservation and partly on transferred personal frustration. His meeting with the enemy soldier 'brought to a climax the whole ghastly misery of his existence. It robbed him of his only solace, the power to hate somebody whom he could injure with impunity'. He is therefore angry with himself when he begins to feel love, a new emotion as powerful as hatred but which he fears because he cannot understand it. To overcome this new fear he reacts violently and kills the alien soldier. He then feels he must escape, but this momentary renewal of fear relapses once more into habitual violent hatred as he dies cursing.

Violence from the tension resulting from sexual frustration appears in physical form in 'The Sinner'. In this story Julia takes Sally the maid's advice: 'Wallop him till he cries. He'll cry like a child. I'll stand by ye. And if that doesn't settle him take him into the courts', and Julia beats her drunken and erring husband. Infanticide caused by the thwarting of natural sex instincts occurs in 'The Ditch'; the sexually frustrated Lydon is seduced and robbed by a prostitute in 'Unclean'; but O'Flaherty is much more successful at suggesting sexual frustration mentally rather than physically as he does in 'Red Barbara', 'The Flute Player' and 'The Wedding'.

Violence in the short stories implying disgust against society is conveyed both by speech which expresses outraged feelings, and by actions. Violent actions can be used ironically, as in 'The Strange Disease' where the priest behaves violently to cover his fear. 'He shuddered with fear, both of the fury of nature and of the strange disease he was going to encounter in the barbarous hamlet among the mountains'. He lashes his mare and later he whips the lovelorn man, but his outraged feelings are more important than his violent actions. Two other stories in which violent action is used ironically to cloak fear and for the purpose of social criticism are 'The Fairy Goose' and 'Mackerel for Sale'.

Mental outrage unredeemed by love but containing no social criticism first occurs in the physically violent story 'Wolf Lanigan's Death'. Wolf terrorises Rosie to hide his own fear and Rosie becomes so terrified of Wolf that she is speechless. When Wolf falls into a drunken sleep, Rosie's eyes show an 'immeasurable hatred' and she kills him. This action, followed by hysterical laughter, releases her hatred which has conquered her fear.

In *The Tent* stories 'The Outcast', 'The Tyrant' and 'Blackmail', mental violence is perpetrated by harsh speech which causes violent emotional reaction in the recipient, and all three stories criticise Irish society. The priest in 'The Outcast' first ignores the girl's plea for pity, and then rebukes her, at which the girl 'began to tremble violently'. She seeks her release from fear in suicide.

In 'The Tyrant' Mrs Sheridan is terrified of her husband. His mental violence is expressed in the phrase 'the underlip raised . . . raised to strike, a thin lip striking upwards'. His words wound her physically 'like a hot iron burning the flesh and causing her body to vibrate painfully with the concussion of the stroke'. By staying she realises she will only 'grow to hate him'. She seeks escape in the peace of nature.

In 'Blackmail' Brunton, the ex-gunman, is out of place in politics where violence, now a sheathed amoral bludgeon, takes the sinuous form repeatedly suggested by Kenneally's reptilian appearance and movements.

In the stories written after 1932 violence to express social criticism disappears; so does brutal violence based on fear, whether expressed by hatred or deliberate cruelty. We are left with violence stemming from the mental and physical frustrations of the characters. Physical frustration leading to inconclusive action occurs, for instance, in 'The Challenge' and the blind man's embrace in 'The Beggars'. Mental frustration leading to violent emotional states often connected with an obsession becomes more common in the later stories such as 'The Wedding', 'The Fanatic', 'Galway Bay' and 'The Eviction'. In this last story frustration also finds physical expression when Miss Newell breaks her umbrella on the skull of Lynch whom she neither fears nor hates but merely despises.

'The Blow', a complex story, is a good example of O'Flaherty's later and more subtle use of violence. The enraged boar whose eyes contain 'bitter hatred' awakens only pity in the boy, for the frustrated animal's violence is actuated by his mating instinct, and is the laudable violence of revolt. When the father and son come to the sow and her piglets the father gives the son an object lesson on the behaviour of the young at their mother's dugs. The boy shows too much sympathy for one weakling piglet and the father, finding him effeminate, strikes him. The blow stiffens the boy's pride, and removes his fear of his father, who he knows struck him not in hate but in anger.

The difference between violence in an animal and violence in a man is that the one can only be based on instinctive self-preservation or preservation of the race. A man's violence can also be of this kind when he is confronted by physical danger and reacts instinctively, but of many other kinds when it is based on mental frustration. Man's violence, if the result of righteous anger or courage, may also be the necessary corrective to love and awaken not fear but respect.

We see in animal stories such as 'The Cow's Death', 'The Wild Goat's Kid', 'The Wounded Cormorant', 'The Hawk', 'The Conger Eel' or 'The Seal' that violence in animals is always related to their instinct to preserve the race, which instinct has been, or is, in danger of being thwarted, whether by injury, death, danger or hunger. In humans, to these same instinctive fears are added a whole range of social frustrations and anxieties. These frustrations, if not rationalised, can cause hatred and fear or anti-social behaviour leading to some form of violence or mental tension, in the same way that trust can lead to love and tranquillity. For O'Flaherty both sequences are complementary; from both art can be created, for both are a part of man's nature and reflected on a differing scale through all forms of life in the world of nature at large.

The cathartic effect on the reader of violence as an aesthetic experience is best shown when man is threatened, whether by natural or human forces, and rises through violent action or sacrifice to selflessness. We see the animal equivalent of this in 'The Cow's Death'; we see it also in stories like 'The Oar' and 'The Landing' in which men threatened by the seas forget their initial fear as do the watchers on the beach. This is a beautiful violence, 'the defiance of humanity hurled in the face of merciless nature'. It is the fierce spirit expressed by Red Barbara who revels in danger and strong emotion. It is the same wild spirit of contention which touches the stories 'The Tent', and 'The Black Mare'. For O'Flaherty life can be no pastel-coloured affair but a joyful acceptance of struggle without which the lyrical aspect of nature, or of life, has no meaning.

As it has been possible to attribute O'Flaherty's use of violence in part to the influence of his own temperament, in part to the historical situation he is describing, so it should be possible to attribute his frequent use of obsessed characters, many of whom become violent or do themselves violence, to the same mixture of causes.

There seem to be several reasons why so many of O'Flaherty's characters suffer from obsessions, or are neurotic, sometimes to the point of insanity. Some characters reflect a neurosis in O'Flaherty himself, the depressed or negative side of his dual personality. In other stories the feelings of characters are so intense that they amount to an obsession and these feelings are usually the result of thwarted desire. He shows us obsessions due to frustrated hatred, love, fear, envy and ambition. These obsessions often take the form of a mental violence which is either directed against others or turns back against itself resulting in derangement and hallucination. O'Flaherty's fondness for obsessed characters shows not only a desire to escape from his own obsessions, but a sympathy with others who fail to do so. These characters, like O'Flaherty himself, find reality unsatisfying so they construct fantasies to take its place. His fantasies resulted in artistic creation but their fantasies remain and fester in the mind. O'Flaherty's characters show a whole range of neurotic obsessions from a temporary condition brought on by suppressed emotion at one extreme to the neurotic illusion which causes insanity at the other.

It is clear, particularly in the 1920s, that O'Flaherty suffered himself from periodic neurosis. Some of this was the result of shellshock. In *Shame the Devil* (pp. 78–83) he gives an account of being shellshocked and the resulting period of insanity. Finally he was discharged from a Dublin hospital after suffering from *melancholia acuta*. Subsequently he had a fear of recurring madness, especially when in a depressive fit from which he at intervals suffered then, and still suffers to this day though less frequently, (see *Shame the Devil* p. 140). When depressed he withdrew and isolated himself from human contact.

In *Shame the Devil* (pp. 201–2) he also gives a description of one of these withdrawal phases during which for two days he shut himself up and became obsessed by a dead spider in the washbasin. He asks himself why he should so fear a spider when he generally exults in situations of physical danger. He concludes that in his case the need to withdraw is connected with a crisis of imagination, and that his creative urge is kindred to insanity. In addition to this tendency to cyclic depression O'Flaherty has extremely powerful visual gifts which enable him for instance to turn the sea into a living thing; to hold an imaginary conversation with his alter ego; to create hallucinations appropriate to the mental aberrations of his characters.

In some of O'Flaherty's early work his own neuroticism based on physical instability and mental frustration finds expression in the open neuroticism or madness of his characters, and in their intensity of feeling which amounts to a fixation. Fergus the neurotic in *The Black Soul*, the two neurotics Finnerty and Deignan in 'The Tramp', Dowling in 'The Doctor's Visit' or the priest in *Thy Neighbour's Wife*, are not only abnormal in various ways but they also suffer from the same inverted pride which O'Flaherty recognises as his besetting sin in *Shame the Devil*. In *The Black Soul* (p. 27), Fergus describes his shellshocked hallucinations and at intervals throughout the book he fears he is going mad. At the end of the 'Spring' section of the book he walks off alone inside the walls of the Fort (Dun Aengus) — where the young curate and Lily also have their last fateful meeting in *Thy Neighbour's Wife*. As he sits there, 'nature seemed to say, "See how beautiful is the world. Fool! You despise peasants, do you? You think you are an intellectual? I'll tell you what you are. You are a charlatan" '.

The priest in *Thy Neighbour's Wife* is also proud of his intellectualism and looks down on the peasants though his grandfather was a Dublin dock labourer. Both Fergus and this priest have to come to terms with their own nature and with nature herself under threat of death before they can accept life without neuroticism, Fergus when he fights with Red John, and the priest when he puts to sea in the oarless curragh. In precisely the same way, but at much greater length, O'Flaherty comes to terms with himself in *Shame the Devil*.

In a few of the short stories the same theme is there in an unexpanded form. In 'The Doctor's Visit' Dowling's neuroticism is based on intellectual pride. He killed the editor because he did not think he was appreciated. In 'The Tramp' Deignan is an educated man whose mind is sick, and Finnerty says 'I often envy those who don't think'. The remnants of their imagined social and intellectual superiority hold them aloof from the tramp. The fullest expression of this intellectual pride theme in a short story is in 'Red Barbara' where Joseph is a neurotic intellectual who attempts to tame nature, whereas Barbara exults in wild nature and fears only sterility. Ferriter in *The Puritan* is another neurotic intellectual; so are Crosbie in *The Martyr* and Lawless in *The Wilderness*. All these characters represent O'Flaherty's alter ego, the warped type of man he might have become if he had not been able to transform his fantasies into fiction, and if he had not learned to come to terms with his own limitations and intellectual pride. Intellectual conceit is not only the weakness O'Flaherty guards himself against but also the trait he detests in others.

O'Flaherty also uses obsession as a means of distorting his characters' feelings in the same way as a painter will give a profile two eyes in order to create a new illusion. Some distortions are slight, others profound. O'Flaherty creates characters removed more or less from the expected norm, by exaggerating their obsessiveness or by making them insane. Such characters can illustrate an abstraction as well as represent a living being whose intensity of feeling makes him larger, or more obtrusive, than life. This (again) can be seen more easily in the fully developed characters of the novels. In *The House of Gold*, for example, Mor Costello is a big man in every sense of the word, but he is obsessed by avarice to such an extent that he is impotent; the neurotic Father Considine is obsessed by guilty lust; both suffer from dreams and visions; in both men their obsessions give rise to intense emotion which needs violent outlet.

In the short stories such a distorted character can be suffering from a temporary emotional crisis resulting in a passing obsession, as in 'Blood Lust', where the emotion erupts in violence against the fish; or he can be distorted by physical weakness such as senility in 'The Stone'. In 'The Old Woman' and 'Galway Bay' the protagonists suffer from fears connected with death. Both these old people illustrate courage, but death is a reality from which they cannot escape. Knowing they cannot avoid death, at least they intend to meet it on their own terms. Old Maggie becomes obsessed with her appearance after death in her clean burial dress. Old Tom pretends to defy death with fierce gestures of independence, but even the sun appears like a threatening eye. His imprecation against the sun, 'May you die without Extreme Unction' reveals his true state of mind. He is obsessed with the fear of becoming helpless before he dies.

In 'The Beggars' the blind man, who lives in an enclosed world of his own, is obsessed by his sightlessness. He has compensated for his physical limitations in other directions by developing a powerful physique about which he can boast, and with which he can threaten those he imagines to belittle him. His face bears an expression of priestly arrogance which hides the deep insecurity caused by his blindness. The obsessive traits of the characters in these three stories are self-defensive compensations against an unpalatable reality, and we become emotionally involved with the characters because we sympathise with their situation.

In other stories, however, such as 'The Salted Goat', 'The Terrorist', 'The Stream', 'The Fanatic' or 'The Wedding' the obsession of the character is an enduring one born of deep-seated frustration which, failing to find a concrete outlet, has turned in upon itself and caused an abnormal mental state. The protagonists of these five stories are frustrated in different ways.[5] With Quigley in 'The Terrorist' frustration, born of his own inadequacy or lack of recognition, takes the form of hatred which has become an obsessive mania. His mania has now given birth to a fixed idea which occupies his whole consciousness, and he thinks only of hurling his bomb. Sitting in the theatre he has paranoiac sensations of grandeur and physical withdrawal. 'It seemed to him that his head was made of iron, it felt so strong. It also seemed to him that he was really sitting alone, an immeasurable distance from everybody; that he was enveloped by a cloud; and that he would hurl a thunderbolt out of that cloud, down upon the drones. An avenging God!' Later he feels that 'nobody else existed in the world but himself and "the horned spectres of the Revelations" down below', The story is a description of an abnormal mental state and what weakens its interest is that we can only guess what has gone before to cause this state in Quigley.

The danger inherent in stories which deal with the insane is that the distortion of their personality is so great that we can no longer recognise them as human. This is the weakness of both 'The Terrorist' and 'The Stream' in which the old woman has been mad since the violent death of her husband on the third day of their married life sixty years before. This tale of frustrated love cannot compare with the obsessive love of the young hero in 'The Mermaid' who is clearly revealed as he was before he became obsessed. To be moved by insanity we must be shown from what heights the character has fallen and this is not revealed in either 'The Terrorist' or 'The Stream'. The psychological and emotional distance of the characters is so great that sympathy, and with it interest in them as people, is impossible.

In 'The Fanatic' and 'The Wedding', both later stories, the emotional distance is well controlled by means of the other characters who set the protagonist in perspective and the setting of the story. In 'The Fanatic' the tavern is so unpleasant inside that 'the sounds of normal healthy life, that came through the open street door from the little country town outside, seem to be unreal and even plaintive'; and the narrator, who is eminently sane, acts as a foil to the alcoholic tavernkeeper. We are first given an objective view of this man from without in great detail and then through his conversation with the narrator, his abnormal state of mind becomes apparent and we learn that he is suffering from pathological loneliness brought on by an inability to love anyone but himself. He has transferred his complicated feelings of inadequacy to his sister at whose door he lays all the blame for his present state. He is at the mercy of conflicting emotions which rule his reason. These are mirrored in his beautiful eyes like those of a woman, which in turn reflect love, hate, savagery and an appeal for pity. The man's yellow greasy face is 'as smooth as a pebble exposed at low tide on a strand'. We may surmise that isolation and disgust at anything to do with sex may be connected in part to hormone deficiency and that his physical abnormality has contributed to his derangement.

In 'The Wedding' the contrast drawn between Nuala's face and her body typifies her mental state. Her face is compared to a death mask, to dry leather and to crushed paper; but her body, though she is over fifty, is like that of an adolescent girl. Her mental and physical development was arrested at the age of sixteen but she has the emotional feelings of a woman which her mind cannot control. In this complex story Nuala's fantasy love affair is given more poignancy by the situation of her sister Peggy who had returned from America years before with an illegitimate daughter. ,

Nuala is a character with whom the reader can sympathise because the reason for her peculiarity is clearly explained. Disgusted with herself she has become physically repulsive in her slovenliness and animal-like behaviour. Her inconsequential whimsical speech is well related to her curious mental state:

> Woe! The miracle has happened. Out comes the sun, hard on the tail of the rain. Up it rises in the sky, with its round face jeering at me like a devil. I can hear the wheels of the priest's jaunt turning on the wet road. Oh! the lustful, villain! She bribed God as well with her money. Ten pounds, I hear, the priest is getting for the wedding. Musha, darling God, you were easily bought.

O'Flaherty thought the state of creative mania to be a disorder akin to insanity (*Shame the Devil*, p. 192), and some of his deranged characters create hallucinations. To Ferriter in *The Puritan*, or the protagonists of 'The Terrorist' and 'The Fanatic' the painful idea from which they must escape is bound up with a real situation they cannot face so they deny reality by creating a fantasy which in each case takes physical shape associated, but transferred in different ways, with the inescapable reality. Ferriter knows if he is condemned for murder he will be hanged so he sees a bloody noose, the emblem of his retribution, in a hallucination. The tavernkeeper thinks his sister has gone to the devil so he has the devil of the flesh in bed with him every night; Quigley has an inferiority complex so he imagines himself imbued with godlike authority over a society to which he is in reality subjected.

Having got rid of his delusions of personal importance and nihilistic philosophical ideas, O'Flaherty goes on in *Shame the Devil* (p. 192) to decide that the most important thing in the universe is love. The protagonists of 'The Terrorist' and 'The Fanatic' are both alienated men who cannot love; the women in 'The Stream' and 'The Wedding' also suffer from frustrated love. In all four characters the cause of their obsession is emotional aridity.

There are also a few stories containing obsessed characters which convey ethical and/or social criticism. This occurs in 'Charity' where the alcoholic is obsessed by his addiction; in 'The Tyrant' where Sheridan is obsessed by ambition; in 'The Eviction' where Festus Lynch is obsessed by revenge; and in 'The Alien Skull' where Mulhall is obsessed by hatred. In these four protagonists the obsession either prohibits or kills love, for each man's obsession has caused him to think only of himself. Each character calls attention to this through self-pity. The alcoholic in 'Charity' bursts into tears; Sheridan in 'The Tyrant' tells his wife he has been slaving for ten years not for himself but for the children she did not give him; in 'The

Eviction' self-pity over his childhood memories causes Lynch's spitefulness; and Mulhall in 'The Alien Skull' is overcome by self-pity because everybody despises him. The social criticism which is a by-product of the ethical criticism is related respectively to the church, social up-starts in post-revolutionary Ireland, the Anglo-Irish aristocracy and the inhumanity of war.

It will be seen that violence and obsession in O'Flaherty's characters not only sometimes occur in the same character, but are related in that both may be used either simultaneously or separately to relieve personal tension, whether physical or psychological, in the author; to express physical or emotional tension in man's relation to himself and to society; as an indirect means of social criticism; and to create an aesthetic reaction in the reader.

Interviewed by a French reporter O'Flaherty once said: 'J'aime les fanatiques, parce qu'ils dérangent'.[6] Presumably he likes violent and obsessed characters for the same reason; they enact the disorder and revolt which is preferable to passivity. They show that the cruel aspect of life has a beauty of its own, and that all struggle has a value either in itself or for the reaction it gives rise to in others.

O'Flaherty occasionally carries violence to the point of crudity by dehumanising his characters as in 'Wolf Lanigan's Death' and 'The Ditch'; as he carries obsession beyond our sympathetic comprehension in 'The Terrorist' and 'The Stream'; but in his more successful stories of this genre the character's particular state of emotional intensity can grip the reader, whether it be the physical horror created by the violent stories, or the mental nightmare created by the insane, and hold him in suspense at emotional arm's length — as it were — from the edge of the emotional vortex by which the character is being engulfed.

At the end of *Shame the Devil* (p. 284) O'Flaherty states, 'my folly is a great concupiscence. I desire first of all the flesh and then the spirit. I reach the spirit through flesh', so that no experience of the flesh, to the limits of emotional sensation or endurance, should be anathema. This statement has a very modern ring.

8 From Ridicule to Contempt

Violence, whether turned outwards against society or repressed inwards against oneself, as described in the last chapter, can be used as a means of releasing tension in the author, or it can express an attempt to release tension in the character. The comic — of course — also acts as a tension reducer. One difference between violence and the comic lies, however, in the reader's response, for violence does not create emotional relaxation but anxiety in the reader, from which he may later obtain release; whereas the comic usually causes an instantaneous impulse of relaxation. O'Flaherty, as we shall see, sometimes juxtaposes violent angry action and the comic visual scene, which can create a confused impression of emotional withdrawal and participation, tension and relaxation, in the reader's mind, the predominant impression often depending on the individual reader's reaction. Some people, particularly, those who dislike an ambiguous emotional response, find this distasteful, and criticise O'Flaherty for being melodramatic.

The melodramatic mode is here defined as one which gives an impression of exaggerated or improbable emotion in which violence or gesture often play an important part. Failure to appreciate a melodramatic action may come about when the nature of the sensations it illustrates is either not made clear by the writer, or not accepted as suitable or sufficiently probable by the reader, or audience. The melodramatic impulse could be compared to laughter which turns to hysteria and becomes tears. It can be expressed through farce or tragedy. It can be associated with the occult at one extreme or with a lurid reality at the other, and to certain categories of persons neither of these extremes is palatable. When successful (as, for instance, in *Macbeth*), melodramatic action can be as therapeutic emotionally as satire is intellectually, but much more difficult to control, and its reception will depend very much on the individual's emotional or conditioned response.

Satire — the term usually applied to mockery which aims to arouse ridicule or contempt for its object — can also cause release of tension when the ridiculous element of satire, which contains pity and some tolerance, rather than satire which contains only anger, is predominant.

O'Flaherty's work reflects the duality in his own nature, and also the inescapable duality within man, which O'Flaherty attempts to illustrate in his allegory 'The Ecstasy of Angus'. This duality could be called the extrovert and introvert facets of O'Flaherty's character; the progressive or regressive states of his mind; the realistic or fantastic tendencies in his work, according to the terminology chosen or the aspect to be investigated. In most writers, as in most readers, one of these moods or means of expression tends to predominate. Reflected in O'Flaherty's early work especially, there is a continual swing between the two which is apparent in his alternating moods of elation and despair; in a style which ranges from lyricism to crudity; in a tone that varies from satire to melodrama.

The biologist Konrad Lorenz says laughter is basically derived from instinctive aggressive behaviour patterns, but he believes that 'humour exerts an influence on the social behaviour of man which, in one respect, is strictly analogous to that of moral responsibility: it tends to make the world a more honest and, therewith, a better place'.[1] I believe this is one of the effects O'Flaherty hoped to achieve when he used humour.

If violence is a necessary correlative to gentleness, as hate is to love, or sadness to laughter, so in O'Flaherty's use of the laughable we can find elements of all these qualities. An analysis of humour of all kinds in his short stories shows, in fact, that it is used in exactly the same way as violence. Humour, in his earliest work particularly, relieves the personal physical tension caused by unexpended energy. In the form of satire it expresses disgust against society. Humour can also cause an aesthetic catharsis, or refinement of emotional response in the reader.

Among the short stories in *Spring Sowing* and *The Tent* volumes and O'Flaherty's uncollected early work there is quite a large group of short stories containing humour of a simple kind with no satiric undertone, where the author is 'having fun', getting rid of his high spirits without ulterior motive. This type of story either ridicules the behaviour of an individual as in 'The Bladder' or 'The Cake', or tells of the subterfuge or verbal adroitness by which the protagonist achieves his aim as in 'A Shilling', 'A Pot of Gold' or 'The Stolen Ass' where Haughy, the name of the accused, is a deliberate pun on a donkey's bray. These stories represent O'Flaherty's use of humour in its simplest form.

Other stories containing simple humour are some of those written about children which form a varied thematic group. They include the serious stories treating the adolescent attitude in 'The Inquisition' and 'The Parting', the childhood animal stories 'The Wren's Nest' and 'Three Lambs', the child—parent relationships explored in 'Mother and Son' and 'The Blow' and four amusing stories revealing the emotional responses of the child in 'Limpets', 'Swimming', 'A Tin Can' and 'The New Suit', in which the amusement arises out of the child's fearful helplessness.

That 'A Tin Can' is based on a childhood memory is shown by its close relationship to Tom O'Flaherty's account of a similar incident published ten years after Liam O'Flaherty's story was written.[2] In both accounts the small boy is sent to Jimmy the drunken village carpenter, to get a new wooden bottom put into his mother's milk can. In Tom's account his mother knows Jimmy is tipsy and will do a bad job, but she is willing to sacrifice the can for the sake of the funny story the boy will tell when he returns. In Liam's account the drunken Jimmy is mending the can when his neglected dog tries to pick a potato out of the boiling pot. Jimmy throws a broken alarm clock at the dog and the boy drops to the floor in terror. The dog returns, mad with hunger, attacks the pot again, upsets it and a can of tea. 'Jimmy did nothing for five minutes but gape at his ruined meal. Then he silently took the rusty old gun, took deliberate aim at the dog, and fired. The shot went out over my body with a deafening roar. But instead of hitting the dog the charge landed over the door, and mortar fell in a shower.

' "Tearing ouns", yelled Jimmy, "I missed him", and began to batter my can with the barrel of the gun. "I missed him", he yelled, as he flattened it to a thin plate of tin like tissue paper. Then he hurled the battered thing at me, crying: "Be off now and see will that hold yer milk, ye . . ." '

We see from this story that Liam O'Flaherty came to associate violence with humour from an early age if, when the child returned home with the flattened can, his mother found the incident as funny as Tom, in his different version of the story, leads us to suppose.

O'Flaherty's tendency to bring physical violence in the form of slapstick or farce into his comic situations is illustrated in 'Colic', a story about a joke at the expense of a publican in which Finnigan gets a free drink on the pretext of agonising colic but gives none to his friend Hanrahan. Hanrahan in his rage bites Finnigan all over the chest and hisses between bites, 'Son of a wanton, robber, may yer bones be sucked dry in hell by hungry little devils, you . . .' Finnigan threatened by Mrs Curran the publican, makes off up the road leaving portions of his clothing behind, and as he runs his hobnailed boots almost meet his half-naked backside. O'Flaherty had a higher opinion of this story than Edward Garnett and told Garnett he considered 'Colic' 'an excellent humorous story'.[3]

'Colic' contains the mixture of verbal dexterity, farce and irony also found in 'The Red Petticoat', another story full of riotous suppressed energy. In spite of all their hardships the Deignan family, 'gifted by the good God who gives all things with the Divine capacity for enjoying life and their good health', are determined to treat life as a joke. The mother, nicknamed 'Mary of the bad verses' is known for her abusive and scurrilous poems. She has a fine gift of invective as she shows when berating

Mrs Murtagh. 'Oh woman that has denied God, Virtue, charity and all the good deeds of the holy ones, you female devil routed from hell because Lucifer himself couldn't sleep under the same roof with such an abomination, you virago of the seven tongues, and they all cancerous with the load of foul words that come each hour across their flabby and pestilential backs; oh, daughter, shared by seven fathers and they all drunkards and vagabonds . . .'

To this verbal play of wit is added violent farce when the two women fight in the shop. The narrator's ironic comments introduce satire into the story against Mrs Murtagh who 'sells everything the peasants can be induced to buy and buys everything they will sell, except cattle and immortal souls'. The humour of the story is therefore provided by Mrs Deignan's tongue, her behaviour, the irony of the narrator and the imagery.

In both 'Colic' and 'The Red Petticoat' the humour overrides the social criticism and O'Flaherty's personal gusto is particularly evident in the devil-may-care attitude of the indigent but carefree Deignan family, for whom no room is left for pity.

In *A Tourist's Guide to Ireland,* as discussed earlier, O'Flaherty satirically outlines his reasons for disliking some roles played by priests, politicians, publicans and peasants in Irish society, criticism which he had already introduced in fictional form into his novels and short stories. In 'Colic' the publican is mocked, in 'The Red Petticoat' the target for wit is the peasant shopowner and in 'Your Honour' it is the upstart politician. When O'Flaherty wrote 'A Strange Disease' in which he makes fun of a priest, he had already written satiric stories about priests in which the angrily contemptuous rather than the pitiful satiric impulse was predominant, namely 'Offerings' and 'The Outcast'. But in an early story 'A Grave Reason' and in 'A Strange Disease', though this last is written under serious impulse, the satire is comical.

In 'A Strange Disease' a young peasant, thinking himself to be on the point of death sends for a priest. The priest sets off at dawn on a wild and lonely ride to the remote mountain village. The priest is shown as separated from the people of whom, after twenty years, 'he was still terrified . . . and considered them to be no whit more civilised than the wild men of the African forests'. The village to which he goes is avoided by the priests because the people are superstitious and 'incapable of understanding the subtleties of the Christian faith, by profession sheepstealers . . . Walled in by their mountain as in a prison, intermarriage had bred lunacy and decadence amongst them'. The priest considers these people 'entirely unnecessary human beings', though from the altar he has to admit the value of their souls.

During the second half of the story a dialogue between the priest and the peasant takes place. The latter confesses his 'illness'. He is in love with the blacksmith's wife. The violent element, already present in the description of the mountain scenery, is now expressed in action as the furious priest whips the man and sets him running up the street. On the way home we see the priest weeping in his hopeless anger, and inveighing against 'this *DEGRADING* passion of love'.

In this brief story O'Flaherty, by the combination of the sublime and the ridiculous has achieved an impression of profundity, for the priest — servant of the God of love — can only hate; the peasant — so idiotic and uncivilised — can only love.

In 'Colic', 'The Red Petticoat' and 'A Strange Disease' O'Flaherty uses humour energetically and with satire, but in the last two stories he also attempts through humour to awaken an aesthetic catharsis, for the basic situation is not funny but pitiful. By the use of humour the situation of the Deignan family is rendered most poignant, and the priest's benighted state of mind more obvious.

The same blend of irony or satire and violent farce can be found either in the form of an isolated incident, or in the predominant tone, of several other stories such as 'The Sinner', 'The Fairy Goose', 'Stoney Batter', 'Mackerel for Sale', or 'The Bath', as it is also present in scenes from the novels such as the drinking shop scene in Chapter XVI of *The Puritan*; the uproarious drunken fight at the end of *Mr. Gilhooley* where Gilhooley hurls the umbrella stand at Macaward, Friel falls downstairs through the banisters, the police take Friel away, and Gilhooley strangles Nellie; or in *The Martyr*, Chapter XII, where Regan raids the hotel bar to find he has been forestalled.

W. B. Yeats once remarked that O'Flaherty's novels *The Informer* and *Mr. Gilhooley* were 'too full of abounding life to be terrible despite their subjects. They are full of that tragic-farce we have invented'.[4] Synge and O'Casey certainly both sometimes use the same brand of humour which is no doubt connected to the Irish attitude towards life.

Arland Ussher, one of those who have tried to define specific Irish characteristics, believes the Irish have an insecure sense of reality and that just because they 'are close to elemental sorrow, they are apt to see little but the ridiculous side of private and particular passion and tragedies ... Like all religious people, Irishmen regard existence rather as a puppet show'.[5] G. A. Birmingham expressed the same idea in another way when he said, 'Irishmen are capable of coming into a room and seeing their own heads grinning at them from a table',[6] and, one might add, then writing a story about it.

Whether O'Flaherty's comic episodes or incidents appear melodramatic and ridiculously exaggerated, or tragi-comic and appealing will depend to a large extent on the individual reader's response. There is sometimes a mere hairline between laughter and agony in O'Flaherty's work, as we see in 'The Fight'. Violent farce is for him a form of physical distraction against the sentimentality which might otherwise ensue, and this paradoxically implies a sympathy with the characters being satirically ridiculed. There is, significantly, no violent farce in O'Flaherty's angrily contemptuous satire. He shrugs off emotional tension in action and converts his own excited bitterness into laughter. Whether or not the reader can accept the violent farce will depend on the extent to which he too can sympathise with the irrational emotional impulse in the character which has given rise to it.

O'Flaherty's taste for melodrama, of which Dostoievsky and Conrad, two of his admired authors, were also accused, has already been remarked.[7] The reasons why he is so fond of farce which sometimes becomes melodramatic, seem to be complex. He finds the farcical situation energetically satisfying, as in 'The Old Hunter' when the rider falls off into the stinking drain; he has learned to laugh at ridiculous physical situations in his childhood, especially those connected with drunkenness, as in 'A Tin Can'; he believes in laughter as an alternative to violence, to overcome fear in a subconscious reaction against circumstances, but the violence sometimes mingles with the laughter. The reaction of the Deignan family in 'The Red Petticoat' would be O'Flaherty's own reaction. O'Flaherty also uses violent farce to deflect his own sentimentality when he feels pity for his character but cannot show it as in 'The Fight'; and to highlight the satiric aspect of the situation as in 'The Fairy Goose' when Mrs Wiggins is felled by the priest.

A person's sense of humour is directly connected to his concept of reality, or way of regarding life. O'Flaherty, it seems to me, has an ideal or concept of reality far beyond life as he sees it being lived. The discrepancy between his ideal and reality causes an abrasive intellectual impatience within him which erupts and rises in aggressively violent humour, or descends to contemptuous satire, depending on whether his intention is to accept as unfortunate but inevitable, or reject as despicable, the situation, person or attitude he describes. For this reason it is not possible to regard his serious satire as anything other than a development, or offshoot of the ridiculous in which disgust has ousted pity.

Because O'Flaherty's concept of reality is so idealistic it easily allows for the entrance of romantic tendencies such as fantasy in the form of a fixed obsessive idea, or farce which verges on melodrama. His vision of reality as he would like it to be, leads him in the direction expressed in lyrical stories such as 'Milking Time' and 'Spring Sowing': but the contrary experience of life as he sees it being led, introduces a revulsion which he tries to overcome by forms of violence and exaggerated laughter. This explains the element of the macabre discernible in stories such as 'Stoney Batter', 'The Fairy Goose' and 'Mackerel for Sale'. Vivian Mercier has explored this aspect of traditional Irish humour. He defines the macabre as 'based on the assumption that a joke or other comic event . . . must inspire laughter which is tinged with terror'.[8] Stoney Batter dies a friendless pauper, in-horrifying contrast to his earlier popularity. The once sacred goose is stoned to death. Tameen's D.T's may amuse the locals but he is really a frightening figure. The same vein of macabre humour can also be found in O'Flaherty's Aran Island novels.

O'Flaherty's concept of reality also explains the grotesque exaggeration of some of his characters, such as the protagonist of 'The Fanatic', whose bizarre appearance and behaviour arouse an emotional response in the reader allied to the absurd; or the grotesqueness of Delaney, the elderly suitor in 'The Caress', where, at the end of the story, he is carried off helpless on the mare's back to the tune of ribald laughter.

This same idealistic concept of reality also often causes O'Flaherty to look upon life as a kind of allegory, or — to repeat Ussher's words — 'as a puppet show' imitating the real thing.[9] Critically speaking however, we can define allegory as any kind of didactic element which emphasises the illustrative meaning of its characters, setting and actions.

The consideration of O'Flaherty's narrative structures in Part I revealed that his artistic development showed an early majority of illustrative or type characters, and a later majority of real or representative characters in his short stories. A suggestion of allegory — in the form of fables — is apparent in some of his animal stories and in his two earliest novels *Thy Neighbour's Wife* and *The Black Soul*, it recurs in *The Wilderness* and *The Puritan* and is strongly present in short stories such as 'The Mermaid', 'The Fairy Goose' and 'Red Barbara' but in only two later stories 'The Mirror' and 'Desire'; while the type-casting of the characters in *Land*, who are nevertheless supposed to be realistic figures, is the reason for the novel's failure.

But if allegory is the form of didacticism which emphasises illustrative meaning, as in 'The Mirror' or 'Desire' where the baby and the girl remain stylised figures whose reactions are supposed to be typical of their kind, satire is the form of didacticism which emphasises the representative meaning of a character or situation.[10] This appears in 'Mackerel for Sale' where the characters are more clearly individualised and act out specific situations. Though O'Flaherty may sometimes have regarded life as a puppet show, at other times the puppets turn into real people and we get a mingling of the allegoric and the satiric. Thus in 'A Strange Disease' the peasants remain type figures but the priest is individualised in order to make his attitude appear more ridiculous. In 'The Fairy Goose' Mary Wiggins and the priest are individualised but the peasants remain types in the background. The behaviour of the peasants emphasises the illustrative or timeless moral meaning of the situation superimposed on which is the comic satire inherent in the specific behaviour of the two protagonists.

Puppets can wear grotesque masks and behave in an exaggerated way but when the puppet takes on a realistic appearance his behaviour has a much stronger social impact, and this — apart from any change in his concept of reality — was, as an artist, what O'Flaherty came to understand. O'Flaherty the man had to be controlled by O'Flaherty the artist. This conclusion is supported by the disappearance of editorial intrusion in his later work noted in Chapter 4, and by his increased use of dialogue. The puppets, even when they remain puppets — must appear to be self-motivated and detached from their manipulator.

As far as the humorous stories are concerned, O'Flaherty wrote thirty-eight short stories which are either humorous or contain some humour. Of these, twelve — all written by 1932 — contain type characters. By this date too he had written all his satiric short stories. In his later stories compassion, which he is now no longer afraid to show, takes the place of anger. A liking for fantasy and farce as in 'The Fanatic' and 'The Bath' — both essential ingredients in O'Flaherty's sense of humour — remains, but the satiric impulse is restricted to irony as in 'The Bath', 'The Pedlar's Revenge' or 'The Post Office'.

Fantasy also appears in 'The Challenge'. In this story O'Flaherty attempts a debased form of the old bardic flyting (*iomarbhaigh*), in which you start by insulting your opponent. The story tells of the challenge to fight issued by a tinker after a fair. His arrogance is contrasted with his ragged appearance. He starts with a passage of rodomontade, 'Come out here one of you, so that I can wipe one of you off the face of the earth'. To his repeated taunts his wife provides an echoing chorus as she beats her tethered asses with a stick and reiterates, 'I could lick the whole fair for a shilling'.

The tinker is answered by a stripling of effeminate appearance who is a Connemara man. The sham-fight then begins. Both men use physical actions to build up their position. The tinker trails his coat and dares his opponent to stand on it. The Connemara man at first remains cool, repeating 'I never start a fight, but I finish one, where I am, I stand!' While the tinker's wife performs ritualistic actions over the young man's jacket.

For some time the challengers continue to circle, jump jackets, spit, leap and brandish their clenched fists. They vie with each other in ferocity and in their simulated rage, which has to be restrained by the bystanders, both utter exaggerated threats about tearing at hearts and drinking blood. Eventually a Civic Guard breaks up the entertainment.

The characters in this story act out a burlesque on the heroic challenge for the amusement of the spectators. By choosing as heroes a tinker and an effeminate youth O'Flaherty has parodied traditional heroism and the historic role of the Celtic bard.

'The Bath' is a comic story containing some irony which — in O'Flaherty's favourite fashion — verges on the melodramatic, as we read about the extraordinary Campbell 'one of the greatest barristers of the times', who can only win a difficult case when roaring drunk, and Paddy the boots who looks like a stable boy and works at Short's which he calls 'the most famous hotel in all Ireland'.

The farce is created by Campbell's attempt to take a bath. The bath — the focal point round which the story is spun — is well described, 'the enamel had worn away from nearly all the bottom of the tub, giving the impression of a small black lake, surrounded by a smooth white precipitous cliff. Into this black lake there now flowed a thick stream of black water from the cold water cock. It did not flow regularly or in volume. It would rumble in the pipe, like a man clearing his throat, a large bubble would form at the mouth of the cock, the bubble would burst, a heavy black clot would drop, followed by a dark ripple, that wound its way around the rim of the cock on emerging sometimes making a semicircular fan, like the upshoot in a gaudy, artificial fountain'.

The mingling of fact and fancy apparent in this passage also informs the dialogue throughout, as when Paddy describes the bath's last occupant. 'He was a loud-spoken class of a man, travelling for a firm of jewellery men in Birmingham; my curse on him, anyway; he must have been roaring with the itch from some awful disease, for he was in and out of that bath from daylight to dark. In the heel of the hunt he broke it and I don't know is it properly mended yet . . . . He was a heavy, gutty sort of a man with a bull neck. Crump was his name. Now, isn't that a funny bloody name for a man to have and he selling rings and bracelets?' Here Paddy's words are supposed to set up a chain of mental associations in the reader's mind. Campbell never gets his bath, for in Paddy's opinion it is much more important for the insides of a person to be scoured daily with fine ale or whiskey.

The undercurrent of irony in the story applies not only to the hotel — as a specimen of modernity with its one bath — but to modern society as when the drunken Campbell says, 'Civilisation is largely, one may say, the art of being graciously insincere', and the joke is also against himself. As noted previously O'Flaherty likes to mock the legal profession.

In the end Campbell is carried off bodily by his friends Reilly and Flanagan still wearing only a shirt and a raincoat. 'Mr Campbell swung his naked legs to and fro. He tried to grab the door jamb as they passed into the street. "My bath", he shouted. "I must have my bath"'. Though the violence here is no longer based on anger, as in the earlier 'Colic', there is a repetition of a similar physically ridiculous situation which O'Flaherty so clearly enjoys.

'The Pedlar's Revenge' on the other hand, contains irony but no farce. There is irony in the casual way the police talk of Paddy Moynihan's dead body which weighs more than three sacks of flour, when he died in a state of semi-starvation. When alive 'all animals loved him', yet when his dead body is hauled out of the ravine into which he fell, the puny sparrows — thinking their nest will be violated — attack his head with beak and claw. It is ironical that his immense size and strength, the glory of his youth, should be the burden of his old age; and that the Pedlar, a little misshapen man, should possess courage and intelligence while Moynihan, the magnificent physical specimen, is simple and a coward.

The expressed laughter in the story comes from satisfied aggression. There is the mocking laughter of Moynihan when he torments the Pedlar by filling his ass's creels with stone; the Pedlar's vindictive laughter when he torments the hungry Moynihan with his beehives and well-stocked garden. It is Moynihan's humorous attitude to life that awakens the Pedlar's hatred. Ironically Moynihan goes off laughing to buy the candles with which he poisons himself, and at the end of the story it is to the tune of the Pedlar's triumphant and mocking laughter that the police leave him.

'The Post Office' is the most subtle of all O'Flaherty's humorous stories. The irony is here conveyed by the narrator and by the characters' speech and actions. The comedy is created first by the mocking attitude of the Gaelic-speaking stranger towards the simplicity of Martin Conlon and the other villagers, and secondly by Conlon's antics on the telephone.

The voiced reactions of the watching peasants provide a chorus to the action of this story. Their first outburst of laughter occurs when Conlon the postmaster is asked to send a telegram to Los Angeles. The villagers know he would rather 'walk twenty miles on bare knees in winter's heaviest frost' than do this, so 'the whole audience now burst out into full-bellied and joyous laughter. The rollicking sound could be heard away out on the road. People stamped on the floor and thumped one another in the sides with merriment. There were tears in their eyes. They became silent, however, after Martin glared at them'.

When Conlon is puzzled by the language the foreign women are speaking, his incomprehension 'brought a tremendous peal of laughter from those present. As the saying goes, the rafters shook'. Later in the conversation between the villagers it is obvious that lukewarm feelings have no part in the emotional reactions of these people. The uproarious laughter has now given way to open-mouthed curiosity as they listen to the telephone conversation between Conlon and Kate about little Tommy. When he puts down the receiver, 'With one voice they shouted savagely; "What little Tommy is that? Is it Little Tommy of the Bottles? Is it Little Tommy of Bohermor? Is it Claddagh Tommy? Which Tommy do you mean, man alive?"'.

When Conlon gives up trying to get connected to Galway he mutters to himself, 'Knock down the house, if you feel like it. Smash, burn, scald, maim and wreck. Steal and ravage to your heart's desire. Lay about you heartily. I don't give a damn what you do. I have no future now, at the end of my life, other than beggary and a miserable wandering from door to door'. This exaggeration of statement is the verbal equivalent of the melodramatic situation, for violent emotional reactions are all part of the game. At the end of the story the people gather round Conlon. 'Ah! You are a kind, good-natured poor devil, when all is said and done. You are the funniest man on earth, into the bloody bargain . . .' And the Spanish girl's serious and passionate recitation of Lorca, which is simultaneously taking place, ends the story on a doubly ironic note for those who realise that to Lorca, and the Spanish tradition, death is a source of inspiration. O'Flaherty is far too attached to this West of Ireland society to mock at it more than gently, as he does here. None of his villagers are 'graciously insincere', and the world would call them uncivilised.

O'Flaherty is a master of the ironic remark which he will often slip into an otherwise serious situation as in 'Two Lovely Beasts' where Kate Higgins becomes so tired she says she has no energy left with which to pick lice out of her children's hair; or in *The Puritan* where the priest asks Ferriter, 'I only asked you if you had murdered her wilfully, because the sin of wilful murder is beyond my power to absolve except in case of extremity or during a Jubilee. Otherwise it can only be absolved by a bishop' (p. 239).

Jonathan Swift said that a reasonable person, when confronted with the disparity between pretended virtue and concealed stupidity and viciousness must be 'tempted according to the present turn of his humour, either to laugh, lament, or be angry'.[11] O'Flaherty's criticism of society can take the form of violence or laughter, used separately or together with satiric implication. The laughter sometimes hides sadness, for in the Irish especially the comic is often in close touch with what mourns in man. It is when anger is predominant, however, that O'Flaherty produces the form of satire in which a passionate indignation sweeps away any desire to be even contemptuously funny. As in general O'Flaherty preferred his satiric implication to be amusing, this does not often happen.

O'Flaherty had written all his satiric short stories by 1932, but the range of satire he used is illustrated by his three full-length satiric novels published in 1929—35. *Hollywood Cemetery* is a caricature of the film world in which 'Holywood is a cemetery where the remains of present day bourgeois intellectuals are buried, after being fattened, like the sacrificial victims in ancient Mexico, on enormous salaries, only to have their hearts plucked out and eaten by the Moguls of modern mammon . . .' (p. 114). *The Puritan* is an ironic satire on the conventional morals of Irish Catholic society. *The Return of the Brute* is a scathing satire on the everlasting futility and savagery of war which does not seem to have been recognised as a satire when it was published.[12]

The bitterness apparent in *The Return of the Brute* is based on the pity O'Flaherty feels for the soldiers and the anger he feels against society for reducing them to brute level. Bitterness is cloaked by humour in most of his satiric work such as the two other novels mentioned, in *A Cure for Unemployment*, written in the vein of Swift's *Drapier's Letters*, and in *A Tourist's Guide to Ireland*; but the bitterness appears naked in two short stories published in *The Tent*, and written at a time when O'Flaherty himself was in a particularly tense emotional state. These stories express emotion which lies too deep for laughter or contempt and therefore display a satiric frontal attack, also used in *The Return of the Brute*, rather than the approach through humorous ridicule.[13] The stories are 'Offerings' and 'The Outcast'.

'Offerings', less than 1000 words long, is similar to a scene in *Skerrett* where, when Skerrett's son is lying dead 'The demon of jealousy found voice in Skerrett's mind. Suddenly it appeared evil to him that the priest, whom he had thought good and pure in all ways, should stand greedily watching coins in the house where his beloved son was dead' (pp. 54–5). Paddy Lenehan is burying his four year old daughter. The priest stands by the door ostensibly reading his breviary but in reality watching the offerings of the mourners being dropped on the table. Paddy too watches the offerings. 'He was not thinking of whether a mass more or less might be said for the dead. But, you know, it is a custom, a measure of a man's social importance: if the offerings are large it is important; if the offerings are small it is an insult'.

In 'Offerings' criticism is implied against the priest, against the publican who has provided Lenehan with porter on credit, and the gombeen man who has advanced him pipes and tobacco. 'And where there is not enough food even to feed two mouths, is not the good God kind to take a third mouth out of the hungry world into the joy of Paradise? So they said at the wake . . .' Lenehan is also known as a wit, for 'when a man is very, very poor and life is very, very miserable, it is a nice thing to be a wit. He could get drinks in public houses for his jokes'. Like Skerrett, as Lenehan sees the priest counting the money just for a moment he hates the priest, but 'then again he thought it was very funny; he was a wit, you know'. No more than the Deignans in 'The Red Petticoat' will Lenehan allow life to defeat him.

'The Outcast', which comes down more heavily against the priest, is ironically subtitled, 'I am the Good Shepherd (Jesus Christ)'. The parish priest, Christ's representative, is a huge fat man with eyes 'scowling behind mountainous barricades of darkening flesh and a paunch that would have done credit to a Roman emperor'.

When Kitty Manion, bearing her new-born son, is brought into the presence of this great man he shows her no pity. She will not declare the father of the child, because there was more than one man. Because the villagers fear the priest's wrath she can obtain no shelter and she has just lost her job as a housemaid. The priest tells her, 'Begone from me, accursed one. Begone with the child of your abomination'. The girl goes and drowns herself with her baby. As in 'The Fairy Goose' and 'A Strange Disease' or 'The Inquisition', the priest is a source of fear rather than love.

'The Outcast' is the vehicle of a satiric message, as the subtitle suggests, but it is more than that. When the girl reaches the sombre lake of Black Cahir, which she has chosen for her end, O'Flaherty uses the pathetic fallacy to stress the fact that the girl and her baby are returning to the elements from which they arose. They have fled from the cruelty man creates when he becomes alien to his nature. In O'Flaherty's words, 'we have grown so tired of priestly cant and hypocrisy that we have turned against the wisdom which their avarice has corrupted by use as a cover for their evil-doing; but we must return to its simple beauty if we wish to save ourselves'.[14] This wisdom, as he shows once more in this story, is the power of love. It is better for the girl to die loving her baby than to live and become broken by fear and hatred.

In Sean O'Faolain's opinion most Irish writers 'see the priest in one of three aspects – the jovial, hunting, hearty priest, who is really a "good fellow" in clerical garb; or the rigorous, unbending saintly and generally rather inhuman ascetic – the patriarch of the flock; or the man whose life is one long psychological problem', and he includes Liam O'Flaherty with other writers to whom this statement applies.[15]

On the basis of the short stories alone O'Flaherty's priests would seem to fall into the third category, but to get a balanced view of O'Flaherty's criticism of priests one would need to take into consideration his treatment of priest characters in his novels such as *Thy Neighbour's Wife*, *The Wilderness*, *The House of Gold*, *The Puritan*, *Skerrett*, *The Martyr*, *Famine* and *Land*, and to relate this to the opinions expressed in *A Tourist's Guide to Ireland*, more than a third of which is devoted to this subject.[16]

In Chapter 3 it was mentioned that Michael H. Murray called 'Charity', 'The Inquisition', 'Offerings' and 'The Outcast' explicitly drawn diatribes against the Irish clergy. It is true that in both 'Offerings' and 'The Outcast' the didacticism is obvious. In 'Offerings' Lenehan is hardly defined as a character and all the satiric impact falls upon the story situation but in 'The Outcast' the satire is directed against the character of the priest. Because in 'Offerings' the satire is directed against the total situation rather than any one character, this story could be interpreted less stringently. The story does not tell us what becomes of the money the priest takes up as he leaves, and those who have read *Famine* know that O'Flaherty also shows priests who beggared themselves to feed the poor. The extremely poor have always had odd ways of spending their money, and might not the same priest who takes this money one day, give it to the hopeless drunkard who begs from him in 'Charity'? Surely it is not only the church, but also the political and social system of Ireland with its many ramifications, which caused poverty and drunkenness to be so prevalent, that is here implicitly criticised.

Behind O'Flaherty's use and control of the ridiculous from its most romantic or fantastic aspect to its most intellectual and satiric, lies his sense of pity to deflect which he uses both bitterness and violence, with or without humour. This is perhaps why O'Flaherty can never maintain a comic situation for long without hinting at tragedy behind it. He magnifies the disorder and absurdities of life to involve his readers and eschew indifference, for without the deep-felt emotional response, whether its expression takes the form of violence, laughter or tears, the world for him is a worthless place.

9 Attitudes towards Death

O'Flaherty is concerned to show that man is a part of nature, but also that man's conscious awareness makes the simple acceptance of this affinity insufficient. Man has to accept his finite physical condition but at the same time he has pretensions to immortality, whether or not it takes the form of individual survival. Human beings have built up a complicated fabric of myth to help resolve this tension caused by the inescapable but unacceptable fact of death; and a man's philosophical beliefs or religion generally include some justification of death. O'Flaherty's beliefs and his attitude to death, must be seen in relation to his own movement from a Catholic upbringing, through a flirtation with Communism to agnostic freethinking.

Death in some form appears in approximately a third of all the short stories O'Flaherty wrote, but the proportion of stories which include death rose in *The Mountain Tavern* volume to thirteen out of twenty and fell in *Two Lovely Beasts* to five out of twenty stories. *The Mountain Tavern* stories were all first published between 1926 and 1929, a time when O'Flaherty was suffering from considerable personal frustration.

The treatment of death in O'Flaherty's writing will first be considered in relation to what autobiographical evidence reveals about his religious ideas, afterwards to the appearance of death in his novels, and in his short stories.

O'Flaherty says in *Joseph Conrad, An Appreciation* (p. 7), 'What is beautiful in man is that he is unhappy as a man and wishes to be a God, to be free from death and the restraint of the earth's balance; ... that he creates gods only in order to break them; that he is a being constantly in revolt ...'

In *Two Years*, looking back to his feelings ten years before, O'Flaherty mentions his early interest in what he calls Bolshevism. He says he had read at college,

> ... some of the works of Marx, Engels, Ferdinand Lassalle, Bebel, Connolly, Proudhon, Bentham and various other writers; but while they

had appealed to my intellect they had not materially affected my attitude towards life. They merely affected what is most vital in the intellectual consciousness of an Irishman, and that is his attitude towards the negative or spiritual part of life; whereas these writers were mainly concerned with the positive or material side of life. They forced me to the conclusion that God, as my mother understood him, was definitely dead . . . and I could not make up my mind which Pretender to support (pp. 70–1).

O'Flaherty continues to tell of the slight effect on him of the Irish Easter Rising, but the profound impression caused by the Russian October Revolution of 1917. By this time, owing to his experiences in the trenches, O'Flaherty says he had a cynical attitude towards life and he no longer believed there was any purpose in human activity. The revolt of the Russian masses encouraged him and he adds, 'man cannot exist without a God of some sort. Despair, cynicism, and atheism inevitably lead to suicide, either of the body or of the mind. A man must have a definite purpose and end in view'. Communism, as he clearly states in *I Went to Russia*[1], was a new form of religion, a religion which denies the existence of God and the immortality of the soul.

After the publication of *The Black Soul*, to write which he says he became a fervent disciple of the religion of artistic beauty,[2] O'Flaherty tells us in *Shame the Devil* how he again visited his family in Aran, and the pain that his social ostracism caused him. Attracted by Communism he thought: 'How comforting it would be to recant my heresies, to bow the knee to the gods of my country and to be taken back into the fold . . . I would feel the joy of forgiveness, of being at one with my tribe. I would have the simple beliefs of my forefathers to shelter me against doubt and tribulation' (p. 22). As an artist, however, he finds this impossible. The sentimental desire for both security of belief and identification with his people returns as a kind of foetal longing in moments of doubt or weakness, but most of the time he rejoices in spiritual liberation from religious obligation, and decides that he is unfitted to be the adherent of any political creed, or to believe in any god, for 'according as the creative impulse grew stronger in me, I found my Communist associates as bigoted, narrow-minded and insufferable as Roman Catholic fanatics or reactionary Conservatives' (p. 28).

Throughout *Shame the Devil* O'Flaherty records his oscillation from the exaltation of artistic achievement and freedom to the despair of alienation and self-doubt. At one moment he believes that it is only by renewing his friendship with nature that he will find peace and at another point he decides that men must humiliate themselves and accept the God of love to find true happiness. 'How strange it is that we have grown ashamed of love! And most ashamed of the love that is loveliest, of suffering little children to come unto us, of being like them! Death is now a monster' (p. 228). This implies that death should not be a monster, and would not be were love to overcome it. However hard he tries, O'Flaherty cannot pin down truth which he calls a slippery whore with many faces, only one of which he may glimpse at a time.

These contradictions, or many faces of truth, appear in his work; but what is clear is that apart from the importance to an Irishman of what O'Flaherty calls the spiritual side of life he considers beliefs of some sort to be essential to man, and these beliefs should help him to love and to die by liberating, not repressing him; without a belief of some kind he is not a complete person.

O'Flaherty's autobiographical writings stop short at 1934 but by following the theme of death through his novels it is possible to see some development beyond this point implied through the mouths of his characters and his attitudes towards them.

In O'Flaherty's first two novels we find that Fergus the Stranger in *The Black Soul* and Father McMahon in *Thy Neighbour's Wife* have to come to terms with death before they can face life. McMahon battles throughout the book with his natural instincts versus his priestly vocation. Finally he decides to put to sea in an oarless curragh — as the holy men of old had done for a penance — to see whether he would be drowned or return safely to shore. A storm blows up while he is defenceless in the boat, equivalent in violence to the personal crisis taking place within him. He is rescued by another curragh as his own breaks to pieces and he emerges from the testing purposeful and sure of himself. Fergus the Stranger in *The Black Soul* has his moment of awakening after his dangerous fight on the cliff-face with naked, mad Red John who dies of a burst heart. Of Fergus the author says 'it was at that moment, when he came face to face with the reality of death that the reality of life assumed a meaning for him', pp. 284–9).

O'Flaherty must have come to terms with physical death in the trenches, as the army also taught him to admire the discipline and valour of the loyal soldier. In *The Return of the Brute* we see the effect on men of the continual presence of death in a violent and horrible form. Gunn in this book is a favourite type of O'Flaherty hero. He has a simple mind, a strong body and 'a spirit that hardship could not conquer' (p. 15). Gunn is aged thirty-two (O'Flaherty's age at the time) and in him, says the author, the fear of death and old age has begun to conquer the arrogance of youth.

The boy Lamont's cowardice saps Gunn's self-discipline and arouses in him a dangerous desire of freedom. He can no longer act as an obedient and thoughtless soldier, and the conflict between desire and circumstance gradually leads to mental breakdown.

Here is the hell-world of the trenches:

All around them the earth lay naked, turned into mud, holed, covered with the horrid debris of war, emitting a stench of rotting, unburied corpses. From the pitch-dark sky the rain fell, unceasing and monotonous, like the droning of brine water falling on a floor of black rocks from the roof of a subterranean cave where moaning seals are hidden and flap about upon their ledges; sounds from a dead world; the mysterious gloom of the primeval earth, where no life had yet arisen; no sap of growing things; nothing but worms and rats feeding on death (p. 23).

A particularly evil form of death this, because dissociated from the life to which it should be complementary.

The men gradually become inured to all miseries except the misery of death — in the midst of death they fear dying, until — under continuous gunfire — even this disappears and they are 'no longer afraid. They no longer thought. They had lost individual consciousness. They had ceased to be human' (p. 116). Corpses in this book are 'things' to be used as packing material for the trench walls, or abandoned without regret. Gunn deteriorates into an animal fighting for survival (hence the book's title) and dies in fear, bellowing like an animal, his reason gone.

In modern urbanised society death is something most people push to the back of their minds. Society does not in general expect them to come to terms with death except as old age approaches or during serious illness. In *Mr. Gilhooley* one gets the impression that O'Flaherty thinks urbanised man tries to ignore death and is as a result personally diminished. O'Flaherty introduces the idea into a conversation between Nellie (who is afraid of death) and Gilhooley (who often thinks of it). In their new flat,

... there was an air of remoteness from primitive life, from the sordidness of poverty, even from the consciousness of life itself, which is always present, even in the fields under a bright sunlight, where the growth and decay of nature, moving conjointly, tinges human joy with a grim realisation of death. But in this room the ingenuity of man had successfully combated these vague premonitions. The hand of nature had been stayed and an effect was procured, of stability, of refinement, of civilisation (p. 164).

When death strikes these urbanised people in the form of sudden accident or murder, the victims are taken unaware as in *The Informer, The Assassin* and *The Puritan*, and the perpetrators are unable to stifle a bad conscience consequent upon committing murder or deliberately causing death. The three protagonists of these novels succeed in coming to terms neither with death nor with their consciences in face of the act, though a great deal of each novel is devoted to their attempts to do so. For all three guilt is in the end more terrible than murder.

Dan Gallagher in *The Informer*, in a rather inconsequential statement made to Mary, would appear to voice O'Flaherty's rationalised beliefs on death at this period when he says' . . . according to my own calculations and discoveries, death brings us back into the great consciousness of the Universe, which is eternal. Therefore death, properly speaking, is not death. It is a second stage of birth . . . Now we see death is not a danger. But defeat is a danger' (London, 1958, p. 163).

O'Flaherty continued to believe that defeat is the real death and lost his Christian belief in the immortality of the individual soul. He replaced this with what at first seems to have been ideas on the unity of all nature including man's life cycle. Nevertheless the nostalgia for the secure beliefs of his childhood emerges not only in the account already mentioned from *Shame the Devil*, but also in an autobiographical short story such as 'The Child of God' and in several novels. In *The Assassin* McDara, after he has killed the politician, makes a sign of the Cross with his victim's blood on the wall. Nolan when he lies dead at the end of *The Informer* stretches out his limbs in the shape of a cross. In *The Martyr* Crosbie is crucified, and in *The Wilderness* Lawless allows Dillon to murder him to show that he has overcome both hatred and fear of death. All these deaths are in the nature of expiating sacrifices willed by the perpetrator, the victim, or sometimes both, but perversely they also seem to illustrate O'Flaherty's own love/hate relationship with Christianity, the belief in which he has mentally cast aside, but which emotionally grips him still.

O'Flaherty's ambivalent state of mind is illustrated in *The Assassin* during McDara's attendance at Mass just after the murder (Chapter XIX). He is at first in a state of mental exaltation which gives him a sense of great superiority: 'he saw himself, like Samson, catching the pillars of the church and crushing them into dust, flying to Saturn and laying it waste and explaining to an enormous multitude a new scientific discovery that would abolish death' (London, 1959, pp. 144—5). Then he remembers his love for his mother is forever lost. Exactly as O'Flaherty must have done he associates his mother with his religious upbringing. The succession of McDara's moods in this chapter could be those of O'Flaherty himself, whose mother had died a few years before. During the consecration McDara suddenly understands that he has lost the innocence, the God and the people of his childhood. 'If he went back among them, rending his garments, like the ancient Jews, they would look at him strangely and then turn away their eyes, just as his mother did' (p. 148), and his mind is filled with a sense of loss. McDara here falls into the category mentioned by O'Flaherty, 'despair, cynicism and atheism lead to suicide of body or mind'.

O'Flaherty has never decried the ideals of Christianity as such, only the Church's interpretation of them. *The Martyr* contains much serious criticism on the difference between the theory and practice of Christianity so that in the end even the crucifixion can become corrupted as a symbol of sacrifice and Tyson says 'all enslaved people worship this fetish of the crucifixion' (p. 275). It is Crosbie's dream, however, which incorporates O'Flaherty's real anger: 'So is Europe and the whole of Christendom waiting for the resurrection, when the brazen gods of money and sensual pleasure shall be hurled in the dust, and Christ our Saviour again enthroned as the King of Kings. Then the church, too, will be regenerated and purified . . . ' (p. 229).

O'Flaherty's early short stories show situations nearly always dominating characters. Characters are often like spindrift caught up in circumstances or overpowering emotion. As O'Flaherty developed as a person, and a writer, this situation was reversed and in his mature work the characters come to dominate the situation; consequently the inevitable shortness of man's earthly span, the inevitability of death, becomes less important. What counts is how a man conducts himself in face of difficulty and death. The hero's contribution to society or the community is measured by the extent to which he realises his potential and makes use of it; something which the protagonists of *The Informer* and *The Assassin* fail to do.

Sometimes the hero's struggles are misdirected (*The Puritan*), or misunderstood (*Skerrett*), or apparently end in defeat (Thomsy in *Famine*). The importance for O'Flaherty is not society's judgeinst of success or happiness but how men succeed in struggling agiainst the frustration and limitation of the circumstances in which they find themselves.

Skerrett had desired to die in his prime rather than become a slave. His aspirations stand throughout the book for life, not the living-death which was that of the superstitious and ignorant island people.

In the short stories there are many glimpses of O'Flaherty's attitude towards death. There are characters taken by death unaware, those who dread death and those who accept or even welcome it. O'Flaherty examines the effect of death on those left behind and the threat of death being used as a test of courage. Above all in the later stories there are a decreasing number of physical deaths portrayed, and an increasing number of characters who are examples of 'living-death', and this again leads to the conclusion that for O'Flaherty the death of the spirit, which should be indestructible, is far more terrible than the inevitable death of the body.

Death in O'Flaherty's animal stories is only tragic when associated with human abuse as in 'Sport: the Kill', or neglect as in 'The Black Bullock'; otherwise it is caused by the animal's instinct to perpetuate life. In 'The Cow's Death' the cow instinctively chooses to die rather than forsake her offspring. 'The Hawk' fights for his mate to the death and there is a similar situation in 'The Wild Goat's Kid'. Death in the animal world is not associated with emotional sadness but the loss of physical presence. The cow leaps after the calf because she misses the presence of the calf which she knows she should nurture. The loss of presence would only otherwise have been borne in upon the cow when the calf had lost its body heat and become inert matter. We see this in 'The Wild Swan' where the male, from habit, stays with the dead female until he sees her body being carried along by the wind 'stiff and without weight' like a kite, and only then does he desert her.

In 'Prey', the only short story O'Flaherty wrote about an animal dying of old age, though death as such is not mentioned in the story we know from the gathering of the carrion crows that the donkey must have died, and it is natural and acceptable that his body should provide food for birds and dogs; yet it may shock the reader when in *Famine* the same thing happens to Thomsy's body.

It is surely the realisation of that spiritual part of life — which O'Flaherty says is particularly important to the intellectual consciousness of an Irishman — that complicates man's attitude towards death, and makes the way in which death is confronted so important. Courage has always been O'Flaherty's most admired quality and many of his best stories are an illustration of this, courage in face of death being the ultimate test.

Of the four stories in the *Spring Sowing* volume which contain deaths, three concern deliberate killing under stress of sudden lust, drunkenness or passion, but the fourth, 'The Sniper', is the most rewarding, for it shows a man's courageous rendezvous with death on the rooftops.

The seat of courage, as O'Flaherty tells us (*Land*, p. 194) lies in the intellect 'as distinct from that of the lower animals', and the eyes of the sniper are described as 'deep and thoughtful: the eyes of a man who is used to looking at death'. His intellect remains master of the fear which threatens to overwhelm him.

The deaths in three other stories 'Wolf Lanigan's Death', 'Civil War' and 'The Alien Skull' are terrible because fear is dominant. Rosie's eyes when she kills Wolf are 'cold and glassy' with fear. In 'Civil War' the fear of death fills Dolan's mind and makes his teeth chatter, and in 'The Alien Skull' Mulhall, having shot the enemy soldier, himself dies in terror.

Courage, by overcoming fear and selfishness, entails integrity of feeling. It can be the instinctive animal courage on a lower plane as shown in 'The White Bitch' and 'The Black Cat', or the intelligent courage shown in stories such as 'The Oar' and 'The Landing' where man pits himself against the elements. Both the men in the curragh and the watchers in 'The Landing' are in control of their fear. In that moment of delirium when their boat bore down on death 'They no longer feared death'.

In 'The Oar' in a similar duel between men and the sea, it is also stated that the men 'no longer feared'. Their only moment of doubt is when Little Martin's boat is swamped and Red Bartly reminds them 'sense comes before courage', but their eyes 'against their cunning life-loving wills, still pierced the darkness behind them'.

Death is viewed by these fisherfolk with a mixture of dread, awe and fatalism. The dread is based on the practical consideration that it is hard enough to support a family in Aran with a husband, let alone without one: the awe is the result of a respect for the power of the sea, fear of the unknown and a superstition that death is unlucky and harmful. There is also a fatalistic acceptance of death as when in 'The Landing' Big Bridget says, 'we only live by the grace of God, sure enough, with the sea always watching to devour us'.

Peasant superstitions connected with death are contradictory for they are dependent both upon familiarity with nature's law that every living thing must seed and die before being reborn, and the Catholic doctrine that though the innocent and the holy will be saved after death, the sinful and the unshriven will go either to limbo, where their souls may be saved after punishment and by the prayers of the faithful, or to hell which is Satan's kingdom. Death is thus equated with evil as well as with good, and as most men are sinful the evil aspect came to be dominant. Contradictory attitudes in which pre-Christian superstitions are mingled with Catholic doctrine about death can be found in stories such as 'The Fairy Goose', 'The Mermaid', 'Red Barbara' and 'Offerings'.

In 'Offerings' the death of the four-year-old child was, the people thought, not really a cause for sorrow 'because they go straight to heaven at that age'. Yet the bitterness of the story hardly implies that this death is a cause for rejoicing. In another wake scene from 'The Child of God' the drunken mourners put the drunken carpenter into the newly made coffin on the floor, while the corpse lies on the table and the rest of the stupefied men lie about in grotesque attitudes beneath a 'sagging black earthen roof', already suggestive of burial. Peter, the artist, draws the scene and shocks the villagers into realising that debauch in the presence of death is desecration.[3] The people react with the same instinct of destruction shown by the birds in 'The Wounded Cormorant', for Peter threatens their sense of security by introducing the idea of evil, so they yell 'sacrilege' and try to kill him. Yet according to their religion they would be guilty of mortal sin by such a murder.

In 'The Mermaid' and 'Red Barbara' the pagan beliefs of the people again prove stronger than their Christian education. At the beginning of 'The Mermaid' Michael is regarded by the people as God's favourite whom the cruel sea would not dare to drown. Michael has all the most admired gifts. When his mother dies he follows her smiling to the grave and deplores mourning for one who has gone to eternal happiness with the saints. He changes, however, after his marriage to the beautiful Margaret who awakens his emotions and his senses. When she suddenly dies he turns against God. It is now God who is cruel. All his shallow Christian ideals are overthrown and his instinct to be reunited with the one person he has ever really loved leads him to commit suicide. This is a grave sin for a Christian, but to Michael his love is more immortal than any myth of happiness in another world. The once cruel sea now welcomes him and his love takes visionary shape and lures him to death.

In 'Red Barbara' the villagers attribute supernatural powers to nature. Seeking to remove the curse of childlessness Barbara sits near the cliffs at the same spot where old men come to die in peace drunk on the potency of the sea air. Because Joseph cannot give her a child Barbara comes to will his death. Death is a reality to these people and their only insurance against it is not the Christian ideal of heaven but the renewal of life and perpetual struggle to postpone the death which they know must come. When Red Barbara remarries she is happy because her new husband is a brave rough fisherman who 'fighting with death' rides the stormy sea, and she sets at nought Joseph who possessed the priestlike and gentle qualities associated with Christianity.

In 'The Child of God' when the people are reminded of their flouting of religious convention, they react violently and their courage is overcome by fear. But in 'The Mermaid' and 'Red Barbara' we have the reverse situation for in both these stories the heroes start off by conforming to the religious ideas of the community and end by submerging their religious loyalties beneath a free and positive acceptance of life as they wish to lead it, in which the courage of conviction overrides fear.

It is clear from these stories that O'Flaherty thinks proscriptive religion as taught to these peasants weakens insteads of nourishing a courageous integrity of feeling which is for O'Flaherty the immortal part of man.

In one of his autobiographical passages O'Flaherty says that it took him years to overcome the melancholy attitude towards life impressed upon him at school,[4] and it was probably not until the early thirties that he resolved his doubt about the purpose of life and overcame some of the fears which had so often emerged in his violent or obsessed characters.

The high proportion of stories containing death in *The Mountain Tavern* volume marks the culmination of the period when violent death appealed to O'Flaherty and the beginning of what may be called a 'cyclic' attitude towards death associated with youth or rebirth, which he later illustrated at length in *Famine*. At the same time he increasingly shows us the death of the spirit in still living persons, illustrated at length in *Hollywood Cemetery*. It is because these three tendencies meet in *The Mountain Tavern* volume that the proportion of stories containing death is so high. Taking these three aspects in turn, violent death; death which is a natural end to a life cycle; and the death of the spirit, it will become evident that in O'Flaherty's short stories the dominance of the first aspect in his early work gives place to the dominance of the third aspect as he matures.

In the *Spring Sowing* volume there are four stories containing violent deaths, 'The Sniper', 'Wolf Lanigan's Death', 'Blood Lust' and 'The Struggle'. All these deaths are murders, though one of the four is committed in self-defence. Among the animal stories in this volume there are five stories containing death, 'The Cow's Death', 'Sport: the Kill', 'Two Dogs', 'The Wild Sow' and 'The Black Bullock' and all five of these deaths are attributable to the carelessness, deliberate cruelty or neglect of man. The cruel aspect of death is therefore dominant. This volume also contains, however, 'The Landing' which shows men fearlessly confronting the possibility of death and 'The Tramp' which is O'Flaherty's first story about men suffering from spiritual death. He brings this out in physical description. The tramp's body 'was after a fashion menacing with the power and vitality it seemed to exude', and he is described as fearless and aggressive; his eyes 'stare you in the face as boldly as a lion, or a child, and are impudent enough to have a gentle expression at the back of them unconscious of malice'. The two paupers on the other hand are described as jaded and terror-striken, dejected and listless, and their eyes envious. The restricting effect of religion on mental freedom also enters this story when the tramp says to Deignan, 'I know why you can't follow me. You're a Catholic, you believe in Jesus Christ and the Blessed Virgin and the priests and a heaven hereafter. You like to be called respectable . . . '

In *The Tent* volume there are six stories containing physical death. Two of these, 'Offerings' and 'The Outcast', again criticise the respectably deadening effect of religion, for in 'Offerings' it is stated 'life does not end with the death of one. There are others who live on and they have customs and a common code of conduct that must be observed'. In 'The Outcast' the girl has lost her social respectability and, the priest tells her 'for the sake of your immortal soul I command you to name the father of your child'. When the girl commits suicide, however, she is spiritually alive as she makes her last prayer, and her act is one of courage not cowardice. Three other stories in this volume, 'The Fireman's Death', 'The Terrorist' and 'Civil War' show men dying, or wanting to die, in abnormal states of mind, for the fireman is sick, the terrorist is mad, and in 'Civil War' the men are either brutalised or paralysed with fear by the horror of warfare.

Also in *The Tent* are three stories which tell of spiritual aridity. 'The Tyrant' and 'Blackmail' both contain callous bullies who are impervious to the feelings of others, filled with personal ambition, and lack self-awareness. 'The Inquisition' shows the spiritual awakening of a young boy. Hitherto Cleary has 'shrunk away in terror from any personal thought, lest it might lead him into doubt and sin'. Cleary is also reminded by the priest to think of his soul, when it is in fact against his soul that the religious dogmas are directed. Like the tramp and the abandoned girl in 'The Outcast' he realises that his only way to spiritual freedom is to cast off the shackles of religious convention which are designed to effect his enslavement not his salvation.

A comparison of the stories in *The Tent* to those in *Spring Sowing* shows that O'Flaherty's idea of death is moving from the dominance of death's cruel aspect to a realisation that death may in certain situations also be willed, and an increasing importance is given to a consideration of spiritual death, caused both by personal selfishness and by the rigidity of the Church.

In *The Mountain Tavern* volume there are examples of stories showing violent and final death in 'The Painted Women', 'The Mountain Tavern', 'The Alien Skull' and 'The Ditch'. In all these stories, as in the earlier *Spring Sowing* group of stories, murder is present, and — as in the *Spring Sowing* volume — there is an animal story 'The Black Rabbit' in which death is directly attributable to the cruelty of man. Two other stories, 'The Stream' and 'The Blackbird's Mate' show death by misadventure, and two more, 'The Stone' and 'Prey', show death as the natural end of the life cycle. There are the stories already discussed, 'The Fairy Goose' and 'The Child of God', which introduce ideas of sin and fear of damnation related to death, and there is 'Red Barbara' and 'The Oar' which illustrate both courage in the face of death and a fatalistic acceptance of it.

In 'Mackerel for Sale' there is another illustration of living death stressed by the still torridity of the weather and the generally derelict and hopeless air of the little town. As Micky Degatty expresses it, 'Won't we all be dead some day?' Someone else asks, 'What were we put into the world for anyway'? and receives the reply, 'to save our immortal souls'. The story is in fact about the death of the soul, or living spirit, of these people.

Finally O'Flaherty's 'cyclic' attitude towards death appears for the first time in both 'The Stone' and 'The Stream'. In these 'cyclic' stories youth is associated with old age and the pattern of birth, maturity, old age and decay emerges to which all living things are subject. In 'The Stream' the water is a symbol of enduring nature, 'the ancient stream that was still young', compared to transitory man. The young woman and child who sit by the stream are frightened away by the ugly aspect of the old woman whom they associate with evil, for this old woman is consumed not only by years but by sorrow. 'Her body withered until it was like her soul . . . when she passed anything young she spat and cursed'. She is jealous of the young and longs for her own youth before sorrow struck her.

In 'The Stone' the doting old man also has a 'mirage of returned youth in his brain'. In this story the stone symbolises the enduring quality of nature which all the young men try to conquer by lifting, but each generation is in turn mastered by old age and death. The evening after the old man's death — caused by trying to lift the stone and get the better of nature — the young men come once more to tussle with the stone.

The later stores contained in *Two Lovely Beasts* show a marked decrease of death themes. Much more attention is paid to spiritual rather than physical death. Death is only actually described in one story, 'Life', where, as in 'The Stone', it is the natural death of the worn-out body once more associated with renewal in the person of the newborn baby whom mentally the old man has come to resemble. In several other stories, however, death is in the forefront of the protagonist's mind. This happens in 'Galway Bay', 'The Old Woman', and 'The Beggars'.

The old man of eighty in 'Galway Bay' is to be admired for his dignity, courage and youthful unconquered spirit. His eyes are described as those of a captured hawk 'unwillingly, they were being captured by approaching death while still in their prime'. Maggie in 'The Old Woman' is, like the old men in 'Life' and 'The Stone', seen in relation to youth — here an eight-year-old child. Maggie also possesses dignity, courage, and a free spirit in which innocence and trust are prominent; but although she accepts her imminent death she is apprehensive of it and dreads the thought of leaving the world she has grown to love for an unknown world where she believes she will face God in judgement.

In 'The Beggars' the blind man reiterates to the passers-by 'I wish you all a happy death', thus playing on the superstitions of the people who believe in the power of a blind man's curse and the potency of his blessing. This reiterated phrase not only stresses his physical helplessness, but also his moral superiority, for this man born blind has overcome bitterness and despair and shows the same fierce determination to remain unconquered by physical limitation as is shown by the older characters in 'Galway Bay' and 'The Old Woman'.

The unbowed spirit, so admired by O'Flaherty, also appears in characters such as Miss Newell ('The Eviction'), and Penelope ('Grey Seagull'), both elderly people who show physical and moral courage; but in this volume O'Flaherty also shows us defeat of young characters in Kate ('The Touch') and Sheila Manning ('The Lament'). Both these girls are caught in frustrating situations which they must somehow learn to rise above if they are to remain spiritually victorious. A different kind of spiritual warping by loneliness causing physical degeneration is shown in Nuala ('The Wedding') and Jones ('The Flute Player') whom love has driven out of his mind and doomed to death.

O'Flaherty shows us that animals let death be a part of life. It is only man who aggressively builds immortal cultures and makes history in order to fight death.

Man's attitude towards death has through fear become as twisted as his interpretation of love. In Ireland the Church, with its many proscriptions and hell-fire sermons has played an important role in interpreting death. A fearless acceptance of the inevitability of death is as difficult for a man to achieve as the true concept of selfless love. Not only the Church, however, is to blame, for scientific discovery has had the effect of altering the earlier concept of man's place as one link in the chain of being and morally isolated him in the centre of the universe, as Stapleton complains in *Insurrection*.[5] His position there was shaky when O'Flaherty was doing most of his writing and has since become even shakier owing to the continued debunking of religious myth, the questioning of ecclesiastical authority and the fact that scientific discovery has increasingly reduced rather than increased man's relative importance on the universal scale.

In his later stories O'Flaherty shows evidence of having arrived at a fearless acceptance of the inevitability of death, and he then turned his attention to the way a man lives. His treatment of death illustrates that a man's attitude towards the spiritual or religious aspect of life is crucial in his mental struggle to arrive at some conception of how he should live — with courage and in continual struggle against odds. This courageous struggle is more important than the physical circumstances of his life and the fact that death will in the end master him.

This belief is summed up in the short final chapter or postscript to *Skerrett*: 'And as Moclair's virtues were of the body, allied to the cunning which ministers to the temporal body's wants, so do they wither quickly into nothingness. Whereas the nobility of Skerrett's nature lay in his pursuit of godliness. He aimed at being a man who owns no master. And such men, though doomed to destruction by the timid herd, grow after death to the full proportion of their greatness' (p. 287).

Immortality or godliness for O'Flaherty consists in an indomitable spirit rather than the perpetuation of a soul after death. The defeat or sickness of the spirit during life which he finds so prevalent in modern society, is far more terrible to O'Flaherty than physical death.

Conclusion

The reasons for the variety of theme, mood and style in O'Flaherty's work as a whole, and in his short stories in particular cannot be separated from a consideration of what he is consciously or subconsciously trying to achieve as a writer. His work charts the long and lonely progress of the author's attempt to understand the earth and become worthy of it. He may use historical or social themes to do this but his vision remains an essentially personal one.[1]

Bravado apart, O'Flaherty is a highly self-conscious person, which makes him feel alienated. This sense of apartness, allied to strong artistic purpose and an effervescent physical energy caused a psycho-physical pressure to build up within him as a young man from which he could only obtain release by writing. He tells us about this in *Shame the Devil*. First he says he tried to flee from himself by roaming the world (p. 12), and later in the book he examines the creative urge related to the desire to withdraw from society which had been his since childhood (pp. 202–3). At other times, however, as we can tell from the picaresque adventures related in his autobiographies, he released this pressure in an extroverted way. The alienated or emotionally maladjusted man is a twentieth century phenomenon that is not, of course, specifically Irish.[2]

O'Flaherty's writing often seems activated by a subconscious desire, through the catharsis of expression, to revert again to the state of internal harmony which would have been his prior to the sensation of self-conscious alienation; a state which animals — except those in captivity — perpetually enjoy. The variety of theme, mood and style to be found in his short stories is the result of differing attempts to regain this harmony which began as a largely personal urge but matured into something more altruistic. From his personal reactions to a hostile or distasteful environment O'Flaherty's concern became related to the problem of man's search for integrity and he attempted to indicate at least some of the hostile forces in modern society which hinder man's development.

O'Flaherty's first five novels, *Thy Neighbour's Wife*, *The Black Soul*, *The Informer*, *The Wilderness* and *Mr. Gilhooley* all contain central male characters who are persecuted by circumstances or their own neuroticism, and he returns to the same pattern in *The Puritan*. These characters are naturally more developed than the type characters of the early short stories. The social or historical detail contained in these novels is subordinate to the personal writhings of the central character.

O'Flaherty is here expressing his own state of alienation through his persecuted characters. They are persecuted not so much by society — though superficially they may appear to be — but by a failure to come to terms with themselves. To stress this O'Flaherty is fond, especially in his early work, of using a limited hero who is incapable of self-awareness, either because he is too stupid like Nolan in *The Informer*, or too neurotic like Ferriter in *The Puritan* or Lawless in *The Wilderness*. Similar characters treated more superficially appear in short stories such as 'Blood Lust', 'Wolf Lanigan's Death', 'The Alien Skull' and many others.

O'Flaherty is rarely an introspective writer. Either he distrusts too much introspection, or feels himself incompetent at reproducing it. In one of his letters to Edward Garnett he said: 'I cannot write about characters, I can only talk about them or create them'.[3]

Even in his novels, where there is more room for introspective development, and which hold the keys to the understanding of his major themes, O'Flaherty often takes delight in exaggerating the thoughts of his characters to melodramatic or fantastic proportions, and what introspection is shown is seldom peaceful, but caused by the spirit of grief, revolt or disgust. Think of the characters in 'Going into Exile' all of whom make determined efforts not to become introspective. In 'The Child of God' Mrs O'Toole is considered queer by the villagers 'because she had a habit of looking out over the cliff tops at the sea . . . for an hour at a time'. It is only in his later work, in stories such as 'The Lament', 'The Fanatic' or 'The Eviction' that introspection appears in unattractive characters who may be sensitive about their own feelings but are not sufficiently sensitive about the feelings of others, and all of them feel persecuted.

What might be called the persecution complex of O'Flaherty's central character, whether he is threatened by forces from without, or from the aberrations of his own temperament, is first weakened in *Skerrett*, in which the eponymous hero is indeed vanquished physically but not morally. The effects of persecution are overcome in *Famine* whose central character-group show incredible moral endurance in the face of the most crushing circumstances which threaten not only their existence but their dignity as human beings.

In his novels O'Flaherty moved away from one central hero, or anti-hero, as his vision of society became more complex and less personal. The splitting of the earlier central figure is first found in *The Wilderness* where, though Lawless is the principal character, Stevens and Macanasa rank closely below him in importance.

The House of Gold is O'Flaherty's first novel written round a group of characters who react upon and victimise each other, each being fixed in the cocoon of his own personal selfishness. *The Return of the Brute* is also centred round a group, united victims of the persecuting circumstances of war, virtually prisoners to their situation.

The Martyr, Land and *Insurrection* also each has a trinity of central figures which represent abstract principles. But an attempt to line up each set of three figures as consistently representing the same principle in each book breaks down for the soldier/poet/monk trio who stand for power, beauty and immortality mentioned specifically in *Land* (London, 1946, p. 53) and who reappear in *Insurrection*, have developed from the peasant/scientist/mystic trio round which *The Wilderness* story is woven. The theses behind these figures are important, however, because they form the only indication we have of O'Flaherty's inconsistent but conscious attempt at answering the question 'What is ideal man?', or 'What is man for?'. The composite answer he gives is an oblique one, but would appear to be that by taking his peasant/scientist/mystic figures of *The Wilderness* and making all three soldiers in *Insurrection* he is suggesting that the contradictory forces within man should not weaken themselves by strife but unite in the face of the common enemy which is defeat. The story of the Irish rising gives an ideal illustration of this theme.

O'Flaherty gave the best answer to his question 'What is man for?' not in those books where he makes the most explicit attempt to do so, but in *Skerrett* and *Famine* in both of which the theme grows out of the action, rather than the other way round. Skerrett and the Kilmartin family in *Famine* also fight against outward circumstances but their true enemy is within themselves.

In a book review O'Flaherty once said: 'Novels would be far more interesting and far more artistic if novelists merely described life instead of trying to change it according to their ideas'.[4] Though this may be a counsel of perfection and it is in general what O'Flaherty tried to do, often his way of showing life also implies that he would like to change it.

Like the doctor in *The House of Gold* O'Flaherty passed beyond his own sufferings to enter into the sufferings of others and he cannot forbear protesting against what he sees. The doctor believes, for instance, that two of the forces which keep man in bondage are greed and superstition. O'Flaherty in his work gives us many different illustrations of both.

Greed may take the simplest form of cupidity, as in 'Patsa or the Belly of Gold'; possessive jealousy, as in 'The Painted Woman'; ambition, as in 'Two Lovely Beasts', or sexual lust as in 'Unclean'.

Superstition may be shown as invested in the power of the Church so that Skerrett's mission is to sow the seeds 'for the growing of a free race' (*Skerrett*, p. 259); or it may be related to paganism as in Aran stories like

'The Fairy Goose' and 'Red Barbara'. Superstition keeps a man in bondage because it stifles or misdirects his humanity, perpetuates ignorance and promotes fear.

It is because O'Flaherty is concerned with large basic issues of universal interest such as these, that the way characters react to a given situation is so often of more importance than the situation itself. As the situation is more often than not an Irish one, a legitimate question is to what extent O'Flaherty can be regarded as a specifically Irish writer.

Without a doubt Aran remains O'Flaherty's spiritual home. 'The island has the character and personality of a mute God. One is awed in its presence, breathing its air. Over it broods an overwhelming sense of great, noble tragedy. The Greeks would have liked it'.[5]

In many of his novels it may at first appear that the situation is very important (think of *The Informer, The Martyr, Land, Insurrection* and *Famine* which are all related to crucial events in Irish history), but it is the basic human reactions which matter most. The fact that O'Flaherty often uses a historical, or quasi-historical situation as in *The Assassin*, lends the plot authenticity and at the same time creates a tension between the actuality or time dimension, and the timelessness of the human reaction to it, which could equally well be transposed into another country or period.

Therefore, though as an Irish writer O'Flaherty uses Irish themes, these are incidental. *The Martyr* is a book about the foolishness of all civil wars in the same way as the non-Irish *The Return of the Brute* is about the futility of all wars. *The Puritan* is a study of hypocrisy, and *The Informer* an exploration of a guilty conscience; in *The Assassin* a man searches for liberty of spirit and in *Mr. Gilhooley* for true love.

O'Flaherty's Irishness is, nevertheless, difficult to forget. It emerges not only in such things as his keen sense of the ridiculous, his rebelliousness, in his alternation of uproarious or pugnacious participation and introspective withdrawal, all of which is not exclusively Irish, though found among many Irishmen, but it is most strongly evident in his love of controversy and struggle.

The detached observation and sincere feeling shown in the best of O'Flaherty's short stories will form his most enduring contribution to Anglo-Irish literature. Here he is able to express a quintessence which by its brevity suggests far more than the diffuse form of the novel states, *Skerrett* with its succession of dramatic situations and *Famine* being exceptions.

The reasons behind the twentieth century Irish writer's liking for and success in the short story are difficult to define but seem to be temperamental, traditional and social.

Temperamentally the Irish are a volatile race. Their gifts are lyrical and imaginative rather than prosaic, logical or philosophic, whimsical rather than serious. They are also naturally loquacious and the discipline of the short story form exerts a control over this. One can, for instance, discern the tendency to be discursive, combined with a genius for words leading to prolixity, in the work of both Joyce and Beckett, and both broke out of the compressed confines of the short story. Many Irishmen have a talent for anecdote and regard the world as a passing show not to be taken too seriously, which also suits the short span of the story. One of the most difficult things to achieve in a novel is the continuity and verisimilitude of the characters, especially if the plot stretches over a period of time, so that the characters have to show not only consistency of mood but also change and development. This requires a persistent control and attention to detail on the part of the writer in which few Irish writers excel. There are, of course, exceptions such as Joyce and Elizabeth Bowen.

The language, the literature and the oral tradition had, together with their Catholic faith, kept alive the sense of identity and fortified the Irish people under British rule. There is a strong poetic tradition in Gaelic literature and the short story is the nearest prose form to poetry. The short story is also a likely form to grow out of the Irish custom of oral story telling,[6] a dying art the demise of which happened to coincide with the rebirth of the Irish nation. The oral stories were often dramatic and this tradition combined with the Irish verbal fluency is reflected in the excellent dialogue commonly found among Irish writers. Some examples are Seamus O'Kelly, Padraic O'Conaire, Frank O'Connor, Sean O'Faolain and a more recent writer Brian Friel, best known for his drama.

There seem to be several contributory social causes. Until very recently the Irish author was writing for a very small and rather provincial audience at home, and a larger English-speaking audience elsewhere whose reaction he could not predict. He could be misunderstood outside Ireland or understood too well and banned at home. The good short story, like the novel, but in a more compressed and fragmentary form, reflects a society's life, manners, morals, national character or aspirations, or may be used as an instrument of psychological insight; but the short story suggests rather than states and it is easier to hint at a theme, scene or situation which would need fuller revelation in the larger framework of the novel. Secondly the practical fact of getting into print favoured the short story.

Another contributing factor is probably that a nation still in the process of formulating, assessing, or re-forming its national image and literary culture, for both cultural and economic reasons tends to produce short story writers. The United States, whose writers excel in the short story, would be the predominant case in point. It was Poe who said, 'We have snapped asunder the leadingstrings of our British Grandmamma, and, better still, we have survived'.

Other new nations show early evidence of the importance of the short story in their emerging literary culture. Canada, suffering in different ways from U.S. and British cultural and economic domination, produced

Stephen Leacock's *Sunshine Sketches of a Little Town* (1912), a Canadian 'Winesburg'. Significantly enough this collection of anecdotes made little impression and was not reprinted again until 1931 and 1960. Since then the collection has run into eight reprints, for Leacock has now been discovered by Canadians as one of their seminal writers. Morley Callaghan's collection of stories, *A Native Argosy* (1929), was first published in New York, as Hawthorne's *Twice-Told Tales* had first been collected and published in London.

In Australia the short story developed from bush ballads and camp fire tales fathered by Henry Lawson whose *Stories in Prose and Verse* (1894), which again made little impression at first, later influenced both Australian and New Zealand writers. Katherine Mansfield, though she lived in England and Europe, wrote her lyrical stories as a New Zealander, but her work has had less influence in New Zealand than that of Frank Sargeson whose stories and sketches began to appear in 1935, but were not collected until 1964. Like Leacock, Sargeson has since been 'discovered'.

The writers of all these countries had at first to struggle to establish their own cultural heritage. None of these countries, unlike Ireland, had an older native literary tradition from which to draw. Their writers were also all restricted in varying ways by readership appeal.

Frank O'Connor's feeling, as recorded in *The Lonely Voice*, that in the short story there is always a sense of outlawed figures wandering about on the fringes of society may come about because the writer's vision of his national image or society is uncertain, or difficult to grasp. Such a writer is also uncertain of his own place in a still fluid, ill-defined, or shifting social structure.

The final effect of a good short story is one of intellectual and moral enlightenment. The nation in the process of formulating, assessing or re-forming its literary tastes and traditions may reveal its national image and emerging or changing cultural patterns by the mosaic of fragmentary impressions embodied in a collection of short stories. Writers, by means of this form, more easily attract pragmatically disposed readers who may be in need of intellectual and moral enlightenment but who have not the habit of obtaining it from prolonged concentration on a longer work.

Similar social criteria could in part account for the resurgence of the short story in recent years, particularly in the United States, for contemporary society is in a continuous state of reassessing itself in the face of fluctuating values and insecurity over the future.

Whatever the temperamental, traditional and social reasons which contributed to O'Flaherty's choice of the short story for such a large part of his total literary output, his success in the short story form comes from the fact that he is at his best when his gifts as a raconteur are disciplined, when he forgets his sense of frustration, or his concern for man at large, and keeps within the limits of either a concentric moment or a dramatic situation. In a short story there is less scope for the illustration of a large basic issue. What is more he enjoyed writing short stories.[7] Without the expansiveness of the novel form, however, into which O'Flaherty put his main effort, the artistic economy of his best short stories might never have been achieved.

O'Flaherty himself likes a fast-moving narrative.[8] His novel chapters are never long. One could compile a volume of short stories from various episodes from the novels which are complete in themselves and have the pith and movement of the more compressed short story form. Take, for example, the curragh race on the last sixteen pages of *Thy Neighbour's Wife*: Chapter XXXIII of *Land* in which Michael meets the old woman; Chapter XIX of *Skerrett* which tells of Father Moclair's inspection of Skerrett's candidates for confirmation, or Chapter XXI of *Skerrett* which is the conversation between the two English coastguards. Chapters VII, XI, XVI, XXIII of *Skennett* are also self-contained narrative episodes.

Among the novels it is only in *Famine* that O'Flaherty maintains a strong narrative progression, an emotional intensity which tires the reader as it must have exhausted the writer. Here it is as if the theme of the book has gripped the author more personally than any of his novels since *The Black Soul*; but by now O'Flaherty has learnt to objectify and control his personal emotion by irony and understatement. *Famine* is superior to *Skerrett* as a novel because it is all of a piece, rather than a succession of scenes; a saga of the unconquerable human spirit.

A long letter written by O'Flaherty to *The Irish Statesman* is revealing for it shows that he believes a writer should have a sense of mission. Here O'Flaherty says: 'No ideal is practical, but all ideals are the mothers of great poetry, and it is only from the womb of an ideal that a great race, or a great literature, or a great art can spring'. Much as he admires the gesture of those who fought in 1916 he refuses to believe in political nationalism. He believes in 'the political union of the human race, in the ideal of human brotherhood. But there will always be strife and struggle . . . But it is certain that always people born in one place will love that place and try to make it pre-eminent by the achievements of its people . . . And always poets will side with the weak against the strong, and not with the strong against the weak and ignorant'.[9]

O'Flaherty is at once both the most peacefully lyrical and the most violent of Irish short story writers. Because of his immense range of theme, mood and style it is difficult to make overall valid comparison between his work and that of other writers. O'Flaherty's work sometimes recalls Katherine Mansfield, Chekov, Maupassant and Joyce. O'Flaherty is a great admirer of Maupassant, especially in his humorous stories. He also admires Joyce, Hemingway and the Russian writers, above all Gogol and Dostoievsky. The influence of the latter may be found in some of his novels such as *The Puritan*, and in a short story 'The Terrorist'. It might, however, be interesting to notice some of the more general differences between the short stories of O'Flaherty and those of Frank O'Connor and Sean O'Faolain, his two most famous Irish contemporaries.

Unlike O'Flaherty, both O'Connor and O'Faolain were raised in a town (Cork). Both enjoy unfolding the nuances of human feeling and recording the ebb and flow of human relationships. They are sociable writers, at home in the provincial Irish scene, and superior to O'Flaherty in their creation of female characters; they use the first person narrative method more often; both write with their audience in mind and both make frequent use of the interior scene. O'Faolain started out as a romantic and O'Connor has an inclination towards sentimentality; neither has the hard, spare, quality to be found in many of O'Flaherty's stories.

An analysis of O'Flaherty's short stories shows that three-fifths of them are set in the open air. O'Flaherty most often writes from the stance of an outsider looking in through the window at his interior scenes, which are often linked with frustration, or abnormal states of mind and body resulting in a feeling of entrapment. He is at his best dealing with simple rural people in a simple way, or writing about animals. It is only in his novels that he attempts deeply drawn characters, and there are no personalities in his short stories as detailed as Frank O'Connor's in 'The Mad Lomasneys' or Sean O'Faolain's 'Teresa'.

O'Flaherty broadcast one of his short stories, 'The Hawk', on Radio Eireann in 1957. He read the story well, rapidly, with very little emphasis, as if completely absorbed in the text. It is the story that matters, not who reads it, or who listens to it. In O'Flaherty's better stories one feels, indeed, that the story has written itself. The author — except when he intervenes in person occasionally in his earlier stories — is forgotten. Neither O'Faolain nor O'Connor, who tried to reintroduce the tone of a man's voice speaking into his stories, gives this impression; they are there, all the time, behind their work. O'Flaherty's early ability to achieve this effect is less marked in his later work. Stories such as 'The Bath' and 'The Post Office' draw nearer to the vein used by his two contemporaries. As O'Flaherty resolved some of his personal difficulties he became more sociable, and identified with his characters. An increased use of dialogue results.

That O'Flaherty spoke Irish from childhood also sets him apart. Like his two speaking voices he has an Irish and an English writing style. His Irish style appears only in some Aran and animal stories. This style uses short simple sentences and very few subordinate clauses. It avoids the relative pronoun which in Irish does not exist, using repetition instead such as in: 'In front there was a vast expanse of falling land, falling in flat terraces to the distant sea' ('Milking Time'), instead of 'which fell in flat terraces . . . '; or 'There were strange shadows on the gently rolling bosom of the sea. The shadows came from the cliffs', instead of 'There were strange shadows which came from the cliffs etc . . . ' ('The Oar'). An Irish scholar would be able to find other distinguishing marks. No detailed study has been made of the effects of O'Flaherty's bi-lingualism and some useful research remains to be done in this field. Although O'Connor later became an Irish scholar, neither he nor O'Faolain have these two styles. They are also more 'literary' writers than O'Flaherty and enjoy analysing their own writing and that of others, whereas O'Flaherty believes primarily in the instinctive response and detests theorising. He has refused all invitations to lecture or broadcast his views.

There is evidence to show that O'Flaherty wrote stories to a tailored length, with a specific market in mind, and others entirely to please himself, and though most of his stories are under 5000 words long he has also written a few stories of twice this length. O'Flaherty is not an easy writer to pigeonhole by exterior criteria and it would be entirely false to do so. His best stories are based on transposed personal experience or memories harking back to his youth. Stories as varied as 'The Sniper', 'The Cow's Death', 'The Child of God', 'The Fairy Goose' and 'The Oar' fall into this category. It is this kind of story which most readily springs to mind as 'typical' of O'Flaherty. He is at his best when he does what he says he set out to do in his first novel, when he does not attempt to preach anything but gives a faithful picture of life as he sees it. It is his personal vision which has contributed most to the short story genre.

O'Flaherty, like James Joyce, started writing at a time when his way of seeing life was considered scandalous and when, what is more, there was a very limited opportunity for Irish writers to be published in Ireland. The warnings contained in *A Tourist's Guide to Ireland* and actuated in his novels are based on the anger of a man who loves his country too well not to see its faults, too well not to want to correct them. But the composite picture which emerges from his work, which most strikes the reader today, now that the acrimonious heat has turned to ash, is one of social revolution in the moral rather than the political sense. This is as O'Flaherty intended it to be, for he is trying to promote a return to enduring values. He has a revulsion against all forms of materialism. He insists on establishing closer contact with nature and between men and on discarding an obsessive concern with things or systems whether religious, political or scientific. Ireland, he is saying, has gained her political liberty but she is not yet mistress of her own soul.

In spite of some overt criticism of Irish society, however, O'Flaherty is wise enough not to write with a specifically Irish audience in mind. It has been pointed out that 'the most hampering of the limitations on the Irish Catholic writers was they had to forge their way in a society officially inimical to their growth'.[10] O'Flaherty is never self-consciously Irish, producing his Irish characters for the amusement of the non-Irish reader. His ideal of human brotherhood makes nationality of secondary importance.[11]

In *Land* Raoul says: 'It is terrible to have lost faith. It is really terrible to be an educated man in our age of transition . . . While we hysterically re-examine the idea of God, with the object of making it conform to our changed conception of the universe, our moral conscience flounders about in the vacuum created by our genius. We cry out desperately for authority, even while we smash all authority' (p. 58), and he concludes that it is to the land, the earth which is the common womb of all humanity, that we must turn for protection.

O'Flaherty does just this in his best short stories. In the end it is what he wrote about the people of Aran, peasants and fishermen, or those animal stories based on observation and memory, which are nearest to his heart and embody his gifts at their best. By writing about simple peasants O'Flaherty has also incidentally helped Ireland to take pride in her peasant stock instead of continually making excuses for it.[12]

It is the revival of man's faith in himself that is O'Flaherty's central message. He sees man through the Irishmen and women he knows best, but they represent all men. No writer with any pretension to greatness only writes for his own people, but because he is intimate with them and reveals their weaknesses he will often be most mocked at home for it is a wise man who knows his own faults and O'Flaherty is no flatterer.

Notes

Unless otherwise stated page numbers given for O'Flaherty's novels refer to the first London edition.

NOTES TO THE INTRODUCTION

1 Liam O'Flaherty, 'Autobiographical Note', *Ten Contemporaries*, ed. John Gawsworth (London, 1933) pp. 139–43.

2 O'Flaherty, 'Jim Larkin the Rebel', *The Plain People* I (18 June 1922). (He also wrote anonymously for this paper.)

3 O'Flaherty says his first published short story was entitled 'Sham Fox'. I have failed to trace its publication.

4 From the dust jacket of the first British edition of *Thy Neighbour's Wife* (London, 1923). This commentary aroused controversy, 'The Blurb Again', *Now and Then*, no. 10 (Dec 1923) 11.

5 *Ten Contemporaries*, p. 143.

6 *The Pedlar's Revenge and Other Stories* (Dublin, 1976) selected by A. A. Kelly, includes these two stories and nineteen others previously uncollected.

7 D.H. Lawrence, letter to Lady Glenavy, 3 February 1928; Harry T. Moore, *The Intelligent Heart: The Story of D. H. Lawrence* (London, 1960) pp. 458–60.

8 D. H. Lawrence, 'John Galsworthy', *Selected Essays* (London, 1950) p. 219.

CHAPTER 1: ANIMAL AND NATURE STORIES

1 This story, according to O'Flaherty based on a childhood memory, was originally entitled 'A Cow's Suicide'.

2 C. E. Montague, *A Writer's Notes on his Trade* (London, 1949) p. 175.

3 George Brandon Saul, 'A Wild Sowing: The Short Stories of Liam O'Flaherty', *Review of English Literature* (July 1963) 108–13.

4 Heinrich Hauser, *Bitter Water* (London, 1930), to which O'Flaherty wrote a short introduction.

5 Henry Williamson, *Tarka the Otter* (London, 1949) p. 7, introduction by Eleanor Graham.

6 J. M. Synge, *The Aran Islands* (Leipzig, 1926) p. 220.

7 Op. cit., introduction, p. 7.

8 O'Flaherty, *Joseph Conrad, An Appreciation* (London, 1925) pp. 10–11.

9 The same symbolic comparison is to be found in 'The Black Cat', *The Humanist* (July 1926) 237–9, an uncollected story.

10 Benedict Kiely, 'Liam O'Flaherty: A Story of Discontent', *Month*, II (Sep 1949) 184–93.

11 Frank O'Connor, *The Lonely Voice* (Cleveland, 1962) pp. 37–8.

12 John Eglington, 'Irish Letter, April 1927', *The Dial*, LXXXII, no. 5, 410.

CHAPTER 2: STORIES OF EMOTIONAL RESPONSE

1 Michael Sheehy, *Is Ireland Dying?* (London, 1968) p. 105.

2 O'Flaherty, autobiographic note in *The Best Short Stories of 1926*, ed. E. J. O'Brien (London, 1927).

3 O'Flaherty, *Darkness* (London, 1926). Shortened version printed in *The New Coterie*, no. 3 (Summer 1962) 42–64. In this play the older brother Daniel is jealous of the younger Brian, who is his mother's favourite, physically attractive and more successful with women. Daniel's 'darkness' is in part psychological and in part sexual frustration. In the end he kills his brother.

4 Tom O'Flaherty, *Cliffmen of the West* (London, 1935) p. 105, or Liam O'Flaherty's remarks about his Irish critics and scandalmongers: 'May they be devoured by the archdevil's itch without a broken bottle within a thousand leagues to scratch their ulcerated haunches' (Letters to Edward Garnett, 20 Jan 1925).

5 H. E. Bates, *The Modern Short Story* (London, 1941) p. 158.

6 O'Connor, *The Lonely Voice*, p. 27.

7 Sean O'Faolain, 'Don Quixote O'Flaherty', *The Bell*, II (June 1941) 28–36.

8 O'Flaherty, *Joseph Conrad: An Appreciation*.

9 M. H. Murray, 'Liam O'Flaherty and the Speaking Voice', *Studies in Short Fiction*, V, no. 2 (1968) 154–62.

CHAPTER 3: URBAN AND WAR THEMES

1 Occasionally however a more sophisticated town-oriented character will be treated comically as in 'The Accident' and 'The Bath', both of which are exceptions within this group and were written after 1932.

2 Edward J. O'Brien, *The Best Short Stories of 1924* (London, 1925) preface.

3 O'Flaherty, *Shame the Devil* (London, 1934) pp. 189–90.

4 William Troy, 'The Position of Liam O'Flaherty', *Bookman*, LXXIV (1929) 10, 7–11.

5 *The Short Story* (London, 1948) p. 197.

6 Also reminiscent of Joyce of whom O'Flaherty is a great admirer, is the falling cadence of the following lines from 'The Tyrant':

> She shuddered, listening stupidly to the distant sounds, shuddering in her thin evening gown with the draught from the window she had opened, listening and looking at the fire that had burned low, now drowsily smouldering in its ashen embers. A dying fire in a deserted room . . .

Compare this with, for instance, the penultimate paragraph of 'The Sisters'.

7 Rhys Davies in the foreword to O'Flaherty, *The Swan and other stories* (London, 1932) p. 7.

8 O'Flaherty, *Two Years* (London, 1930) p. 217.

> Therefore when I arrived in Canada my mind urged me to be *good*. But what should I do? How could I do good? There was no tool or weapon to my hand. My mind held but a tongue to pour forth words that lacked subtlety, words written in the air by my body's vapours, dying at their birth and striking with the feebleness of a moth's wings against the inhospitable ears of their hearers. My helplessness produced a gloom that drove me off to seek the waste places of this wild country, that I might think in solitude.

9 Michael H. Murray, 'Liam O'Flaherty and the Speaking Voice', *Studies in Short Fiction*, V, no. 2 (1968) 156.

10 Michael H. Murray, op. cit.

11 Michael Sheehy, *Is Ireland Dying?* pp. 103–4.

12 James Joyce, *A Portrait of the Artist as a Young Man* (London, 1965) p. 179.

13 Roland Barthes, 'Criticism as Language', *The Times Literary Supplement* (27 Sep 1963) 740

14 Sean O'Faolain, *The Finest Stories of Sean O'Faolain* (New York, 1957) Foreword, ix and x.

15 Op. cit., p. 223.

CHAPTER 4: MAN IN COMMUNITY: THE TELLER AND THE TALE

1 The term used by Norman Friedman in his valuable article on narrative points of view, 'Points of view in fiction; the development of a critical concept', *PMLA*, LXX, no. 5 (Dec 1955) 1160—84.

2 It was only after completing this study that I was able to go to Texas and read O'Flaherty's letters to Edward Garnett in the Academic Center Library, Austin. In a letter marked (May ?) 1923 he mentions that 'The Black Mare' was written in Irish and translated into English using Aran phraseology.

3 J. H. Delargy, 'The Gaelic Story-Teller', *Proceedings of the British Academy*, XXXI (London, 1945) 24.

4 Quoted by H. E. Bates in *The Modern Short Story*, p. 21.

5 Quoted by Richard Ellmann in *James Joyce* (New York, 1959) p. 107. What Yeats meant by 'the spirit' is complex but in 'The Spirit Medium' he advocates a return to earthy things in 'I bend my body to the spade or grope with a dirty hand' and in 'Those Images' he claims that the real material for poetry is found directly in nature. 'See those images that constitute the wild'.

O'Flaherty in *Shame the Devil* (p. 217) 'The Earth, the sea and the air are man's substance and his sustenance. What man builds on earth and his contraptions for mastering the elements are ephemeral and alien to nature. Renew your friendship with nature. In that lies your chance of regaining peace'.

6 O'Connor, *The Lonely Voice*, p. 38.

7 Rhys Davies, Foreword to Liam O'Flaherty, *The Wild Swan and Other Stories* (London, 1932) p. 7.

8 Roland Barthes, 'La Littérature aujourd'hui', *Essais Critiques* (Paris, 1964) 159—60.

One can give literature an *assertive* value either through satisfaction, according it the conservative values of society, or through tension, using it as an instrument in the struggle for liberation; on the other hand, one can give literature an essentially interrogative value; . . . this interrogation is not *what is the meaning of the world?* nor perhaps, *has the world any meaning?* ; but only *here is the world, does it contain any meaning?*

9 O'Flaherty, *A Tourist's Guide to Ireland* (London, 1930) p. 132.

10 Op cit., pp. 113 and 116.

11 George Brandon Saul, 'A Wild Sowing: The Short Stories of Liam O'Flaherty', *Review of English Literature* (July 1963) 112.

CHAPTER 5: THE CONTROL OF STYLE AND LANGUAGE

1 Letter from O'Flaherty to Edward Garnett, 5 May 1923. An exploration of what O'Flaherty calls 'that feeling of coldness' is made by the French critic Roland Barthes in *Writing Degree Zero*, trans. Annette Laven and Colin Smith (New York, 1968). The 'cold' writer does not try to communicate something to the rest of the world, but only to define correctly the relation between his writing and the world.

2 Letter to Edward Garnett, 4 June 1923.

3 Letter to Edward Garnett, 2 Apr 1924.

4 Letter to Edward Garnett, 31 July 1925.

5 Letter to Edward Garnett, 18 Sep 1924.

6 O'Flaherty decried the public taste: 'if there is no sentiment in it they say it is not true to life'. Letter to Edward Garnett, 20 Aug 1923.

7 Letter to Edward Garnett, 16 July 1925.

8 Richard Church reviewing *Spring Sowing*, *Spectator Literary Supplement*, *Spectator* (4 Oct 1924) 468.

9 O'Flaherty, *I Went to Russia* (London, 1931) p. 225.

10 In *The Black Soul*, p. 62, O'Flaherty also uses guns as a comparison for the sea

when he says 'the people feared the resting bilious sea as the soldier fears the silence of the guns in an interval between two engagements'.

11 Mark Schorer, 'Technique as Discovery', *Hudson Review* (Spring 1948). Reprinted in *Critiques and Essays on Modern Fiction 1920—1951*, sel. John W. Aldridge (New York, 1952) p. 72.

12 The autograph MS. of 'The Oar' in The Academic Center, University of Texas, is marked 'Written in Gortnacapall, August 14th—15th, 1927'.

13 This story, adapted by Eoin O'Suilleabhain, was televised in Ireland on 7 March 1969.

14 O'Flaherty has two speaking voices, one Irish and one received pronunciation. He will drop into his Irish accent when telling a story involving Irish characters.

15 It is interesting to note that J. Conrad also uses many repetitive devices including repetition to act as a thematic refrain. An interesting discussion of J. Conrad's repetition is to be found in Elma A. Ordonez, 'The Early Joseph Conrad: Revision and Style', *Philippine Social Sciences and Humanities Review, XXXIII* (Mar / June 1968) nos. 1—2 (part of a doctoral dissertation written for the University of Wisconsin, 1963).

16 J. M. Synge, *The Aran Islands*, J. M. Synge, *Collected Works*, II (London, 1966) p. 75.

17 Tom O'Flaherty, *Aranmen All* (London, 1934) Ch. X 'Wrack'.

18 Vivian Mercier, 'The Irish Short Story and Oral Tradition', *The Celtic Cross*, ed. Ray B. Browne, William John Roscelli and John Loftus (West Lafayette, Indiana, 1964).

CHAPTER 6: MAN AS PART OF NATURE

1 Alfred Nutt, p. liv of the postscript to Douglas Hyde, *Beside the Fire* (London, 1890).

2 Teilhard de Chardin, *Human Energy* (London, 1969) p. 32, first published in French in 1962. (Essays written between 1931 and 1939.)

3 It is interesting to note that the first papal encyclical to deal with evolution was *Humani generis* (1950). This allows belief in the evolutionary origins of man's body, but insists on the special creation of Adam's soul.

4 Vivian Mercier, introduction to *The Stories of Liam O'Flaherty* (New York, 1956).

5 William Troy, 'The Position of Liam O'Flaherty', *Bookman, LXIX* (Mar 1929) 7 and 11.

6 O'Flaherty, *Shame the Devil*, p. 242.

7 Letter from O'Flaherty to Edward Garnett, 16 May 1924.

8 The editors of *Tomorrow* were H. Stuart (Francis Stuart) and Cecil Salkeld, an artist. The first issue, printed in London, included poems by F. R. Higgins, Joseph Campbell, Yeats' 'Leda and the Swan' which had been refused publication by AE in *The Irish Statesman* because of its revolutionary implications; short stories by Lennox Robinson and Margaret Barrington (then Mrs Curtis, later to marry O'Flaherty), and O'Flaherty's short story 'A Red Petticoat'. There was also a review by L. K. Emery of *The Black Soul* in which O'Flaherty's hero is stated to have rid himself of the 'malaise' of the century, for he is not afraid of passion or instinct.

9 O'Flaherty's letters to *The Irish Statesman* were entitled and published as follows:—

'National Energy', III (18 Oct 1924) 171.

'A View of Irish Culture', IV (20 June 1925) 460—1.

10 *The Humanist*, editor Herbert Devine, the journal of the British Humane Society, was published Mar 1924—Aug 1927. Henry Ford was also associated with this magazine.

11 This is of course one of the burning issues of today. A good discussion of man

related to his environment will be found in René Dubos' *So Human an Animal* (New York, 1968; London, 1970).

12 Maurice Shadbolt, 'The International Symposium on the Short Story — Part Two', *Kenyon Review*, XXXI, no. 1 (1969) 70.

13 Letters from O'Flaherty to Edward Garnett dated 2 May 1924, and 6 June 1923.

14 The *Irish Statesman*, X (1928) 295.

15 Edward Shanks in *The London Mercury*, XV, 88 (Feb 1927) 434.

16 O'Flaherty, *The Assassin* (London, 1959) p. 119.

17 O'Flaherty, *The Informer* (London, 1968) pp. 167 / 8.

18 *The Wilderness* (about 52,000 words) was published in *The Humanist*, IV in six instalments as follows: Jan 1927, 17—25; Feb 1927, 69—78; Mar 1927, 121—9; Apr 1927, 175—82; May 1927, 225—34; June 1927, 275—85.

19 This full stop where a comma would be more correct is an example of O'Flaherty's sometimes odd punctuation. Here he intends the speaker to make a long pause.

20 G. B. Shaw, *John Bull's Other Island* (London, 1921) p. 116.

21 This allegory may owe something to James Stephens' *Crock of Gold* (London, 1912) in which Angus Og tells Caitlin that the world has forgotten him and Caitlin tears herself away from Pan — the spirit of desire, lust and death — to follow Angus.

22 'The Touch', *Irish Writing*, I (1946) 50—8, text A; 'The Touch', *American Mercury*, LXIV (May 1947) 549—56, text B. This story was also published in Irish entitled 'Teangabháil', *Comhar* (July 1946).

Thomás de Bhaldraithe, 'Liam O'Flaherty — Translator (?)', *Eire—Ireland* (Summer 1968) 149—53 (the author's adaptation of his article in Irish in *Comhar* (May 1967) 35—7). He says of 'The Touch', that 'it is fairly certain from internal evidence that the original was in Irish, as well as from the fact that it was written in answer to a request by the Irish-language periodical *Comhar*, that it appeared in Irish before it appeared in English'. Mr O'Flaherty himself, however, says he is certain he first wrote this story in English in Connecticut in 1940 and has no recollection of translating it into Irish. I have been unable to obtain any explanation of the two different English versions. Text B, according to Mr Bhaldraithe is nearer to the Irish version. Quotations are from text B.

23 T. S. Eliot, *The Idea of a Christian Society* (London, 1939).

24 D. H. Lawrence, 'Democracy', *Selected Essays* (London, 1950) p. 88.

CHAPTER 7: VIOLENCE AND OBSESSION

1 O'Flaherty, book review of T. F. Powys, *Mr. Tasker's Gods*, *The Irish Statesman*, III, no. 26 (7 Mar 1925) 827.

2 Letter from W. B. Yeats entitled 'Irish Ban on a novel', *Manchester Guardian Weekly* (26 Feb 1932) 176.

3 Sean O'Faolain, 'Don Quixote O'Flaherty', *The Bell* (June 1941) 30—1, an adapted version of a previous article of the same title published in *The London Mercury*, XXXVII, no. 218 (Dec 1937) 170—5.

4 Benedict Kiely, 'Liam O'Flaherty: A Story of Discontent', *Month, II* (Sep 1949) 184—93.

5 Old Patsy in 'The Salted Goat' suffers from insanity 'akin to that of the ancient hermits' because he is poor, old, ostracised by the primitive community in which he lives. When the goat, his only companion, dies, he cuts up the body and puts it in brine and locking himself into his hovel refuses to leave the goat's remains and is found starved to death.

6 Jeanine Delpech, 'Aux Courses avec O'Flaherty', *Les Nouvelles Littéraires* (1 May 1937).

CHAPTER 8: FROM RIDICULE TO CONTEMPT

1 Konrad Lorenz, *On Aggression* (New York, 1967) p. 287.

2 Tom O'Flaherty, *Cliffmen of the West*, Ch. X, 'The Old Tin Can'.
Liam O'Flaherty's 'The New Suit' bears an equally strong resemblance to his brother's 'My First Suit', Tom O'Flaherty, *Aranmen All* (London, 1934).

3 O'Flaherty's letter to Edward Garnett, 23 May 1924.

4 Letter from W. B. Yeats to Mrs Shakespear, Mar 13 1927, quoted by A. Norman Jeffares, in *W. B. Yeats, Man and Poet* (London, 1949) p. 241.

5 Arland Ussher, *The Face and Mind of Ireland* (London, 1949) p. 105.

6 G. A. Birmingham, *Irish Short Stories* (London, 1932) introduction, p. 15.

7 Gordon Phelps, *The Russian Novel in English Fiction* (London, 1956) considers that both Dostoievsky and Gorky had some unconscious influence on O'Flaherty (p. 175). O'Flaherty's doss house scene in *Two Years* is compared to Dostoievsky's bath house in *The House of the Dead* and (p. 136) to Gorky's *The Lower Depths* and (p. 176) *The Informer* is compared to Dostoievsky's *The Possessed*. In a letter to Edward Garnett (31 July 1925) O'Flaherty said 'I read nothing now but Joyce, and Dostoievsky and Gogol'. John Eglington, 'Irish letter April 1927', *The Dial*, LXXXII (May 1927) 407–10, calls O'Flaherty 'a Carleton who has read the Russians'.

8 Vivian Mercier, *The Irish Comic Tradition* (London, 1962) p. 47.

9 This could not be claimed as an exclusively Irish attitude, but it is interesting to note that it is shared by Frank O'Connor who said, 'Life is an allegory to which you and I belong — the allegory that God knows, the saints live by, and the poets expound'. Quoted by Maurice Sheehy in his essay 'The Platonist', *Michael Frank: Studies on Frank O'Connor*, ed. Maurice Sheehy (London, 1969) p. 127.

10 For a discussion of the difference between illustrative and representative meaning see Robert Scholes and Robert Kellogg, *The Nature of Narrative* (New York, 1966) pp. 82–92.

11 Jonathan Swift, *Of Public Absurdities in England, The Prose Works of Jonathan Swift*, ed. Temple Scott (London, 1907) p. 179.

12 L. P. Hartley reviewing *The Return of the Brute* in *The Saturday Review* (7 Dec 1929) 686, said:

> The details are convincing enough, but the general impression is of a nightmare based, indeed, on actuality, but so transmuted by the author's characteristic besetting fancies, that as a contribution to history (whatever may be its relation to art) it is not trustworthy.

The Times Literary Supplement (21 Nov 1929) reviewed this book as repulsive in detail and 'a more savage picture of war than has yet appeared in a British or German novel. The wit is absent, the asperity is reinforced and there is an air of unreality about the whole scene'.

13 O'Flaherty's satire has not always been understood by critics. O. D. Edwards, 'The Burden of Irish History' from *Conor Cruise O'Brien Introduces Ireland*, ed. Owen Dudley Edwards (London, 1969) pp. 21–9, attempts to define the peculiar character of Irish satiric humour and the ambiguity of the hero — and of the anti-hero — in Irish history.

14 O'Flaherty, *Shame the Devil*, p. 228.

15 Sean O'Faolain, *The Irish* (London, 1947) p. 113.

16 Sean McMahon in 'The Priest in recent Irish Fiction', *Eire—Ireland* (Summer 1968) 105–14, published by the Irish-American Cultural Institute, St Paul, MA., claims that no Irish writer has written a novel with a priest as main character. In fact in *Thy Neighbour's Wife* O'Flaherty wrote a novel with a priest as principal character, so did Richard Power in *The Hungry Grass* (New York, 1966; London, 1969).

CHAPTER 9: ATTITUDES TOWARDS DEATH

1 *I Went to Russia*, p. 292.

2 Letter from O'Flaherty to Edward Garnett, 6 June 1923.

3 Seán O'Súilleabháin in *Irish Wake Amusements* (Cork, 1967) gives an account of church opposition to wake abuses, Ch. X, pp. 146—58.

4 O'Flaherty, 'My Life of Adventure', *T. P's Weekly* (20 Oct 1928) 756.

5 O'Flaherty, *Insurrection* (London, 1959) p. 157:

I'm in revolt against the whole concept of good and evil current in our age. I'm in revolt against all forms of government, because they are all based on the same false concept of morality. Above all, I'm in revolt against the idea that man is the centre of the universe and that he is made in God's image.

CONCLUSION

1 Benedict Kiely, *Modern Irish Fiction* (London, 1950) p. 18:

It is the understanding of the earth, of animals worthy and human beings not always worthy of the earth, that makes O'Flaherty's work important.

2 O'Flaherty's variation of mood is very evident from his handwriting which in his letters to Edward Garnett is at times flowing and energetic and at other times cramped and uncertain. When he is suffering from a depressive fit the calligraphy shrinks, the words dither to and fro and the 'I' becomes especially shrivelled.

3 Dated 31 July 1925.

4 Book review by Liam O'Flaherty of Sinclair Lewis's *Free Air* in *The Irish Statesman* (5 Apr 1924) 116. But O'Flaherty also believed that literature should be based on an ideal, see note 9 below.

5 Letter to Edward Garnett, 17 June 1927.

6 *Great Irish Short Stories*, ed. and introduced by Vivian Mercier (New York, 1964). In his introduction the editor discusses this possibility.

7 'One might as well write for the love of the thing. My short stories you see fill that instinct'. Letter to Edward Garnett dated 'July sometime 1925'.
'I am eagerly looking forward to the drunken pleasure of writing more sketches when I finish my novel'. Letter to Edward Garnett, 21 July 1926.

8 Book review by O'Flaherty of T. F. Powys' *Mr. Tasker's Gods* in *The Irish Statesman* (7 Mar 1925) 827: 'There is a lack of speed in the development of the story which jars on a man like myself'.

9 Letter to the editor entitled 'The Plough and the Stars', *The Irish Statesman* (20 Feb 1926) 739 in which O'Flaherty protests against Yeats' demonstration in the Abbey Theatre when O'Casey's play was badly received by the audience.

10 Michael Sheehy, *Is Ireland Dying?* p. 36.

11 O'Flaherty remains, however, very aware of his nationality. At one point he wrote to Edward Garnett that he could not write for an Irish audience neither did he feel acceptable to the British public. 'Added to the racial prejudice that is in England against an Irish writer there is the added prejudice of puritanism and unless one becomes both a buffoon and a charlatan there does not seem to be any possibility of overcoming these two prejudices' (1 Nov 1926).

12 Some interesting Aran background material will be found in P. Sheeran's *The Novels of Liam O'Flaherty* (Dublin, 1976).

Bibliography

LIAM O'FLAHERTY'S WRITINGS

A. NOVELS

B. SHORT STORY COLLECTIONS

C. AUTOBIOGRAPHY

D. BIOGRAPHY

E. BOOKLETS

F. DRAMA

G. INTRODUCTIONS

H. ESSAYS, LETTERS AND BOOK REVIEWS

I. PUBLICATIONS IN IRISH

(1) Short story collection
(2) Short stories in periodicals
(3) Poems
(4) Essays and letters
(5) Translation from Irish

SECONDARY SOURCES

A. ABOUT LIAM O'FLAHERTY (A SELECTION OF CRITICAL ARTICLES)

B. FULL-LENGTH STUDIES

C. SOME CRITICISM IN IRISH OF LIAM O'FLAHERTY'S WORK

D. BIBLIOGRAPHY

E. OTHER WORKS REFERRED TO IN THE FOOTNOTES

APPENDIX

ALPHABETICAL LIST OF SHORT STORIES

LIAM O'FLAHERTY'S WRITINGS

A. NOVELS

Thy Neighbour's Wife, London: Cape 1923; New York: Boni & Liveright, 1924.

The Black Soul, London: Cape, 1924, 1936; New York: Boni & Liveright, 1925; Travellers' library edition, 1928, 1931; Lythway Press, Bath, 1972.

The Informer, London: Cape, 1925, 1929, 1949; John Lane (Penguin Books no. 17), 1935; Landsborough Publications (Four Square Books no. 42) 1958, 1964; The Folio Society, 1961; New York: Knopf, 1925; New American Library (Signet book), 1961, 1970, 1971.

Mr Gilhooley, London: Cape, 1926; New York: Harcourt, Brace, 1927.

The Wilderness, London: serialised in *The Humanist*, IV, Jan 1927, 17–25; Feb, 1927, 69–78; Mar 1927, 121–9; Apr 1927, 175–82; May 1927, 225–34; June 1927, 275–85.

The Assassin, London: Cape, 1928, Landsborough Publications (Four Square Books no. 129) 1959; New York: Harcourt, Brace, 1928.

The House of Gold, London: Cape, 1929; New York: Harcourt, Brace, 1930.

The Return of the Brute, London: Mandrake Press, 1929; New York: Harcourt, Brace, 1930.

The Puritan, London: Cape, 1931; New York: Harcourt, Brace & Co., 1932.

Skerrett, London: Gollancz, 1932; New York: Long & Smith, 1932.

The Martyr, London: Gollancz, 1935; New York: Macmillan, 1933.

Hollywood Cemetery, London: Gollancz, 1935.

Famine, London: Gollancz, 1937, Landsborough Publications (Four Square Books no. 162) 1959, 1966; New York: Random House, 1937.

Land, London: Gollancz, 1946: New York: Random House, 1946.

Insurrection, London: Gollancz, 1950, Landsborough Publications (Four Square Books no. 174) 1959; Boston: Little, Brown, 1951.

(Unpublished novel)

Stack, MS. 173 pages quarto, bound, undated, in the Academic Center Library, University of Texas, Austin.

B. SHORT STORY COLLECTIONS

SS1 *Spring Sowing*, London: Cape, 1924, Travellers' library edition, 1927, 1929, 1931, 1935; New York: Knopf, 1926.

SS2 *The Tent*, London: Cape, 1926.

SS3 *The Mountain Tavern*, London: Cape, 1929; New York: Harcourt, Brace & Co., 1929.

SS4 *The Short Stories of Liam O'Flaherty*, London: Cape, 1937, 1948, Four Square Books, the New English Library Ltd., 1966 (contains 22 stories from SS1, 20 from SS2, and 16 from SS3).

SS5 *Two Lovely Beasts*, London: Gollancz, 1948; Consul Books, paperback, 1961; New York: Devin-Adair, 1950.

SS6 *The Stories of Liam O'Flaherty*, New York: Devin-Adair, 1956 (selection from SS1, SS2, SS3 and six previously uncollected stories).

SS7 *Liam O'Flaherty: Selected Stories*, ed. Devin A. Garrity, New York: Signet book, the New American Library, 1958.

SS8 *Selected Short Stories of Liam O'Flaherty*, London: New English Library, 1970 (an abridged edition of the first Four Square edition SS4, 1966).

SS9 *Irish Portraits: 14 Short Stories by Liam O'Flaherty*, London: Sphere Books,

1970 (selection of stories from SS1, SS2 and SS3 not included in SS4).
SS10 *The Short Stories of Liam O'Flaherty*, London: Brown, Watson, 1961 (Digit Books).
SS12 *More Short Stories of Liam O'Flaherty*, London: New English Library, 1971 (contains the rest of the stories from SS4 not included in SS8).
B.M. Naughton / Liam O'Flaherty Short Stories, compiled R. Mansfield and K. Newson, London: Pergamon Press, 1968, Pergamon English Library, Contrast series (14 stories from each writer compared for secondary school pupils).
SS13 *The Pedlar's Revenge*, Dublin: Wolfhound Press, 1976.
Limited editions of short stories. Details are included in the short story appendix.

C. AUTOBIOGRAPHY

Two Years, London: Cape, 1930; New York: Harcourt, Brace, 1930. (Ten excerpts from this book were published in *Everyman* between 2 Jan and 27 Mar 1930.)
I Went to Russia, London: Cape, 1931; New York: Harcourt, Brace, 1931.
Shame the Devil, London: Grayson & Grayson, 1934.

Autobiographical articles

'My experiences (1896–1923)', *Now and Then*, no. 10, Dec 1923, 14–15.
The Best Short Stories of 1926, ed. Edward J. O'Brien, London, 1927, autobiographical note by Liam O'Flaherty, pp. 406–7.
'My Life of Adventure', *T.P's Weekly*, 20 Oct 1928, 756.
'Autobiographical Note', *Ten Contemporaries, Second Series*, edited John Gawsworth, London, 1933, pp. 139–43.
'I go to Sea', *Esquire*, Sep 1952, 38–9, 85, 86, 88 (adapted from Chapter 6 of *Two Years*).

D. BIOGRAPHY

The Life of Tim Healy, London: Cape, 1927; New York: Harcourt, Brace, 1927.

E. BOOKLETS

A Tourist's Guide to Ireland, London: Mandrake Press, 1929, 1930.
A Cure for Unemployment, London: Blue Moon booklets, no. 8, E. Lahr, 1931; New York: Julian Press, 1931. (In addition to the regular issue, E. Lahr also published a special spoof edition in 1931.)
Joseph Conrad: An Appreciation, J. Conrad Memorial Library: The Collection of George T. Keating, New York, 1929; London: Blue Moon booklets, no. 1, Lahr, 1930.
The Ecstasy of Angus, London: Joiner and Steele, 1931.

F. DRAMA

Darkness: A Tragedy in Three Acts, London: Archer, 1926, also published slightly cut in the *New Coterie*, III, Summer 1926, 42–64.

G. INTRODUCTIONS

'Introduction', *Six Cartoons by Alfred Lowe* (sketches of Barrie, Bennett, Chesterton, Kipling, Shaw, and Wells) London, 1930, pp. 7–8.
'Foreword', Rhys Davies, *The Stars, The World, and the Women*, London, 1930, pp. 7–9.

Introduction', Heinrich Hauser, *Bitter Water*, trans. from German by Patrick Kirwan, London, 1930 (five pages).

H. ESSAYS, LETTERS AND BOOK REVIEWS

'Jim Larkin the Rebel', *The Plain People*, 1, 18 June 1922, 4.

Thy Neighbour's Wife' (explanation of why this novel was written), from the dust jacket of the first London edition. This commentary aroused controversy; cf. 'The Blurb Again', *Now and Then*, X, Dec 1923, 11.

'Sinclair Lewis's *Free Air*', *The Irish Statesman*, II, 5 April 1924, 116 (a book review).

'Adrien Le Corbeau's *The Forest Giant*', *The Irish Statesman*, II, 5 Apr 1924, 116, 118 (a book review).

'Vera Britain's *Not Without Honour*', *The Irish Statesman*, II, 5 Apr 1924, 118 (a book review).

'H.G. Wells' The Dream', *The Irish Statesman*, II, 19 Apr 1924, 178, 180 (a book review).

'Maupassant's A Life', *The Irish Statesman*, II, 7 June 1924, 402, 404 (a book review).

'National Energy', *The Irish Statesman*, III 18 Oct 1924, 171 (letter to editor).

'Trimblerigg, by Laurence Housman', *Now and Then*, XIV, Christmas 1924, 29–30 (a book review).

'Mr. Tasker's Gods', *The Irish Statesman*, III, 7 Mar 1925, 827–8 (book review of a novel by T.F. Powys).

A View of Irish Culture', *The Irish Statesman*, IV, 20 June 1925, 460–1 (letter to editor).

"Peadar O'Donnell's *Storms* and H.N. Brailsford's *Socialism for Today*', *The Irish Statesman*, V, 9 Jan 1926, 556, 568 (a book review).

'The Plough and the Stars', *The Irish Statesman*, V, 20 Feb 1926, 739–40 (letter to editor).

'Fascism or Communism', *The Irish Statesman*, VI, 8 May 1926, 231–2 (an article).

'Review of *Ethel Manning's Sounding Brass*', *The Irish Statesman*, VI, 5 June 1926, 360, 362.

'Literary Criticism in Ireland', *The Irish Statesman*, VI, 4 Sep 1926, 711 (letter to editor).

'Art Criticism', *The Irish Statesman*, IX, 1 Oct 1927, 83 (letter to editor).

'The Waratahs', *The Irish Statesman*, IX, 19 Nov 1927, 253–4 (a commentary on a rugby match).

'Writing in Gaelic', *The Irish Statesman*, IX, 17 Dec 1927, 348 (letter to editor).

'Red Ship', *New Republic*, LXVIII, 23 Sep 1931, 147–50.

'Kingdom of Kerry', *Fortnightly Review*, CXXXVIII, Aug 1932, 212–18.

'The Irish Censorship', *The American Spectator*, 1, Nov 1932, 2. This article is also available in *The American Spectator Yearbook*, ed. G. Jean Nathan, Theodore Dreiser et al. (New York, 1934) pp. 131–4.

'Irish Housekeeping', *New Statesman and Nation*, XI, 8 Feb 1936, 186 (letters to editor).

'Good Soldiers Play Safe', *Esquire*, XVII, May 1942, 23, 120–2.

'Village Ne'er-d-well', *Esquire*, XXIV, Sep 1945, 53–4.

'Personalities by Nimrod', *Irish Tatler and Sketch*, Apr 1949, 36, 75.

Approximately 160 letters from Liam O'Flaherty to Edward Garnett, written between 5 May 1923 and 3 Mar 1932, not all of which are precisely dated, are in the manuscript collection of the Academic Centre Library of the University of Texas, Austin.

I. PUBLICATIONS IN IRISH

(1) *Short story collection*
Dúil (Desire), Baile Atha Cliath (Dublin): Sáirséal and Dill, 1953 (18 stories), 1962, 1966.

(2) *Short stories in periodicals*
'Bás na Bó' (The Cow's Death), *Fáinne an lae,* 18 Lul 1925, 5,
'Fód' (The Sod), *The Dublin Magazine,* 1 May 1924, 882–3.
'An t-aonach, (The Fair), *Fáinne an lae,* 5 Meán Fómhair 1925.
'An Fiach' (The Hunt), *Fáinne an lae,* 27 Meitheamh 1925, 5.
'Daoine Bochta' (Poor People), *Fáinne an lae,* 29 Lúnasa 1925, 3.
'An Cula Nua' (The New Suit), *The Irish Press,* 21 June 1946, 2.
'Teangabháil' (The Touch), *Comhar,* Lul 1946.

(3) *Poems*
'Smaointe i giéin' (Distant Thoughts), *The Dublin Magazine,* 11 Dec 1924, 330.
'Na Blátha Craige' (Cliff Flowers), *Nuabhéarsaíocht,* 1938–49, ed. Séan O'Tuama, Dublin, n.d., 35.

(4) *Essays and letters*
'An Braon Broghach' (The Dirty Drop), *Comhar,* VIII, Bealtaine 1949, 5, 30 (a book review).
'Briseann an Dúchas' (Nature Breaks), *The Irish Press,* 30 May 1946, 2.
'Throideamar Go Fíochmhar' (We Bravely Fought), *The Irish Press,* 6 June 1946, 2.
'Ag Casadh Le Padraig O Conaire' (Meeting Padraig O Conaire), *Comhar,* XII, Aibrean 1953, 3–6.

(5) *Translations from Irish*
Padraig O Conaire, 'The Agony of the World', *The Adelphi,* III, Sep 1925, 250–60 (short story).

SECONDARY SOURCES

A. ABOUT LIAM O'FLAHERTY

(Critiques, including a few of the more interesting book review articles.)

Bates, H.E., *The Modern Short Story,* Boston, 1941, pp.157–9.
Bhaldraithe, Thomas De, 'Liam O'Flaherty—Translator(?)', *Eire—Ireland,* Summer 1968, 149–53.
Broderick, John, 'Liam O'Flaherty: A Partial View', *Hibernia,* 19 Dec 1969, 17.
Church, Richard, review of *Spring Sowing, Spectator Literary Supplement, Spectator,* 4 Oct 1924, 468.
Davies, Rhys, 'Introduction', *The Wild Swan and Other Stories,* London, 1932, pp. 7–10.
Delpech, Jeanine, 'Aux Courses avec O'Flaherty', *Les Nouvelles Littéraires,* May 1937.
Greene, David H., 'New Heights', *Commonweal,* LXIV, 29 June 1956, 328.
Griffin, Gerald, 'Liam O'Flaherty', *The Wild Geese: Pen Portraits of Famous Irish Exiles,* London 1938, pp. 191–5.
Hackett, Francis, 'Liam O'Flaherty As Novelist', *On Judging Books,* New York, 1947, pp. 288–93.
Hampton, Angeline A., 'Liam O'Flaherty: Additions to the Checklist', *Eire—Ireland,* VI, Winter 1971, 87–94.

Hampton, Angeline A., 'Liam O'Flaherty's Short Stories, Visual and Aural Effects', *English Studies*, 55, no. 5, Oct 1974, 440—7.

Hughes, Riley, 'Two Irish Writers', *America*, LXXXIII, 2 Sep 1950, 560—1.

Hynes, Frank J., 'The Troubles in Ireland', *Saturday Review of Literature*, XXIX, 25 May 1946, 12.

Kelleher, John V., 'Irish Literature Today', *Atlantic Monthly*, Mar 1945, 70—6, and *The Bell*, X, 1945, 337—53.

Kelly, Angeline A., 'O'Flaherty on the Shelf', *Hibernia*, 20 Nov 1970, 8.

Kiely, Benedict, 'Liam O'Flaherty: A Story of Discontent', *The Month*, II, Sep 1949, 184—93.

Kiely, Benedict, *Modern Irish Fiction — A Critique*, Dublin, 1950, pp. 17—18, 32—8, 88—90.

Kiely, Benedict, 'The Literary Vision of Liam O'Flaherty: by John Zneimer', *The New York Times*, 3 Jan 1971, 4 (a book review).

MacDonagh, Donagh, 'Afterword', *The Informer*, New York, 1961, pp. 183—8.

Mercier, Vivian, 'Introduction', *The Stories of Liam O'Flaherty*, New York, 1956, pp. v—viii.

Mercier, Vivian, 'The Irish Short Story and Oral Tradition', *The Celtic Cross*, edited by Ray B. Brown, William John Rocelli and John Loftus, West Lafayette, Indiana, 1964, pp. 98—116.

Mercier, Vivian, 'Man Against Nature: the Novels of Liam O'Flaherty', *Wascana Review*, I, no. 2, 1966, 37—46.

Moseley, Maboth, 'The Humanity of Liam O'Flaherty', *The Humanist*, May 1927, 223.

Murphy, Maureen, 'The Double Vision of Liam O'Flaherty', *Eire—Ireland*, VIII, 3, 20—5.

Murray, Michael H., 'Liam O'Flaherty and the Speaking Voice,' *Studies in Short Fiction*, V, no, 2. 1968, 154—62.

O'Connor, Frank, 'A Good Short Story must be News', *The New York Times Book Review*, 10 June 1956, 1, 20.

O'Faolain, Sean, 'Don Quixote O'Flaherty', *The London Mercury*, XXXVII, Dec 1937, 170—5. This article appears with additions and deletions in *The Bell*, II, June 1941, 28—36.

O'Faolain, Sean, 'Fifty years of Irish writing', *Studies*, LI, Spring 1962, 102—3.

O'Faolain, Sean, 'Speaking of Books: Dyed Irish', *The New York Times*, 12 May 1968.

Paul-Dubois, L., 'Un romancier réaliste en Erin: M. Liam O'Flaherty', *Revue des Deux Mondes*, XXI, 15 June 1934, 884—904.

Reynolds, Horace, 'A Man, A Mouse and a Wave', *The New York Times*, 16 July 1950 (a book review of *Two Lovely Beasts*).

Rosati, Salvatore, 'Letteratura Inglese', *Nuova Antologia*, Anno 69, 16 Sep 1934, 317—19.

Ryan, Richard, 'Liam O'Flaherty: A Blackened Soul', *Hibernia*, 10 May 1974, 24.

Saul, George Brandon, 'A Wild Sowing: the Short Stories of Liam O'Flaherty', *Review of English Literature*, IV, July 1963, 108—13.

Troy, William, 'The Position of Liam O'Flaherty', *Bookman* (New York), LXIX, Mar 1929, 7—11.

Troy, William. 'Two Years', *Bookman* (New York), LXXII, Nov 1930, 322—3.

Von Sternemann, J. 'Irische Geschichten: Novellen von Liam O'Flaherty', *Die Neue Rundschau*, XLII, Apr 1931, 521—39.

Warren C. Henry, 'Liam O'Flaherty', *Bookman* (London) LXXVII, Jan 1930, 235—6.

B. FULL-LENGTH STUDIES

Doyle, Paul A., *Liam OFlaherty*, Twayne's English Authors Series, New York, 1971 (contains additional biographic material).

O'Brien, James H., *Liam O'Flaherty*, Bucknell University Press, Irish Writers Series, 1973 (an introductory monograph).

Sheeran, Patrick F., *The novels of Liam O'Flaherty. Background profile analysis*, Wolfhound Press, Dublin 1976.

Zneimer, John N., *The Literary Vision of Liam O'Flaherty*, Syracuse: Syracuse University Press, 1970.

C. SOME CRITICISM IN IRISH OF LIAM O'FLAHERTY'S WORK

Neol (Leon O'Broin), 'An Dorchadas (The Darkness), an original play by Liam O'Flaherty', *Fáinne an lae*, 13 Márta 1926, 6.

Theo, 'Dorchadas — tuairim eile' (Darkness — another opinion), *Fáinne an lae*, 13 Márta 1926, 6.

Bhaldraithe, Tomas de, 'O Flaithearta — Aistritheoir' (O'Flaherty — Translator) *Comhar*, 25, Bealtaine, 1967, 35—7.

O Buachalla, Breandan, 'O Cadhain, O Ceileachair agus O Flaithearta' (Kyne, Kelleher and O'Flaherty), *Comhar*, 25, Bealtaine, 1967, 69—73.

O Cuagáin, Proinsias, 'Dúil san Ainmhí Téama I Scéalta Liam O Flaithearta', *Irisleabhar Mhá Nuad*, 1968, pp. 49—55, 57—9.

D. BIBLIOGRAPHY

Doyle, Paul A., *Liam O'Flaherty: An Annotated Bibliography*, New York: Troy, 1972.

E. OTHER WORKS REFERRED TO IN THE FOOTNOTES

(only the edition or source used is quoted.)

Barthes, Roland, 'Criticism as Language', *The Times Literary Supplement*, 27 Sep 1963. 740; 'La littérature aujourd'hui', *Essais Critiques*, Paris, 1964; *Writing Degree Zero*, trans. Annette Lavers and Colin Smith, New York, 1968.

Bates, H.E., *The Modern Short Story*, London 1941.

Birmingham, G.A. (ed.), *Irish Short Stories*, London, 1932.

Delargy, J.H., 'The Gaelic Story-Teller', *Proceedings of the British Academy*, XXXI, London, 1945.

Dubos, René, *So Human an Animal*, New York, 1968; London, 1970.

Edwards, Owen Dudley, 'The Burden of Irish History', *Conor Cruise O'Brien Introduces Ireland*, ed. O.D. Edwards, London, 1969.

Eglington, John, 'Irish Letter, April, 1927', *The Dial*, LXXXII, May 1927, 407—10.

Eliot, T.S., *The Idea of a Christian Society*, London, 1939.

Ellmann, Richard, *James Joyce*, New York, 1959.

Friedman, Norman, 'Point of View in Fiction: the Development of a Critical Concept', *PMLA*, LXX, Dec 1955, 1160—84.

Hyde, Douglas, *Beside the Fire*, London, 1890.

Lawrence, D.H., 'Democracy' and 'John Galsworthy', *Selected Essays*, London, 1950.

Lorenz, Konrad, *On Aggression*, New York, 1967.

McMahon, Sean, 'The Priest in Recent Irish Fiction', *Eire—Ireland*, Summer 1968.

Mercier, Vivian, *The Irish Comic Tradition*, London, 1962; (ed.), *Great Irish Short Stories*, New York, 1964.

Montague, C.E., *A Writer's Notes on his Trade*, London, 1949.

Moore, Harry T., *The Intelligent Heart: the Story of D.H. Lawrence*, London, 1960.

O'Brien, E. J. (ed.), *The Best Short Stories of 1924*, London, 1925 (refer to preface).

O'Connor, Frank, *The Lonely Voice*, Cleveland, Ohio, 1962; *The Backward Look*, London, 1967.

O'Faolain, Sean, *The Irish*, London, 1947; *The Finest Stories of Sean O'Faolain*, New

York, 1957 (refer to foreword).

O'Flaherty, Tom, *Aranmen All*, London, 1934; *Cliffmen of the West*, London, 1935.

O'Malley, Ernie, *On Another Man's Wound*, London, 1936 (Later entitled *Army Without Banners*).

O'Suilleabhain, Sean, *Irish Wake Amusements*, Cork, 1967.

Phelps, Gordon, *The Russian Novel in English Fiction*, London, 1956.

Scholes, Robert and Kellogg, Robert, *The Nature of Narrative*, London and New York, 1966.

Schorer, Mark, 'Technique as Discovery', *The Hudson Review*, Spring 1948. Reprinted in *Critiques and Essays on Modern Fiction* 1920—51, selected by John W. Aldrige, New York, 1952, pp. 67—82.

Shadbolt, Maurice 'The International Symposium on the Short Story — Part Two', *Kenyon Review*, XXXI, no. 1, 1969, 70.

Shaw, G.B., *John Bull's Other Island*, London, 1921.

Sheehy, Maurice, (ed.), *Michael/Frank: Studies on Frank O'Connor*, London, 1969.

Sheechy, Michael, *Is Ireland Dying?* London, 1968

Stephens, James, *The Crock of Gold*, London, 1912.

Swift, Jonathan, *Of Public Absurdities in England, The Prose Works of Jonathan Swift*, cd. Temple Scott, London, 1907.

Synge, J.M., *The Aran Islands*, Leipzig, 1926.

Ussher, Arland, *The Face and Mind of Ireland*, London, 1949; *The Vanishing Irish*, London, 1954.

Williamson, Henry, *Tarka the Otter*, London, 1949.

Yeats, W.B., 'Irish Ban on a novel', *Manchester Guardian Weekly*, 26 Feb 1932, 176. Letter to Mrs Shakespear, 13 Mar 1927 quoted by A. Norman Jeffares in *W.B. Yeats, Man and Poet*, London, 1949, p. 241.

APPENDIX

ALPHABETICAL LIST OF SHORT STORIES

Short stories published in periodicals, anthologies, short story collections and limited editions. The code numbers used are listed under *Short Story Collections*.

'Accident', *Fortnightly Review*, CXLIII, Feb 1935, 155—67.

'Alien Skull, The', SS3, SS4, SS12.

'All things come of Age', *Esquire*, III, Jan 1935, 43, 184; SS13.

'Arrest', *Weekly Westminster*, 5 Sep 1925, 476; SS13.

'At the Forge', *The New Leader*, 14 Aug 1925; SS2, SS9.

'Backwoodsman's daughter', *Mademoiselle*, XXII, ,Apr 1946, 150, 230—1, 241, 243 (adapted from chapter 19 of *Two Years*).

'Bath, The', *Story*, XVI, May—June, 1940, 9—19; SS5.

'Beauty', SS1.

'Beggars, The', *The Bell*, XIII, Mar 1947, 5—23; SS5, SS6.

'Benedicamus Domino', SS1.

'Birth', *The Humanist*, Oct 1926, 361—2. *The Fairy Goose and Two Other Stories*, London and New York: Crosby Gaige limited edition 1927; SS3, SS4, SS6, SS7, SS12.

'Black Bullock, The', SS1, SS4, SS8.

'Black Cat, The, *The Humanist,* July 1926, 237—9.

'Blackbird, The', *The Nation* (London), XXXV, 2 Aug 1924, 563—4; SS1, SS4, SS6, SS8.

'Blackbird's Mate, The', SS3, SS4.

'Blackmail', SS2, SS9.

'Black Mare, The', *New Statesman*, XXII, 3 Nov 1923, 110—11; *Great British Short*

Stories, ed. E. and E. Huberman, New York: Bantam, 1968; SS1, SS4, SS6, SS7, SS8.

'Black Rabbit, The', SS3, SS4, SS12.

'Bladder, The', *The Nation* (London), XXXI, 22 Mar 1924, 887; SS1, SS9.

'Blow, The', *The Bell*, XIX, May 1954, 9—22; *Esquire*, XLII, July 1954, 32—3, 110—13; *Great Irish Short Stories*, ed. Vivian Mercier, New York: Dell, 1964; SS6.

'Bohunk', SS13.

'Cake, The', *The Irish Statesman*, V, 19 Dec 1925, 455—7.

'Caress, The', at the end of Liam O'Flaherty's autobiography *Shame the Devil*, pp. 252—83; SS13.

'Challenge, The', SS5.

'Charity', *Weekly Westminster*, 4 July 1925, 256; SS2, SS4.

'Child of God, The', limited edition, London: Archer, 1926; *The New Coterie*, V, Spring 1927, 43—60; SS3, SS4, SS6.

'Christmas Eve', *Weekly Westminster*, III, 20 Dec 1924, 246.

'Civil War', limited edition, London: Archer, 1925; *The New Coterie*, 1 Nov 1925, 60—6; *Irish Short Stories*, ed. G. A. Birmingham, London, 1932; SS2, SS4.

'Colic', SS1, SS9.

'Conger Eel, The', *The Nation* (London), XXXVI, 1 Nov 1924, 183—4; *The Dial*, LXXVIII, Jan 1925, 5—7; SS2, SS4, SS6, SS7, SS8.

'Cow's Death, The', *New Statesman*, 30 June 1923, 364; SS1, SS4, SS6, SS7, SS8.

'Crow Fight, A', *The Dublin Magazine*, II, Sep 1924, 102—6; SS13.

'Cutting of Tom Bottle, The', *Charles Wain: A Miscellany of Short Stories*, London: Mallinson, 1933, pp. 137—60.

'Desire', *Evening News* (London), 2 Nov 1948, 2; *The Bell*, XIX, July 1954, 48—50; SS6, SS7.

'Ditch, The', SS3.

'Doctor's Visit, The', SS1, SS9.

'Dublin Eviction, A', *Weekly Westminster*, III, 13 Dec 1924, 216.

'Enchanted Water, The', *Yale Review*, XLII, Sep 1952, 46—53; SS13.

'Eviction, The', *Maranist*, XLII, Apr 1951, 11; SS5.

'Fairy Goose, The', *The Humanist*, Aug 1926, 275—7. Limited edition, London: Faber and Gwyer, 1927; New York: Crosby Gaige, 1928; *This Week in Ireland*, 5 Dec 1969, 29—33; SS3, SS4, SS6, SS7, SS12.

'Fall of Joseph Timmins, The', SS3, SS9.

'Fanatic, The', *The Bell*, XVIII, Summer 1953, 16—26; *Esquire*, XL, Dec 1953, 90, 194, 196, 198; *Pick of Today's*, 5, ed. John Pudney, London, 1954; SS13.

'Fight, The', *Manchester Guardian*, 28 Aug 1923; SS1, SS4, SS6, SS7, SS8.

'Fireman's Death, The', *Weekly Westminster*, 24 Oct 1925; SS2, SS9.

'Fishing', *The Irish Statesman*, III, 6 Dec 1924, 392—4; SS13.

'Flood, The', *The Dublin Magazine*, II, Jan 1925, 408—10; *Living Age*, CCCXXV, 20 June 1925, 642—3.

'Flute Player, The', *Esquire*, XXVII, Mar 1947, 41, 127—9, SS5.

'Foolish Butterfly, The', *The Adelphi*, II, Nov 1924, 474—7; *The Dial*, LXXVIII, May 1925, 402—4; SS2, SS4, SS12.

'Fresh Mackerel', *Weekly Westminster*, III, 6 Dec 1924, 176.

'Galway Bay', *London Mercury*, XXXIX, Jan 1939, 297—307; SS5, SS6.

'Going into Exile', *The Dublin Magazine*, I, Apr 1924, 789—96; *The Irish Press*, XVI, 22 Apr 1946, 10; 23 Apr 1946, 7; *1000 Years of Irish Prose*, ed. Vivian Mercier & Greene, New York, 1952; (under the title of 'The Exiles', *This Week in Ireland*, 12 Dec 1969, 29—35); SS1, SS4, SS6, SS7, SS8.

'Good Samaritan, The', *The New Leader*, 27 Aug 1926, 8.

'Grave Reason, A', *The New Leader*, 16 Oct 1925, 12.

'Grey Seagull', SS5.

'Hawk, The', *Town & Country*, CIII, Mar 1949, 57, 100—1; *44 Irish Short Stories*, ed. Devin A. Garrity, New York: Devin-Adair, 1955; SS6, SS7.

'His First Flight', *Manchester Guardian*, 5 Oct 1923 (entitled 'First Flight'); *The Lilliput Annual*, I, July 1937, 1—3; *Ireland of the Welcomes*, XVII, Mar—Apr 1969, 32—9; SS1, SS4, SS6, SS8.

'Hook, The', *The Dublin Magazine*, I May 1924, 871—3; SS1, SS4, SS8.

'Idle Gossip', *The New Leader*, 19 Feb 1926, 11.

'Indian Summer', *Good Housekeeping*, CXX, May 1945, 34—5, 225—33.

'In each beginning is an end' (otherwise entitled 'Greenwich village') *Fascination*, I, July 1946, 32—3, 66 (adapted from Chapter 23 of *Two Years*).

'Inquisition, The', *The Adelphi*, III, Mar 1926, 666—73; *The Best Short Stories of 1926*, ed. E. J. O'Brien, London, 1927; SS2, SS9.

'Intellectual, The', *Weekly Westminster*, IV, 22 Aug 1925, 428.

'Irish Pride', *Nash's Pall Mall Magazine*, XCVII, June 1926, 39—45; *Forum*, XCIV, Dec 1935, 343—51; also appears as a shortened version with the title 'King of Inishcam', *Living Age*, CCCLVII, Nov 1939, 236—43; SS13.

'It Was the Devil's Work', *The Wild Swan and Other Stories*, London: Joiner & Steele, 1932.

'Jealous Hens, The', *Weekly Westminster*, 18 Oct 1924; SS2, SS4, SS12.

'Josephine', SS1.

'Lament, The', *Harper's Bazaar*, LXXV, Apr 1941, 58—9, 114—17; *The Bell*, XII, July 1946, 283—300; SS5.

'Landing, The', *T P's & Cassell's Weekly*, 24 May 1924; *Living Age*, CCCXXII, 19 July 1924, 136—9; SS1, SS4, SS6, SS7, SS8.

'Letter, The', *The Criterion*, VII, June 1928, 58—63; SS3, SS4, SS12.

'Life', *American Mercury*, LXIV, Feb 1947, 156—61; SS5, SS6, SS7.

'Light', SS5.

'Limpets', *Weekly Westminster*, 30 Jan 1926, 312.

'Little White Dog, The', *Manchester Guardian*, 24 Oct 1927; *The Bookman* (New York), LXVII, Apr 1928, 145—7; SS3, SS4, SS12.

'Lost Thrush, The', *The Chapbook (A Yearly Miscellany)*, ed. Harold Monro, no. 40, 1925, pp. 14—17; SS2, SS4, SS12.

'Lovers', *Harper's*, CLXII, Apr 1931, 528—32; *English Review*, LIII, Sep 1931, 437—45; *The Best Short Stories of 1932*, ed. E. J. O'Brien, London, 1933; *Great Irish Short Stories*, ed. Vivian Mercier, New York, 1964; SS13.

'Mackerel for Sale', *London Mercury*, XV, Feb 1927, 354—61; SS3, SS9.

'Matchmaking', *Cassell's Weekly*, 20 June 1923, 443.

'Matter of Freedom, A': (otherwise entitled 'Timoney's Ass') *Tomorrow Magazine*, VI, June 1947, 36—7; SS13.

'Mermaid, The', *John O'London's Weekly*, 26 Oct 1929, 101; SS13.

'Milking Time', *Manchester Guardian*, 14 Aug 1925; *The Dial*, LXXXIX, Dec 1925, 491—4; SS2, SS4, SS6, SS7, SS8.

'Mirror, The', *Esquire*, XL, Nov 1953, 58, 146; SS6, SS7.

'Mother and Son', *Weekly Westminster*, 28 Nov 1925; SS2, SS4, SS6, SS12.

'Mountain Tavern, The', *The Monthly Criterion*, VI, Aug 1927, 118—27; limited edition, *Red Barbara & Other Stories*, London: Faber & Gwyer, New York: Crosby Gaige, 1928; SS3, SS4, SS6, SS7.

'Mouse, The', *Lilliput*, III, 1938, 248—50, 252—3; *Coronet*, V, Jan—Feb 1939, 7—10; SS5.

'Moving', *Manchester Guardian*, 16 Nov 1925, 16.

'New Suit, The', *The Household Magazine*, XLIII, Sep 1943 4, 9; *Irish Press*, 21 June 1946, 2; SS5, SS6, SS7.

'Night Porter, The', *Story*, XXX, Jan—Feb 1947, 23—32.

'Oar, The', *Outlook* (London), LXI, 14 Jan 1928, 54—5; limited edition, *Red Barbara & Other Stories*, London: Faber & Gwyer, New York: Crosby Gaige, 1928; SS3, SS4, SS6, SS7, SS12.

'Offerings', *Outlook* (London), LVII, 13 Mar 1926, 191; SS2, SS4, SS12.

'Old Hunter, The', *Golden Book Magazine*, VI, Oct 1927, 443—6; *Irish Writing*, no. 21, Nov 1952, 17—23; SS2, SS4, SS12.

'Old Woman, The', SS5, SS6, SS7.

'Ounce of Tobacco, An', *TP's Weekly*, VIII, 8 Oct 1927, 739—40.

'Outcast, The', *The Adelphi*, II, Feb 1925, 725—30; SS2, SS9.

'Painted Woman, The', SS3, SS9, SS12.

'Parting, The', *Irish Writing*, no. 6, Nov 1948, 35—43; SS6, SS7.

'Patsa or the Belly of Gold', *The London Aphrodite*, I, Aug 1928, 29—34; SS13.

'Pedlar's Revenge, The', *The Bell*, XVIII, June 1952, 148—61; *Collier's*, CXXXII, 25 July 1953, 38—43; *Ellery Queen's Mystery Magazine*, VIII, Nov 1956, 56; SS13.

'Pig in a Bedroom, A', *The Irish Statesman*, II, 29 Mar 1924, 71—3; SS1.

'Poor People', *Weekly Westminster*, 26 Sep 1925; SS2, SS4, SS12.

'Post Office, The', *The Bell*, XIX, Apr 1954, 5—26; SS6.

'Pot of Gold, A', *The Irish Statesman*, II, 26 July 1924, 615—17; SS1, SS4, SS8.

'Prey', *Outlook* (London), LIX, 4 June 1927, 711—12; *Bookman* (New York), LXVI, Oct 1927, 193—5. Limited edition, *Red Barbara & Other Stories*, London: Faber & Gwyer, New York: Crosby Gaige, 1928; SS3, SS4, SS12.

'Proclamation', *Yale Review*, XXI, no. 1, Sep 1931, 158—66; SS13.

'Public House at Night, A', *TP's and Cassell's Weekly*, 15 Nov 1924, 151.

'Public Scandal, A', *Manchester Guardian*, 9 Sep 1925, 16.

'Reaping Race, The', *The Dublin Magazine*, II, Nov 1924, 257—61; *The Best Short Stories of 1926*, ed. E. J. O'Brien, London, 1927; SS2, SS4, SS12.

'Red Barbara', *The London Aphrodite*, II, Oct 1928, 78—83; limited edition, *Red Barbara & Other Stories*, New York: Crosby Gaige, London: Faber & Gwyer, 1928. SS3, SS4, SS6, SS7, SS12.

'Red Petticoat, A', *Tomorrow*, I, Aug 1924, 1, 3—4, 6. (Two numbers of this magazine appeared in Dublin, the other issue being Sep 1924.) SS2, SS4, SS6, SS12.

'Rockfish, The', SS1, SS4, SS6, SS8.

'Salted Goat, The', *The Irish Statesman*, I, 26 Jan 1924, 616—17; SS13.

'Seal, The', SS5.

'Secret Drinking', *This Quarter*, II, July—Aug—Sep 1929, 109—14.

'Selling Pigs', *TP's and Cassell's Weekly*, 19 Jan 1924; *The Golden Book Magazine*, XII, Sep 1930, 54—6; SS1, SS9.

'Sensualist, The', SS2.

'Shilling, A', SS1, SS4, SS6, SS7, SS8.

'Sinner, The', SS3, SS4.

'Sniper, The', *The New Leader*, 12 Jan 1923; *Scholastic*, LXIX, 18 Oct 1956, 18; SS1, SS4, SS8.

'Sport: the Kill', SS1, SS4, SS8.

'Spring Sowing', *TP's and Cassell's Weekly*, 8 Mar 1924; *The Best Short Stories of 1925*, ed. E. J. O'Brien, London, 1926; *Golden Book Magazine*, XI, May 1930, 36—8; *Irish Press*, 28 Mar 1946, 7; SS1, SS4, SS6, SS7, SS8.

'Stolen Ass, The', *Manchester Guardian*, 3 Dec 1925; *Lilliput*, II, 1938, 397—8, 400; SS2, SS4, SS12.

'Stone, The', SS3, SS4, SS12.

'Stoney Batter', SS2, SS4.

'Strange Disease, The', *The Bermondsey Book, A Quarterly Review of Life and Literature*, V, Mar/May 1928, 32—7; later included in *Seven Years Harvest: an anthology of the Bermondsey Book 1923—1930*, ed. Sidney Gutman, London, 1934; SS3, SS4, SS12.

'Strange Hen, The', *Lilliput*, II, 1938, 146—8.

'Stream, The', SS3, SS4, SS12.

'Struggle, The', SS1, SS9.

'Swimming', *Weekly Westminster*, 27 Dec 1924, 274.

'Tent, The', *The Calendar of Modern Letters*, II, Oct 1925, 104—11; *Irish Writing*, no. 16, Sep 1951, 11—17 (a slightly different version of the story); *44 Irish Short Stories*, ed. Devin A. Garrity, New York: 1955; *Irish Stories and Tales*, ed. Devin A. Garrity, New York: 1956; SS2, SS4, SS6, SS7, SS8.

'Terrorist, The', *The New Coterie*, II, Spring 1926, 52—6; limited edition, London: Archer, 1926; SS2, SS9.

'Test of Courage, The', *Esquire*, XIX, Feb 1943, 28, 129—30, 132, 134; SS13.

'Three Lambs', SS1, SS4, SS8.

'Tide, The', SS5, SS6, SS7.

'Tidy Tim's Donkey', *Weekly Westminster*, 5 Jan 1924, 316.

'Tin Can', *Weekly Westminster*, 3 Jan 1925, 302; SS13.

'Tinker Woman's Child, The', *TP's and Cassell's Weekly*, 3 Oct 1925, 759.

'Touch, The', *Irish Writing*, I, 1946, 50—8 (text A); *American Mercury*, LXIV, May 1947, 549—56 (text B); SS5, SS6, SS7.

'Tramp, The', SS1, SS4, SS6, SS7, SS8.

'Trapped', SS2, SS4, SS12.

'Two Dogs', *Spectator*, CXXXI, 8 Dec 1923, 893; SS1, SS4, SS8.

'Two Lovely Beasts', *The Bell*, XIII, Dec 1946, 4—30; *Story*, XXXI, Nov—Dec 1947, 30—46; SS5, SS6.

'Tyrant, The', *Bookman* (New York), LXV, Aug 1927, 691—4; SS2.

'Unclean', *The Wild Swan*, London: Joiner and Steele (W. Jackson), 1932.

'Waterhen, The', *Esquire*, X, Aug 1938, 59, 147; SS5, SS6, SS7.

'Wave, The', SS1, SS4, SS8.

'Wedding, The', *The Bell*, XIII, Oct 1946, 40—59; SS5, SS6.

'White Bitch, The', *Weekly Westminster*, 7 June 1924, 176; SS13.

'Wild Goat's Kid, The', *The Dublin Magazine*, II, July 1925, 793—8; *Dial*, LXXIX, Aug 1925, 137—43; *Golden Book Magazine*, V, Apr 1927, 451—4; SS2, SS4, SS6, SS7, SS12.

'Wild Man of County Galway, The', *Collier's*, CXXXI, 18 Apr 1953, 54—63. (This is a cut and altered version of the story entitled 'The Post Office'.)

'Wild Sow, The', *New Statesman*, XXIII 26 Apr 1924, 65—6; SS1, SS4, SS8.

'Wild Stallions', SS13.

'Wild Swan, The', *The Wild Swan*, London: Joiner and Steele, 1932; *The Evening Standard Book of Best Short Stories*, second series, London, 1934; SS6.

'Wing Three quarter, The', SS2, SS4, SS6, SS12.

'Wolf Lanigan's Death', *The Irish Statesman*, II, 7 June 1924, 391—3; SS1, SS4, SS8.

'Wounded Cormorant, The', *The Nation* (London), XXXVIII, 28 Nov 1925, 317—18; *1000 Years of Irish Prose*, ed. Mercier and Greene, New York, 1952; SS2, SS4, SS6, SS7, SS12.

'Wren's Nest, The', *The New Leader*, 9 May 1924; SS1, SS4, SS8.

'Your Honour', *Manchester Guardian*, 24 Dec 1925; *Living Age*, CCCXXVIII, 20 Mar 1926, 643—5; SS2, SS9.

Index